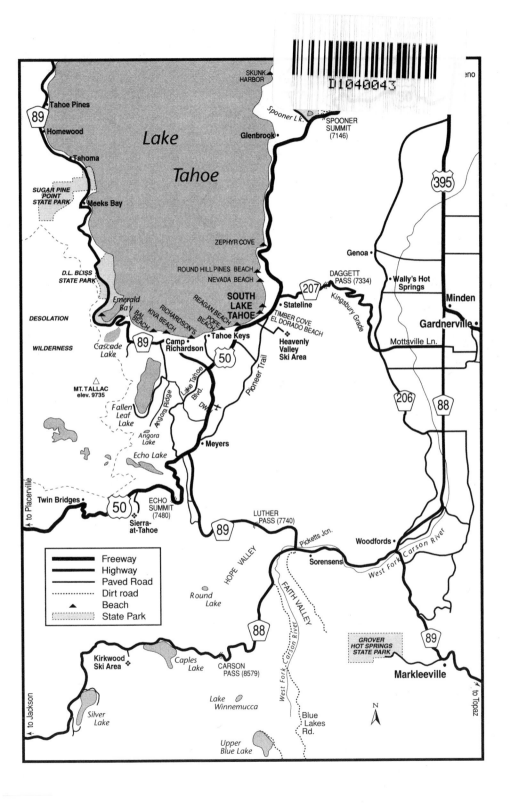

"Oh the exquisite beauty of this lake!—its clear waters, emerald green, and the deepest ultramarine blue; its pure shores, rocky or cleanest gravel, so clean that the chafing of the waves does not stain in the least the clearness of the waters ..."

Joseph Le Conte, on a visit to Tahoe, 1870.

What Shall We Do Tomorrow At

LAKE TAHOE

5th Edition

The Complete Activites Guide
for Lake Tahoe, Truckee and Carson Pass

by Ellie Huggins

Coldstream Press
Truckee, California

Cover Photo: An April day at Sand Harbor. © Ellie Huggins

Book Design: Ellie Huggins
Cover and Logo Designs: Andrea Hendrick
Drawings: Andrea Hendrick
Maps: Sue Irwin
Editor: Dan Wendin
Contributing Editor: Robert Frohlich
Printing: Central Plains Book Manufacturing

Publisher's Cataloging-in-Publication
Huggins, Ellie
  What shall we do tomorrow at Lake Tahoe : a complete
  guide for Lake Tahoe, Truckee and Carson Pass / by
  Ellie Huggins.— 5th, 2000-01 ed.
   p. cm.
   Includes index.
   Preassigned LCCN: 00-090401
   ISBN: 1-893057-02-X
   1. Tahoe, Lake, Region (Calif. and Nev.)—Guidebooks.
  2. Truckee Region (Calif.)—Guidebooks. I. Title.

  F868.T2H836 1998   917.94'380453
             QBI98-445

Second Printing

Published by:
  Coldstream Press
  P.O. Box 9590
  Truckee, California 96162
  toll free: (800) 916-7450
  fax: (530) 587-9081
  e-mail: info@coldstreampress.com
  www.coldstreampress.com

Table of Contents

Winter dawn at Donner Lake.

Area Bus Service

Lake Tahoe and Truckee have year-round bus service that connects in winter with shuttles to ski areas and in summer to the special summer trolleys. Schedules for all services are at Visitor Information Centers, retail outlets and bus stops.

YEAR-ROUND SERVICE

TART

One TART bus line runs between Squaw Valley and Emerald Bay with stops at the Resort at Squaw Creek, River Ranch, Tahoe City, Sunnyside, Homewood and Tahoma. A second line runs between Squaw Valley and the Hyatt Regency in Incline Village and between Sugar Pine Point and Incline Village. There is regular TART service between the Truckee Train Depot and the Tahoe City Y. In July and August San Francisco-style trolleys run hourly between the West Shore and Carnelian Bay and every half-hour between Carnelian Bay and Crystal Bay. (530-581-6365)

TRUCKEE TROLLEY

The trolley routes connect the town and Northstar-at-Tahoe via the airport. Another line runs between the Depot in Truckee out Donner Pass Road to Gateway and Crossroads Shopping Centers, to the Factory Stores and Donner Memorial State Park. Evenings the trolley connects Truckee and the Stateline casinos. In summer the trolley extends to West End Beach at Donner Lake. (530-587-7451)

STAGE in South Lake Tahoe

STAGE buses have regular service every fifteen minutes on two routes up and down Highway 50 between the South Tahoe Y and the casinos, along Pioneer Way and up Ski Run Boulevard. Maps are on the buses. (530-573-2080)

Area Bus Service

WINTER SERVICE

TART

TART connects with shuttles to Northstar-at-Tahoe and Alpine Meadows. (530-550-1212)

THE TRUCKEE TROLLEY

The Truckee Trolley offers service between Northstar-at-Tahoe and Truckee downtown. A bus runs on Donner Pass Rd. between Truckee and Sugar Bowl and Donner Ski Ranch on the summit, weather permitting. (530-587-7451)

SOUTH LAKE TAHOE

Free shuttles run from the casinos and all major hotels to Heavenly all day. Sierra-at-Tahoe has shuttles that leave in the morning from the hotels and return in the afternoon. Reservations are required for the shuttle service to Kirkwood Resort. (209-258-6000) Zephyr Cove Resort offers free shuttles between the casinos and their snowmobile rides.

January to early April Hornblower Cruises runs a paddlewheeler ski shuttle to North Shore with connecting buses from your hotel and to Squaw Valley.

SUMMER ONLY — SOUTH LAKE TAHOE

The NIFTY 50 TROLLEY runs two routes from 10:00 a.m. to 11:00 p.m. every hour. **Route A** runs from the casinos and motels along Highway 50 to the Factory Stores at the South Tahoe *Y* out Emerald Bay Road to Camp Richardson's Resort, the Tallac Historic Site and the U.S. Forest Service Visitor Center. **Route B** offers service from Zephyr Cove to the Casinos and to the Heavenly Valley Tram. (530-542-6077)

Resource Phone Numbers

TRANSPORTATION

Amtrak	800-872-7245
Caltrans Highway Information Network	800-427-7623
Nevada Highway Department	877-687-6237
Greyhound Bus Lines	800-231-2222

Local Bus Lines

TART – Tahoe Area Regional Transit	530-581-6365
North Tahoe TMA	530-581-3922
South Tahoe TMA	530-542-6076
Truckee Trolley and Dial-A-Ride	530-587-7451
STAGE – South Tahoe Ground Express	530-573-2080
Bus Plus (on demand service - So. Lake Tahoe)	530-542-6077

Taxi Companies

Domino Taxi - South Lake Tahoe	530-544-6666
Paradise Taxi – South Lake Tahoe	530-577-4708
Sunshine Taxi Company – South Lake Tahoe	530-542-1234
Tahoe Truckee Taxi - Truckee & North Shore	530-583-8294
Yellow Cab	
North Lake Tahoe	530-546-9090
Incline Village	775-831-8294
South Lake Tahoe	530-544-5555
ZZ Cab - Northshore	530-581-0222

Reno-Tahoe Airport Shuttles
See "Airport Transportation Service" in the Yellow Pages.

PARKS

California State Parks

Sierra District California State Parks	530-525-7232
Donner Memorial State Park	530-582-7892
Tahoe State Recreation Area (Summer)	530-583-3074
Kings Beach State Recreation Area	530-546-7248
D.L. Bliss State Park (Summer)	530-525-7277
Emerald Bay State Park (Summer)	530-525-7277
Sugar Pine Point State Park	530-525-7982

Resource Phone Numbers

Nevada State Parks

| Lake Tahoe Nevada State Park | 775-831-0494 |
| Kahle Park | 775-588-0271 |

Regional Parks and Parks and Recreation Departments

Truckee Donner Recreation and Parks	530-582-7720
North Tahoe Regional Park	530-546-7248
Tahoe City Parks	530-583-3796
Incline Village IVGID	775-832-1100
South Lake Tahoe Recreation and Parks	530-542-6055

Unites States Forest Service

Big Bend Visitor Information (Summer)	530-426-3609
Truckee Ranger Station	530-587-3558
Tahoe National Forest	530-265-4531
Lake Tahoe Basin Management Unit	530-573-2600
Visitor Information Center (Summer)	530-573-2674
Desolation Wilderness Permits	530-573-2600

VISITOR INFORMATION

Baby Sitting

See "Baby Sitters" in the Yellow Pages or the concierge at your hotel.

Visitors and Convention Bureaus

North Tahoe	530-583-3494
Truckee	530-587-0476
North Tahoe Resort Association	800-824-6348
Incline Village Crystal Bay	775-832-1606
Tahoe Douglas Visitor Center	775-588-4591
South Lake Tahoe Reservations	800-288-2463
South Lake Tahoe Chamber of Commerce	530-541-5255

© Ellie Huggins

"As it lay there with the shadows of the mountains photographed upon its surface, I thought it must surely be the fairest picture the whole world affords."
Samuel Clemens, alias Mark Twain, 1861.

Introduction

You have come to Lake Tahoe to ski; it's storming and you wonder what you can do. You're attending a conference. You have a free day and want to go out on the lake. Who offers tours of the lake? You're renting a cabin for two weeks and the kids are tired of the beach. What can you plan for tomorrow? Where can you find out more about the emigrants who brought their wagons over Donner or Carson Pass, visit a museum or hike somewhere interesting for a picnic?

This book will help you discover the many options that will make your visit to Lake Tahoe, Truckee and the Carson Pass region an enjoyable and fun-filled time. Would you like to take a balloon ride, or kayak on the lake? Do you want to try your hand at fishing, take a bike ride, find a meadow with wildflowers, or cross-country ski free? In short, What Shall We Do Tomorrow? The many choices open to you are described in this book.

The book is arranged in four chapters, each with a tab on the outside edge of the page. The first one describes historic lodges and B&B's, lodging reservation services for homes and condominiums and dining. The next three chapters feature summer, winter and year-round activities. Each category of activity has a logo, shown on pages 8 and 9. Just turn to the pages with the logo at the top to find out where to water ski, take a cruise, fish on Lake Tahoe, hike or do any one of 31 different activities covered in this book. The locations of all activities are listed in the following geographical order: Donner Summit, Truckee, Highway 89, Tahoe City, West Shore, North Shore and Incline Village, South Lake Tahoe north to Sand Harbor, then Echo Summit and Carson Pass.

The outside column of each page includes fees, season and hours of operation plus addresses, phone numbers, websites and special features. The bottom of each page sites the locations of the activities.

Summer Activities

Adventures

Excursions

Beaches

Boating

Cruising Lake Tahoe

Fishing

Fishing Charters

Fly Fishing Guides

Rafting

Bicycling

Horseback Riding

Tennis

Golf

Historical Walks

Special Hikes

Just For Kids

Ranger Programs

Winter Activities

Downhill Ski Areas

X-Country Skiing

Ice Skating

Snowmobiling

Snowplay

Winter Adventures

Year-Round Activities

Kids at Casinos

Art Galleries

Shopping

Museums

Photo and Vista Points

Special Events

Dining Out

Lodging

History

The Region's Earliest Inhabitants

Human history of the Truckee, Lake Tahoe and Carson Pass region goes back many thousand years when the Washoe and Paiute tribes of Nevada traveled to the mountains to hunt and fish and escape the summer heat of the desert. Evidence of Paiute summer encampments can be found in various places near Truckee. Perhaps as early as five thousand years ago, Native Americans from Nevada created petroglyphs on the granite rocks just east of Donner Pass, and obsidian arrowheads have been discovered on the west shore of Donner Lake. The Paiutes worshiped the rocking stone perched on top of a flat rock above Truckee. This rock was so perfectly balanced that the wind could set it to rocking. The Paiutes believed that the wind spoke to them through its movements. It is presently enclosed in a cupola located next to the Veterans Building. At the turn of the century the town fathers cemented the rocking stone into place to prevent it from rolling down upon unsuspecting citizens.

For thousands of years Washoe tribes came to Lake Tahoe every summer to meet and reaffirm their tribal unity. The Washoe climbed up from the Carson Valley to their summer villages along the shores of the lake. They called these places *da ow a ga*, which means "edge of big waters." Although the Washoe believed that the remains of Ang, a much-feared, monstrous bird, lay at the bottom of the lake, they still believed that *da ow* was sacred. The lake was the giver of life, for it fed fish, animals and humans. The tribe fished and gathered seeds, roots, strawberries, gooseberries and sugar pine sap. Deer and rabbit were favorite meats. In the fall they moved to lower elevations along the eastern slope of the mountains. Here they gathered the nuts of the piñon pine. By winter they retired to villages in the Carson Valley where the women spent long hours weaving beautiful baskets and the men prepared arrowheads.

The arrival of white men signaled serious changes for the Washoe. Settlers claimed their hunting and fishing grounds, felled their piñon trees for building and fuel, and brought cattle that destroyed the meadow plants upon which the Washoe depended. Unable to withstand the invasion, the native population dwindled. Most tribes

History

stopped coming to the lake for the annual migration and stayed in Carson Valley. Their descendants settled in small colonies on their ancient lands. A number of years ago, the Washoe were instrumental in creating a Washoe Indian Cultural Exhibit at the Tallac Historic Site. They now operate the Meeks Bay Resort as well. This gives the Washoe tribe a modern-day presence on the lake and an occasion to revive their historic summer experience.

Opening the Trail to California

The Spaniards who settled in California in the eighteenth century did not venture into the mountain range they called the *Sierra Nevada*, or Snowy Range. When Americans began looking westward to settle California's fertile valleys, emigrants attempted to find a route west across the Sierra Nevada to Sutter's Fort. The first group to succeed crossed the forbidding barrier in 1841, but without their wagons which they had abandoned in the Nevada desert. Their route is believed to have been near Sonora Pass.

The initial branch of the California Emigrant Trail was opened in 1844 by a group known as the Stephens-Townsend-Murphy party, led by Elisha Stephens. Their herculean effort must be admired, for this wagon train had traveled in unknown country ever since leaving the established Oregon Trail in Idaho. While traversing the Nevada desert, they encountered a Paiute who scratched a map in the sand that showed a route following a river (the Truckee) to the summit.

The Stephens party reached the site of present-day Truckee on November 14, discovering to their dismay that the Truckee River bent south, not west toward the visible summit. They discussed the problem, deciding to split up. Six men and two women on horses and mules followed the Truckee River south, and it can be assumed that they were the first Americans to walk along the shores of Lake Tahoe. Their probable route to the Sacramento Valley followed the Rubicon River, bringing them safely to Sutter's Fort in early December.

The other group of emigrants decided to leave all but five wagons on the shores of Donner Lake. Moses Schallenberger and two other young men offered to stay

History

with the abandoned wagons and their contents until they could be brought over. As winter storms raged and their supplies dwindled, Schallenberger's two friends decided to attempt the pass on crudely fashioned snowshoes. Moses, too weak to accompany them, was left entirely alone until his rescue in February.

The remaining emigrants in five wagons made it over the pass in two feet of snow but only reached Big Bend before they were forced

Courtesy of Donner Memorial State Park

Hauling a wagon over the granite walls of Donner Summit.

to make camp for the winter. A baby was born to one of the Murphy women, and the women, children and two men were left at this campsite. The able-bodied men continued on foot to Sutter's Fort.

Moses Schallenberger and those at Big Bend were not rescued until late in February. The miracle of this tale is that all survived. Because of the determination of the group and the cool leadership of Elisha Stephens, a route to California was found.

In 1994, a mountain overlooking Donner Pass was named Mount Stephens, celebrating the 150th anniversary of the first wagons over the Sierra.

The Ill-fated Donner Party

The tragic story of the 1846 wagon train known as the Donner Party is memorialized in the names Donner Lake, Donner Summit, Donner Peak and Donner Memorial State Park.

Illinois farmers George and Jacob Donner and their friend James Reed set out for California in the summer of 1846. They were taken in by glowing reports in Lansford Hastings' *The Emigrants' Guide to*

History

California and Oregon that described wild clover five feet high and hollyhocks and sweet william blooming everywhere in winter. Harsh Illinois winters and summers filled with sickness convinced the Donners that California was the only place to spend the remaining years of their lives. They were neophytes on the trail but did not employ a guide, preferring instead the written word of author Hastings that promised to shave 200 miles off any previously used route. Nor did they accept the advice of experienced mountain men who warned them that no wagons could pass through the country described in Hasting's shortcut. This decision cost them dearly, for they spent a month hacking their way foot by foot through steep canyons in Utah, taxing men and animals almost to the breaking point. A disconsolate wagon train with no leader crossed the Nevada desert weeks later than planned.

It was early November with snow already on the peaks at the pass when most of the group began the ascent from Truckee Meadows (Reno) toward the summit of the Sierra. They were forced to return to Donner Lake after failing to cross Donner Pass during a fierce snowstorm. One family used Moses Schallenberger's cabin and others made crude shelters nearby. Their suffering is hard to comprehend. Many died either from starvation or attempting to cross the mountains.

The Donner family and their drivers were the last to leave Truckee Meadows. Six miles northeast of Donner Lake a wagon overturned while descended toward Alder Creek. While fixing a broken axle, George Donner cut his hand badly. The injury and a snowstorm forced the group to make camp immediately. All but a few children would spend their last days at the camp, starving to death in inadequate, cold, shelters.

Archaeologists and historians continue their research of this tragedy and identification of the sites of the winter encampments. Donner Memorial State Park and the U.S. Forest Service Donner Day Camp both offer interpretive exhibits describing the travails of these ill-fated emigrants.

Early Days in Truckee

In 1863, seventeen years after the Donner tragedy, Truckee was first settled when Joe Gray built a cabin near the turnpike road on which

History

he arrived. This was the year that the Central Pacific Company began building the country's first transcontinental railroad. The cabin was known as Gray's Station and became a way station for travelers over the Sierra. The next year J. McConnell built another cabin not far away which he sold to S. S. Coburn before the year was out. Coburn added more buildings, and the little town became known as Coburn's Station serving the construction crews of the Central Pacific Railroad between 1864 and 1868.

The Dutch Flat to Donner Lake Toll Road was built along sections of the former emigrant road and the railroad right-of-way in 1866. It brought railroad workers and supplies and even a few hardy tourists to see the beauty of the Sierra Nevada up close. At the east end of Donner Lake, a small town soon boasted two hotels, a general store and sawmill. This cluster of establishments had the proud name of Donner Lake City.

Ten thousand Chinese laborers braved summer dust and winter snows in 1867 and 1868 to lay the tracks and hack thirteen tunnels through the granite at a rate of seven inches a day. The Chinese,

as well as lumbermen and construction workers, built their shanties along the Truckee River near Coburn's Station.

When the first trains rolled through town in June of 1868, thousands lined the tracks to cheer. A month later, the town burned to the ground. It was soon rebuilt and christened Truckee, in honor of the Paiute who showed Elisha Stephens where to find the pass over the Sierra.

Gold in California

When gold was discovered in 1848, the world rushed to California. Those already in the West headed for the hills to pan for gold, among them a group of Mormons. They did not stay long, however, for Brigham Young called them home to Salt Lake City. Their journey east established the route over Carson Pass that soon became the preferred trail to reach Hangtown (Placerville). Thousands of wagons were hauled over the Sierra via the Carson Emigrant Trail which followed the Carson River from Carson Valley into Hope Valley. From there it skirted the shores of Red Lake to a fearful climb over the first pass. A second summit was traversed at

History

a point between Thimble and Covered Wagon Peaks in present-day Kirkwood Ski Resort. This pass above 9,200 feet is the highest crossed by any wagons on the trek west.

The town of Genoa, Nevada, at the eastern edge of the Sierra became an important trading post for thousands of emigrants. This small settlement was also home to one of the area's legends, "Snowshoe Thompson," who strapped on his 10-foot skis and carried the winter mail across the mountains between Genoa and Placerville from 1856 to 1876.

Settlers at South Lake Tahoe

The first major road was built to encourage emigrants to come to Placerville from the Nevada territory. Called the Placerville Road, it was completed in 1858. By 1859 with the discovery of gold and silver in Virginia City, commerce picked up as wagon masters and ranchers ferried supplies to feed the miners of the Comstock mining bonanza. A toll road, named the Bonanza Road by newspapers, crossed the Tahoe Basin near the route of today's Pioneer Trail to Daggett Pass (Kingsbury Grade) and north to

Genoa in the Carson Valley. By 1863 traffic was routed along the lake and over Spooner Summit. In that year it was estimated that 5,000 teamsters were employed hauling everything from machinery and dairy products to silk for ladies' gowns through South Lake Tahoe to Virginia City. That same year Glen Brook House opened its opulent rooms to travelers along the road and remained one of Tahoe's most famous hostelries for a decade. When the Central Pacific Railroad through Reno was completed in 1868, a faster more reliable way for goods and people to reach the mines signaled the end of the Bonanza Trail. However the Glen Brook House still lured travelers by advertising that you could reach its front portal in 20 short hours from the Bay cities.

Lumbering Decimates Tahoe's Forests

Small operators established lumber mills surrounding Lake Tahoe to build the local communities along the lakeshore. But it was the insatiable demand for wood to shore up the Virginia City silver mines that brought entrepreneurs to the area. Among the most famous was the Bliss family who founded the Carson and Tahoe

History

Lumber and Fluming Company. Trees were felled at a horrifying rate, sent downhill in flumes, then rafted across the lake to the Bliss mill at Glenbrook. Here Bliss built a railroad up to Spooner Summit where finished lumber was put into flumes for a speedy journey to the Carson Valley. There it was loaded onto the Virginia and Truckee Railroad bound for Virginia City. Incline Village takes its name from the Sierra Nevada Wood and Lumber Company's Incline Tramway. With a length of 4,000 feet and vertical lift of 1,400 feet the tramway carried lumber from the shores of the lake east up to the summit on the first leg of the journey to the Virginia City mines. It is estimated that 30 million board feet of lumber was supplied by the Glenbrook and Incline mills annually during the 1870s. At the same time four local lumber companies invested $3.5 million in 21 miles of pipeline and 45 miles of flumes to carry millions of gallons of water daily from Marlette Lake to the Virginia City mines.

By the end of the century the character of the forest around the lake had been changed forever. Sugar pines disappeared and the finest fir, yellow pine and Jeffrey were cut, leaving many areas absent of seed stock for new pines and open to an invasion of chaparral brush. Smaller white fir, not desirable for lumber, remained. Their seedlings proliferated, growing well in shade and leading to the single species forest seen in many South Shore locations today. It is estimated that more than 60 percent of the white fir were victims of the eight-year drought from 1987 to 1994. The task facing the U.S. Forest Service and the communities of the lake is to find a way to remove the dead trees without producing scars on the land and roads that create erosion runoff that will reduce Lake Tahoe's famous water clarity.

The Railroad Center of Truckee

Truckee has known good times and hard times over the years, but because of the railroad, it has remained a center of commerce in the Sierra Nevada. In the 1870s lumbermen swarmed to the area to fell local forests to feed the steam engines of the railroad and to support the deep silver mines in Virginia City, Nevada. In winter, frozen ponds provided ice to keep fruit shipments cold on their trip to market and to cool miners in the hot tunnels of Virginia City's

History

mines. When the hills near town were barren of trees and the silver mines played out, Truckee was in a decline. One of the town's leading citizens, C.F. McGlashan, decided to put Truckee on the map as a tourist mecca. He created an ice palace in the center of town and talked the railroad management into running excursion trains to Truckee for winter carnivals. The Dutch Flat to Donner Lake Road was taken over by the state to create a proper road for the fast growing number of automobiles. In 1928 the automobile era began in earnest when State Highway 37 was realigned and paved to create U.S. 40. This transcontinental highway brought traffic jams to Truckee's main street. The area became a stopping place but not a particularly desirable resort. Recession and war brought tough economic times until the 1960 Winter Olympic Games at Squaw Valley ushered in ski resort development. When Interstate 80 was completed in 1964, traffic bypassed the town bringing peace to Downtown Truckee and to summer vacationers at Donner Lake.

Truckee Ice Palace.

Courtesy of Donner Memorial State Park

History

Lake Tahoe Beckons Summer Visitors

Meanwhile, along Lake Tahoe's South Shore, deforested land became available for grazing or small summer settlements. While the end of the logging era depleted the permanent population of the area, the lake was being discovered as a summer tourist haven. Bliss dismantled his Glenbrook railroad operations and moved them to Tahoe City where he established the Lake Tahoe Railway and Transportation Company to carry passengers from the Central Pacific in Truckee to Tahoe City. He brought in *The Tahoe*, a lovely 169-foot steamship which soon became the "Queen of the Lake," carrying passengers and mail to homes and hotels along the shore. In 1900 rail service from Truckee to Tahoe brought tourists to the Tahoe Tavern, a magnificent hotel that opened in that year. The railroad connection provided yet another summer excursion possibility. Travelers could ride the train from San Francisco to Truckee then on to Tahoe City where a steamer delivered them to Glenbrook and a stagecoach bound for Carson City. Here the Virginia and Truckee Railroad offered service back to the main rail line in Reno.

With ship transportation around the lake assured, fine hostelries and more modest summer camps appeared. Rubicon Park Lodge and Lucky Baldwin's famous Tallac Hotel opened their doors to wealthier tourists. Dance floors were built over the water with casinos for evening entertainment. Boating on the lake, swimming, fishing and horseback riding were the sports of the day. Tallac Hotel was known as the "Saratoga of the Pacific." By 1927, however, Lucky Baldwin's heirs demolished the buildings, sold off the salvage and placed "Keep Out" signs on the neighboring property. Years later the land was sold to the U.S. Forest Service, along with other private lodges and buildings on nearby properties. This entire section of the South Shore between Highway 89 and the lakeshore is now the Tallac Historic Site. Just east of the historic site, Richardson's Resort at Camp Richardson continues to host visitors as it has since 1926.

New Tourists, Automobiles and New Roads

The advent of automobiles and, in the 1930s, paved roads to the lake brought a new wave of summer tourists. Summer cabins were built at Fallen Leaf, Angora and Echo

History

Lakes. The developments at both Fallen Leaf and Echo Lakes were owned primarily by professors' families from both Stanford and the University of California. At Fallen Leaf a lodge was created with rustic accommodations and a central dining hall. Now known as the Stanford Camp, it is run by the Alumni Association of Stanford University and the cabins in all these locations have been passed down to descendants of the original owners.

Winter Tourists and Gaming

Hardy skiers had been coming to Tahoe Tavern and Granlibakken Ski Area near Tahoe City to enjoy the slopes since 1928. The Sierra Club Clair Tappaan Lodge began hosting skiers at the Ski School Klein, started by Bill Klein and his brother, Fred. In 1939, Sugar Bowl opened its pioneer ski resort with the area's first chair lift. On the South Shore Sierra Ski Ranch offered downhill skiing in the early 1950s. But it was the 1960 Winter Olympic Games at Squaw Valley that ushered in ski development on a large scale. On the North Shore developers built lifts and homes in beautiful Alpine Meadows, and Northstar-at-Tahoe was built as the area's first full-service resort, complete with golf course, homes, condominiums, and recreation facilities. Heavenly Valley Ski Area became well known when its founder Chris Kuraisa invited Stein Eriksen to direct the ski school.

Early motoring at Lake Tahoe.

Courtesy of the Lake Tahoe Historical Society

History

Kuraisa also put in the area's first tram to open runs with some of the best views of Lake Tahoe. The Hugh Killebrew family bought the resort from Kuraisa and expanded it to include trails on the Nevada side of the mountain. In 1977, when Hugh was tragically killed in a airplane accident, his twenty-three-year-old son Bill took over. He nursed the corporation through droughts and made it profitable. In 1990, he sold it to the Kamori Kanko Company of Japan. A few years later the resort, one of the premier ski resorts in the world, was bought by Les Otten's American Ski Corporation. Major expansion includes condominiums and hotels at the bottom of the new gondola to be completed before 2004.

Year-round tourism fueled a building boom of condominiums and homes in the 1960s and 1970s. Highrise casino hotels sprang up filling the skyline on the Nevada side of the South Shore. When citizens discovered degradation of Lake Tahoe's famous water clarity, they mobilized to form the League to Save Lake Tahoe. The group has worked hard to make the Tahoe Regional Planning Agency live up to its charter to protect the Tahoe Basin's environmental health. The South Shore grew so rapidly in the 1970s that a new California city, South Lake Tahoe, was established by the voters.

In 1993, Truckee, the oldest town in the Sierra, finally became an incorporated city. The current population is nearing 14,000. The Truckee Donner Land Trust was founded in 1990 to preserve the area's historical, recreational and scenic lands. Among its many projects is a major expansion of Donner Memorial State Park to be completed in 2002. It has already preserved sections of the Emigrant Trail and is building a Donner Lake Rim Trail.

The Tahoe Conservancy

To fund efforts needed to keep Lake Tahoe blue and clear, California voters created the Tahoe Conservancy. It began operation in 1985. Close to $200 million has been dispensed to acquire more than 7,000 acres of environmentally sensitive lands and wildlife habitat as well as to provide funding for erosion control projects to prevent further degradation of the legendary blue waters. Lands are being restored and public access to lakefront areas has been provided in 34 projects.

History

Recognizing the need for expanded recreation opportunities in the basin, the Conservancy has helped with acquisition of rights-of-way and construction of many miles of hiking, biking and cross-country ski trails.

The Tahoe Summit

President Clinton and Vice President Gore attended the first environmental forum for the future of Lake Tahoe in the summer of 1997. The meeting ended with a precedent-setting pledge to fix drought-damaged forests and continue the efforts of the Conservancy to keep the lake's fabled blue waters clear. The Environmental Improvement Program was established to bring together private and public monies totalling $1 billion toward these important tasks.

Carson Pass and Hope Valley

Carson Pass and Hope Valley have remained relatively untouched by development and, with the exception of the Kirkwood Resort just west of Caples Lake, the area is known best for its beautiful scenery, superb hiking and fishing. Two small lodges, Caples Lake Lodge and Sorensen's Resort, continue to attract overnight guests who want a quiet retreat in a wilderness setting. Kirkwood Resort has become a premier year-round recreation site offering tennis, swimming, riding, hiking, and mountain biking to a growing number of summer visitors.

Naming Lake Tahoe

Lake Tahoe was of only passing interest to early emigrants who struggled over the Sierra Nevada in the 1840s. It was first mentioned by John Charles Frémont in the report of his 1844 expedition who named the body of water Lake Bonpland in honor of a French botanist. Maps of the 1850s and 1860s carried the name Lake Bigler, honoring a governor of California. There were those who did not like the name because Governor Bigler was a sympathizer of the South in the Civil War, and Unionists did not want the lake named after him. Finally, citizens and several newspaper editors christened the lake "Tahoe," a corruption of a Washoe Indian word meaning *big waters*. But, it was not until 70 years later, in 1945, that the California State Legislature officially changed the name to Lake Tahoe.

© Ellie Huggins

Donner Lake from Donner Summit.

Natural History

Geologic History

The geologic story of California began when the sea covered the land. Three times, over eons, the mountains rose, were eroded, and sank beneath the sea. The last period of great uplift produced the Sierra Nevada we see today. The 400-mile Sierra Nevada is one of the longest single mountain ranges in the world. For this reason it is correct to use the singular *Sierra*. The southern peaks are the highest and include Mount Whitney at 14,495 feet.

The granite bedrock of the Sierra was formed when two plates of the earth's crust, an ocean plate (Pacific Plate) and a continental plate (American Plate), moved toward each other. A process called subduction began. The thin but heavy plate of ocean floor slid under the lighter, higher riding continental plate and remelted in a crustal recycling system. The resulting molten rock either rose to the surface in volcanic eruptions or cooled slowly underground into a mass, or pluton, of crystalline rock. In this way, the batholith of granite became the bedrock of the future Sierra Nevada range.

The plates of the earth's crust are never still. They continue to move up and down, slide past each other, and thrust upward as in the devastating 1994 Los Angeles earthquake. The Sierra Range is still rising, a few centimeters a year, not so that we would notice, but in mostly small quakes that only sensitive instruments can detect. Occasionally though, the earth rumbles and you can feel a quake. In 1872 a major quake produced a vertical displacement of 17 feet in the Owens Valley. The mountains of California are beautiful because of the activity of its earthquakes.

Between 15 and 30 million years before humans settled California, a series of cataclysmic events took place. Volcanoes along the Sierra crest spewed clouds of ash and sent rivers of lava and volcanic mud across the landscape. Many of the peaks in the Truckee and Carson Pass area are remnants of those ancient volcanoes. Then a series of movements along faults uplifted the entire block of the range, creating a steep escarpment along the eastern edge. About three million years ago, a block of the earth's crust dropped down creating a deep rift where Lake Tahoe now lies. Subsequent lava flows dammed its drainage, setting the stage for filling the lake.

Natural History

Starting one million years ago, the Ice Ages brought a series of glaciers to the region scooping out bowls at Donner Lake, Emerald Bay, Fallen Leaf and Cascade Lakes. These same glaciers scraped across the bedrock granite of the Desolation Wilderness, polished it smooth and left erratic boulders dotting the granitic landscape like giant bowling balls. Moraines of rock and rubble at the outermost edges of the glaciers dammed the outlet of Lake Tahoe. In one glacial period an ice dam formed at the outlet to the Truckee River, allowing the water level to rise 600 feet. The ice dam broke and a flood of water, rock and ice cascaded down the Truckee River, carving the canyon north and east toward Reno. Only 10,000 years ago, the last of the great glaciers began to melt, sending torrents of water to fill Lake Tahoe and gouge out river valleys flowing east and west from the crest. The stage was set for the arrival of the flora and fauna we see today.

Plants and Animals of the Region

The land in this region varies in elevation from about 6,000 to 10,000 feet, forcing plants and animals to survive with an average growing season between 60 and 120 days. Snow can cover the ground from early November until mid-July. At lake level the dominant tree species are white fir, Jeffrey and lodgepole pine. Between 1860 and 1900 loggers clear-cut the basin of the finest fir, yellow pine and Jeffrey pine that shared the forest with the sugar pine, a stately tree with outstretched branches holding foot-long cones. Sadly, only a few virgin stands of sugar pine remain today. Above the lake at 7,000 feet red fir trees grow forming a cathedral-like canopy that does not allow much undergrowth, making it a perfect place to hike or ski. Graceful hemlocks and western white pine grow in clusters at tree line along with lodgepole and whitebark pine.

For those willing to climb, beautiful gardens of miniature alpine flowers hug the rocky terrain above 9,000 feet, turning it into a painter's palette of color during July and August. The Sierra juniper, that ancient giant that stands sentinel on windswept ridges, can be found along the Pacific Crest Trail. Summer visitors to the area will most often be greeted by fields of blue lupine near roadsides and along trails, while open meadows glow with yellow

sugar pine

red fir

hemlock

Natural History

mule ears. Wildflower lovers will find many trails into the high country where they can enjoy a multitude of colorful gardens to please the eye and thrill any photographer.

The animals who remain all year must be hardy, hibernating in winter or able to store or find food when snow covers the ground. Most-often encountered are perky chipmunks dashing across the forest floor and ground squirrels standing outside their holes ever-watchful for danger, a well as an occasional marmot or porcupine. Mule deer are everywhere in the summer, and black bears raid unprotected garbage cans. Coyotes and raccoons are frequent foragers in residential areas. They appreciate the easy dining on dog food and garbage. Very occasionally, you might be surprised by the winter visit of a bobcat. (See below) Resident ducks and Canada geese are omnipresent, while overhead, the lucky observer may spot an osprey or bald eagle. The eagles nest in some locations along the southwest shore of Lake Tahoe, while ospreys can be seen on top of pine snags along the West Shore and at Donner Lake. Nests can be seen from some vantage points in D.L. Bliss State Park or from an Emerald Bay cruise.

© Peg Paul

Rare winter visit of this handsome bobcat at the author's house. Notice the tufts on the ears. This is its identifying feature.

Natural History

Lake Tahoe is not the highest nor is it the deepest lake in the world, but its setting, nestled in a deep valley between towering mountains, makes it one of the most beautiful. The clarity of its water is legendary, taking on the color of cobalt during summer days.

Lake Tahoe lies at 6,223 feet with one third of the lake in the state of Nevada and two thirds in California. It is 22 miles long and 12 miles wide with a maximum depth of 1,645 feet. When full it holds approximately 122 million acre feet of water, enough to cover Texas 8.5 inches deep or the state of California 14.5 inches. The Lake Tahoe Basin is roughly 480 square miles, larger than the state of Rhode Island. Average snowfall is 300 inches. With an estimated 250 sunny days per year, it is a vacation paradise.

Starting in 1986 and continuing through 1992 a drought forced the ski industry to install snowmaking, a costly endeavor for resorts that used to rely on Mother Nature for 10 to 12 feet of snow per season. Lake Tahoe fell to an historic low below the natural rim in 1991, drying up the Truckee River below Tahoe City. The winter of 1994-95, however, became one of the wettest winters in recorded history, only 1951-52 and 1982-83 being wetter. The winter of 1996-97 brought another disaster; so much rain fell between Christmas and early January that the Truckee River jumped its banks, flooding homes, carrying away trees, propane tanks and parts of decks and forcing evacuation of riverside residents. Donner Lake rose so high that many docks were destroyed. Reno experienced the worst flood in its history.

The snow pack and its water content are important not only to the plants and animals of the region, but as water supplies for thirsty Nevadans. A fact not usually understood is that Lake Tahoe has been dammed to raise the water level six feet above the natural rim of 6,223 feet above sea level. Water released from the dam is a primary source for residents and farmers of the Reno region. In 1993 the lake spilled over the natural rim for the first time since September 1991 and regular releases followed the wet winter of 1994-95. However, the dam could not hold back enough water to prevent the floods of 1997. Since then Pacific currents known as El Niño and La Niña have created unusual weather patterns.

Lodging

When planning a trip to Lake Tahoe, Truckee or Carson Pass, there are three central numbers to call for information about hotels, motels and condominiums. You can ask for the summer or winter planners that have detailed information on most of the facilities. Their websites have links to a variety of accommodations.

North Shore Reservations
888-434-1262 — www.tahoe-4-u.com

South Shore Reservations
800-288-2463 — www.virtualtahoe.com

Incline Village/Crystal Bay
800-468-2463 — www.gotahoe.com

If you know what price range, location and kind of facility you want, this may be the only call you need to make.

Truckee, Squaw Valley, Northstar-at-Tahoe and Kirkwood have central reservations, and will gladly send brochures or connect you to a property management service that handles private homes.

Truckee Chamber of Commerce
530-587-2757 — www.truckee.com

Northstar-at-Tahoe - Central Reservations
800-466-6784 — www.skinorthstar.com

Squaw Valley - Central Reservations
800-403-0206 — www.squaw.com

Kirkwood - Central Reservations
800-967-7500 — www.skikirkwood.com

Lodging

Vacation Rentals – Lake Tahoe
Here are some of the larger management companies.

Vacation Station
800-841-7443 www.vacationstation.net

The 120 homes and condominiums with Vacation Station are located in Incline Village and Crystal Bay.

Lake Tahoe Accommodations
800-544-3234 www.tahoeaccommodations.com

The company offers the largest selection of luxury vacation rentals around the lake. They have four offices, in South Lake Tahoe, Stateline, Incline Village and Tahoe City. The office in South Lake Tahoe is open seven days a week. The units are located in prime locations.

Lake Tahoe Lodging
800-654-5253 www.vacationsatlaketahoe.com

Their 100 special units range from cabins to corporate or celebrity retreats, some on the lake or with fabulous lake views. Their homes have from one to eight bedrooms, and can accommodate from two to 20 guests.

Lake Tahoe Lodgings
800-242-5387 www.tahoe-estates.com

The company manages 200 privately owned properties on the South Shore. Their properties can handle from two to 24 people in executive homes, condominiums and chalets.

Tahoe Management
800-624-3887 www.at-tahoe.com

Their 125 properties are all on the South Shore in Nevada.

Lodging

Squaw Valley, Truckee, Donner Summit Vacation Rentals

Squaw Valley Accommodations — 800-330-3451 is run by Squaw Valley Realty, and books the Christy Inn and manages about 70 homes and condominiums in the valley. www.tahoesbest.com/Lodging/svr.htm

Donner Lake Realty — 800-392-5253 specializes in mountain homes on and around Donner Lake. Many homes have privileges at the private beach and some have their own docks on the lake. www.donner-lake.com

Martis Valley Vacation Rentals — 800-287-7685 specializes in Northstar homes and condominiums with access to all the Northstar facilities. www.mvvr.com

Ski West Vacation Rentals — 800-339-5535 manages 110 homes and condominiums at Tahoe Donner and Northstar. www.skiwestvacations.com

Soda Springs Rentals — 530-426-1031 manages properties on one of the Serene Lakes or other woodsy retreats in the Soda Springs area.

Castle Peak Vacation Rentals — 888-253-5551 specializes in homes at Serene Lakes, some on the lakes. They offer tender loving care, shovel the driveway and entrances, turn on the heat and even leave a bottle of wine in the refrigerator. www.castlepeak.com

Second Home Care — 530-582-0220 specializes in homes in the Tahoe Donner area. www.tahoe2ndhomes.com

Truckee Mountain Vacation Rentals — 800-805-8199 manages homes in the Tahoe Donner area. www.tmvr.com

Vacation Property Management — 800-748-6725 specializes in homes in the Tahoe Donner area. Each home is opened before you arrive, preheated in winter with driveways plowed. www.vpmrentals.com

Lodging

North Lake Tahoe and Truckee have been tourist meccas since the Central Pacific started train service in 1869. The region boasts of several historic lodges and bed and breakfast inns that offer delightful accommodations. South Lake Tahoe and Carson Pass/Hope Valley have been welcoming summer tourists since the late 1800s. We have listed inns that offer unique overnight experiences year-round. Lodging is listed alphabetically by location.

Always Inn - Tahoe Bed and Breakfast

Located on the banks of the Yuba River in old Soda Springs, the former Traverse Inn has been remodelled inside. Three rooms are on the main level. One room features a queen bed with an electric free-standing stove and bath with a jacuzzi tub and shower. Another has a king-size bed and a large bathroom with tub and shower. The downstairs bedroom is perfect for a family, with a king bed and a trundle that makes two singles. All rooms have TV/VCRs and the inn has a large collection of videos. The great room features a copper floor-to-ceiling gas fireplace with a picture window and a large deck facing the Yuba River and the Soda Springs ski slopes.

Always Inn
P.O. Box 861
Soda Springs, CA 95728
530-426-3010 877-56-TAHOE
Fax 530-426-1100
www.alwaysinn.net

Special Features:
The inn is only minutes from the four Donner Summit downhill ski areas and the extensive Royal Gorge cross-country trails.

The full country breakfast will start your day and mid-day complimentary hot soup, tea and coffee is always available. They will even provide dinner from a selected menu with advance notice.

Lodging

Ice Lakes Lodge
1111 Soda Springs Road
P.O. Box 805
Soda Springs, CA 95728
530-426-7660 888-462-2683
Fax 530-426-7667
www.icelakeslodge.com

Special Features:
The large dining room with its wrap-around porch is sure to become a favorite. The lodge has conference rooms and can schedule weddings and corporate retreats at this prime location on Donner Summit.

All of the outdoor activities of the area are just steps from the lodge. Winter guests can ice skate on the lake. In summer the lake has a nice beach for swimming, while hiking and mountain biking opportunities abound nearby.

Ice Lakes Lodge

Vicki and Matt Williams, 28-year residents of Soda Springs, tore down the old Serene Lakes Lodge to build the new Ice Lakes Lodge right on the shores of Serene Lake. There are twenty-six rooms, twenty with lake views and the rest with creek views. Two rooms on the ground floor have handicap access. One has a king and the other two queen beds. Rooms feature custom woodwork and old photos of the days when ice was harvested at the lake. Each room has either a private balcony or patio. The restaurant on the premises is described on page 57.

© Dan Wendin

Ice Lakes Lodge.

Lodging

Rainbow Lodge

The Big Bend of the Yuba River is filled with history. The original part of this beautiful mountain lodge was built in the 1880s and served as a stage stop on the Dutch Flat to Donner Lake Road. When the Lincoln Highway was built in 1931, additions to the hotel were made to accommodate the growing number of visitors to the area. The current lodge, operated by Royal Gorge, retains the feeling of the past while offering comfortable lodging and excellent cuisine in the Engadine Cafe. See page 57 in "Dining." There are 32 cozy rooms, a bridal suite and a family suite for two adults and two children. Breakfast is included in the room price.

After your day of activity, you can sit in the guest lounge by a roaring fire, or visit the bar with the original spittoon at its base and look at the historic photos adorning the walls.

The lodge keeps a large supply of games and books to fill the evening in front of the fire.

Rainbow Lodge
530-426-3871 800-500-3871 also 800-666-3871 www.royalgorge/ accommodation/rainbow.htm

Directions:
Take I-80 to the Rainbow Rd. exit. Drive west one-half mile to the lodge.

Special Features:
The historic location on the banks of the Yuba offers spectacular hiking, fishing and skiing right from the front door. On winter weekends free shuttle buses take nordic skiers to Royal Gorge, where experienced skiers can take the 22-mile interconnect trail from the summit direct to the lodge at the end of the day, snow conditions permitting. The four Donner Summit downhill areas are less than 20 minutes away.

Lodging

Sugar Bowl Resort
P.O. Box 5
Norden, CA 95724
530-426-9000
www.sugarbowl.com

Directions:
Take the Magic Carpet Gondola on Donner Pass Rd. one-half mile east of Donner Summit.

Special Features:
Ski weeks are described in "Downhill Skiing" on page 222. Photos of early-day skiing at Sugar Bowl adorn the walls of The Belt Room bar where you can relax after a day on the slopes, while the dining room serves up sumptuous meals at dinner.

Sugar Bowl Lodge

The Bavarian-style lodge was built in 1939 for this first destination resort in the Sierra Nevada. In the 1940s, skiers, including famous Hollywood stars, boarded the "Snowball Express" train from San Francisco to Norden where a tractor-drawn sleigh took them on a 40-minute ride to the resort. Today guests ride the Magic Carpet Gondola from the parking garage on Donner Pass Road to a world away from the hustle, bustle and stresses of today's life. When you stay here, there is no waiting for buses or chaining up the car in the morning. You can hit the slopes as soon as they open.

© Ellie Huggins

Winter lodging at the historic Sugar Bowl Lodge is steps from the slopes.

Lodging

Bock's 10064 House

Kent and Monica Bock invite you into their Victorian home which they constructed on the banks of the Truckee River. They have three rooms, each with private bath. Two bedrooms have double beds and the master bedroom features a queen-size bed. They offer a full breakfast as well as wine and cheese in the afternoon.

Their home is just across the river from downtown Truckee with its many dining opportunities and interesting shops.

Bock's 10064 House
10064 South East River Rd.
P.O. Box 1863
Truckee, CA 96160
530-582-1923
Weekends and holidays only.

Special Features:
The Bocks are outdoor enthusiasts and can give advice about hikes, bike rides and skiing. While you are out enjoying your skiing or hiking, they will make dinner reservations for you.

Hania's Bed and Breakfast Inn

You can stay with Hania Jarmoc in her lovely white house with blue trim on High Street overlooking Truckee. Hania speaks English, Polish, German and Russian. She offers very special American and European breakfasts with many specialties such as Polish-style potato pancakes with vanilla sugar or crêpes with cinnamon apples or cream cheese. If you prefer, she will serve you breakfast in bed. Three rooms have log furniture, queen beds, private baths and TV with VCR.

Hania's Bed and Breakfast Inn
10098 High St.
Truckee, CA 96161
530-582-5775 888-600-3735
www.truckee.com/hania

Richardson House

Richardson House
10154 High Street
Truckee, CA 96161
530-587-5388 888-229-0365
www.richardsonhouse.com

Special Features:
A full continental breakfast with baked goods and a hot dish is served in the Victorian dining room, complete with a breakfront that once belonged to Mr. Florsheim of Florsheim shoes. Wine and cheese are in the parlor that features a player piano as well as a modern TV with VCR. You can walk to dinner at any of the many wonderful Truckee restaurants.

The Richardson House was built in the 1870s by Warren Richardson, a lumber baron of Truckee. The Victorian residence has undergone a complete restoration to bring the property back to its nineteenth century splendor. Much of the beautiful woodwork is original, as is the wainscot created to look like tooled leather in the front hall and up the stairs.

Eight rooms feature genuine antiques, and each with a different theme. The Tamsen and George Donner Room has a queen bed and private bath with a claw foot tub for two. There are two, two-room suites that share a bath. All other rooms have private baths.

Richardson House is on High Street above town.

Lodging

The River Street Inn

The stone building on the corner of River Street and Highway 267 has a rich history that includes a boarding house for ice cutters, a bordello and even a clandestine site for making bootleg liquor during prohibition. New owners have redecorated the eleven rooms and front parlor. Ten rooms have queen-size beds with cozy down comforters and one room has twins. All rooms have private baths, TV and VCR.

The River Street Inn
10009 East River Street
Truckee, CA 96161
530-550-9290 fax 530-582-2391
www.bbhost.com/theriverstreetinn

Special Features:
Morning breakfast features fresh bagels, muffins and fruit plus coffee and tea. Although they don't serve wine and cheese, many groups bring their own into the comfortable parlor. Truckee's great restaurants are just steps away.

The Truckee Hotel

The Truckee Hotel in downtown Truckee has been in continuous operation since the 1870s. The owners have completely renovated the building to reflect its Victorian heritage and were awarded the prestigious 1994 California Heritage Council Award of Merit for historic preservation. You really can step back into Truckee's past in rooms that are uniquely decorated in nineteenth-century style. Eight rooms or suites have private baths. The rest of the rooms come with sink, mirror and towels in the room and share a bath across or down the hall.

The Truckee Hotel
P.O. Box 884
Truckee, CA 96160
530-587-4444 800-659-6921
www.truckeehotel.com

Directions:
At the corner of Highway 267 and Bridge Street in downtown Truckee.

Special Features:
The management thoughtfully provides ear plugs for those unaccustomed to a downtown location next to the railroad, but then that is part of the charm of the place.

Breakfast is served every day in the parlor on the first floor. Hors d'oeuvres and wine are served before dinner on weekends and holidays.

Christy Inn
1604 Christy Lane
Olympic Valley, CA 96146
530-583-3451 800-330-3451
www.tahoesbest.com/Lodging/
svr.htm

Special Features:
There is at present no breakfast service. Graham's restaurant is in the front of the building and can handle wedding parties of up to 100 people, particularly in the summer when the deck is available. See "Dining Out" on page 62.

Poole's Guest House
1509 Sandy Way
P.O. Box 3768
Olympic Valley, CA 96146
Voice and message phone:
530-412-5436
www.lodgingusa.com

Special Features:
The best way to make a reservation is on the web but before you do, you can make a virtual tour of the house.

The two upstairs bedrooms, one with a king and one with a queen bed can be rented as a suite. The views from these rooms are spectacular. Guests may access the internet at any time.

Christy Inn

This historic lodge was formerly the home of the Poulsens, who founded Squaw Valley. They built the home for their large family with one of the valley's choicest mountain views. The inn has seven rooms, each decorated in a different theme.

One large room with a king-size bed plus a trundle has its own electric fireplace. Four rooms have queen-size beds and private baths with showers. Two rooms have two queens and bathrooms with tub and shower.

Poole's Guest House

Located above Squaw Valley with fantastic mountain views, hosts Herman and Ann Poole offer three very special guest rooms in their mountain chalet. It is not a traditional bed and breakfast, rather the gourmet kitchen is available for guests to use and the Pooles have coffee, tea and hot chocolate ready at any time in the morning. You are treasured guests in their home.

Each room has satellite TV, although the beautiful livingroom with its cathedral ceiling beckons most guests, particularly if they have decided to cook in.

Lodging

River Ranch Lodge

This historic lodge on the Truckee River dates back over a century when the Deer Park Inn became a fashionable watering place on the narrow gauge railway from Truckee to Tahoe City. The current lodge was rebuilt in 1950 into a fishing lodge. During the 1960 Winter Olympics, diplomats and other officials stayed here. Now completely renovated with American antiques, you can stay on the banks of the Truckee River in an atmosphere of "Old Tahoe." The dining room is described in "Dining Out" on page 63.

River Ranch Lodge
P.O. Box 197
Tahoe City, CA 96145
530-583-4264
In California: 800-535-9900
www.riverranchlodge.com

Directions:
On Highway 89 at Alpine Meadows Rd.

Special Features:
The Truckee River rafting companies end their four mile journey from Tahoe City at River Ranch, so the patio is a great place to watch rafters and kayakers maneuver the last rapids into the pool in front of the lodge.

You can access the Tahoe City to Truckee Bike Trail, or take the bus to Alpine Meadows Ski Area just up the road. Summer afternoons will find guests on the riverside patio, where musical groups play on weekends.

Courtesy of Poole's Guest House

The airy kitchen and dining area where guests assemble in the evening.

Chaney House
4725 West Lake Blvd.
Homewood, CA 96141
530-525-7333
www.chaneyhouse.com

Special Features:
The Honeymoon Suite is a one-bedroom apartment over the garage with a separate sitting area, TV, kitchen, queen bed and bath.

The beautiful dining room, used for breakfast in winter and cooler seasons, features a mahogany table and sideboard filled with the family's own silver, which Lori uses to serve you. In summer guests can eat breakfast on the side patio with a view of the lake. The house has its own private pier and beach. It is hard to imagine a more dignified and elegant place to stay.

Chaney House

Lori and Gari Chaney's bed and breakfast is truly their own home. You will be treated like a valued guest in this historic Old Tahoe house nestled in a grove of Jeffrey pines. The house has eighteen-inch-thick stone walls, Gothic arches and a massive stone fireplace in the livingroom. Furniture to fit the scale of the room is just right for relaxing with afternoon wine or to read a book on a quiet evening. Three guest rooms in the house formerly were used by the Chaney's children. One suite has a king-size bed and sitting area. All have private baths.

The Chaney House was built by the stonemasons who built Vikingsholm at Emerald Bay.

Lodging

The Cottage Inn at Lake Tahoe

The Cottage Inn features renovated cottages, each with a distinctive exterior and decor, clustered under century-old pine trees. The charming cottages dating back to 1938 were built by the Pomin family, with lots of knotty pine, stone fireplaces and the feeling of having retreated from the world. With fifteen cabins to choose from, there is one for every taste.

The Bit O' Bavaria, for instance, offers a two-room fireplace, kitchen, private balcony with a view and a sofa bed for an extra person. The Bird Nest, a suite with a lake view, has a loft bedroom for two extra persons.

Honeymooners or couples looking for a romantic weekend will find the solitude they desire in a suite with a two-story fireplace and natural rock jacuzzi with a waterfall.

The Cottage Inn
1690 West Lake Blvd.
Tahoe City, CA 96145
530-581-4073 800-581-4073
www.thecottageinn.com

Special Features:
A hearty country breakfast is served in the dining room or on the deck in summer. A sauna is available to relax muscles after your day of activity, and best of all, guests can walk to one of Tahoe's finest private beaches. If all you want to do is stay in front of the fire and read or watch a video, the management will leave breakfast on your doorstep and hold any messages in the office. There is a fine selection of books and videos for borrowing.

Mayfield House
236 Grove St.
Tahoe City, CA 96145
530-583-1001 888-518-8898
www.mayfieldhouse.com

Special Features:
The small cottage in back with a queen bed offers a secluded location. Wine and cheese or tea and cookies are served every afternoon and wine and brandy are available in the evening. The inn is within walking distance of Tahoe City's finest restaurants and all the activities of the harbor. Stan and Colleen continue the tradition that, "there are no strangers at Mayfield House, only friends who have not yet met."

Mayfield House

Built in 1928 as the home of Norman Mayfield, a pioneer contractor at Lake Tahoe, Mayfield House and its new owners Colleen McDevitt and Stan Scott welcome guests to enjoy the quiet charm of this old Tahoe home on a quiet side street in Tahoe City. There are six newly decorated rooms, three with Queen beds and private baths. Julia's room is where famous architect Julia Morgan stayed. She was a personal friend and associate of Norman Mayfield. It has a king-size bed and private bath. The Mayfield Room is a suite with large sitting and dining area, king-size bed and private bath.

Courtesy of the Mayfield House

The Mayfield House in Tahoe City.

Lodging

Meeks Bay Resort and Marina

For centuries before Europeans came to Lake Tahoe, Meeks Bay was a sacred place for the Washoe tribe, a source of sustenance and spirituality. In 1934 the Kehlet family built a summer home here. Later the property became a lodge. Thanks to an agreement with the U.S. Forest Service the Washoe have returned to manage the historic lodge on their beautiful bay.

Here you will find a group of cabins and lodging units that sleep from two to six people, each with kitchen and bath. The campground on the premises has been a favorite for generations of campers.

Meeks Bay Resort and Marina
P.O. Box 787
Tahoma, CA 96142
530-525-6946 877-326-3357
www.meeksbayresort.com

Directions:
Ten miles south of Tahoe City and eight miles north of Emerald Bay.

Special Features:
The Kehlet Mansion is rented for special occasions and weddings.

The Marina offers boat rentals, fishing excursions and a high speed shuttle to South Shore.

© Dan Wendin

Some of the lakeside lodging units at Meeks Bay Resort.

Norfolk Woods Inn
6941 West Lake Blvd.
Tahoma, CA 96142
530-525-5000
www.norfolkwoods.com

Special Features:

Amy's Cottage is a historic 100-year-old log cabin, updated to make the perfect honeymoon hideaway. After a day of active pursuits in the area, be sure to check out the homemade pastries, fruit smoothies and shakes, espresso or capuccino at the Ice-House. Your stay should always include a romantic dinner in the gourmet restaurant, described on page 68 in "Dining Out."

Norfolk Woods Inn

The inn and cabins have been renovated and redecorated. Plenty of knotty pine will take you back in time to relaxed mountain vacations of a bygone era. Two rooms in the inn share a bath — perfect for a family. Two suites each have two bedrooms, bath, kitchen and living room with TV. On this beautiful wooded property with heated swimming pool and spa for summer guests, there are five separate cabins, four with fireplaces, that can accommodate up to six people.

© Dan Wendin

The beautiful shoreline view at Meeks Bay.

Lodging

Rockwood Lodge

Here is a chance to stay in one of Tahoe's grand 1930s summer chalets, built of rock and knotty pine with hand-hewn beams. The rockwork was done by Austrian stonemasons who had finished working on the Kaiser Estate, now Fleur du Lac. Step back in time to a gracious home — removing your shoes at the door — and enjoy the hospitality of Lou Reinkins and Connie Stevens who have operated their lodge since 1985. They lovingly restored the house, put in modern bathrooms and decorated it with antiques. The spacious livingroom beckons for a chat in front of the stone fireplace with a glass of Riesling or Cabernet that is always available. All guest rooms have private baths, with down comforters on the queen-size beds.

Rockwood Lodge
5295 West Lake Blvd.
Homewood, CA 96141
530-525-5273 800-538-2463
www.rockwoodlodge.com

Special Features:
The house is set back from the road and across the street from the lake. The front patio has an outside fireplace to take off the chill of early summer evenings at the lake. For those with an interest in wildlife, Connie has been operating the Wildlife Rescue for the Lake Tahoe region for several years in a small building at the back of the property.

Tahoma Meadows Bed and Breakfast
6821 West Lake Blvd.
Tahoma, CA 96142
530-525-1553 800-355-1596
www.tahomameadows.com

Tahoma Meadows Bed and Breakfast

Nestled among sugar pines on the west shore are eleven historic cabins of the Tahoma Meadows Bed and Breakfast. Lovingly redecorated with themes of local wildflowers, most have queen-size beds and all have TV. Some bathrooms have claw foot bath tubs to bring back memories of grandmother's house. One two-bedroom cabin sleeps six, but doesn't include breakfast. However, have no fear, because the Stony Ridge Café out front offers scrumptious breakfast and lunch. The Tahoma location is close to Sugar Pine and Bliss State Parks with all the beautiful beaches and trails that they offer.

Courtesy of Haus Bavaria

Haus Bavaria, a European-style guest house.

Lodging

Byrn'nn Bed and Breakfast

The Byrn'nn is located convenient to summer and winter activities in Tahoe Vista. The inn was built as a bed and breakfast with four rooms plus a one bedroom cottage with a complete kitchen and living room next to a private yard. One large suite with a queen bed has a jacuzzi and oversized tile shower on the second floor. Two downstairs bedrooms have queen beds, while a third has a queen and a twin. The community room features a very large leather sectional and big screen TV, although two of the rooms have their own TV's.

The Byrn'nn Bed and Breakfast
Anderson Ave. at Highway 28
P.O. Box 94
Tahoe Vista, CA 96148
530-546-9472 888-888-3848
www.byrn.qpg.com

Special Features:
Your host, Hugh Byrn, serves a full continental breakfast of bagels, cereal and fruit.

Haus Bavaria

You don't have to travel to Bavaria to be stay in an alpine chalet. The inn was built in 1980 as a European-style guest house, complete with German bric-a-brac in the panelled living room with views of the mountains. It is located in a residential area high above Incline Village. There are five rooms, each with private bath, two with king-size beds and three with queens, and all have private balconies.

Haus Bavaria
593 North Dyer Circle
Incline Village, NV 89451
775-831-6122 800-731-6222
www.hausbavaria.com

Special Features:
Your host, Bick Hewitt, serves beverages when you arrive, and a breakfast of home-baked goods and fresh fruit in the pleasant dining room each morning. He is happy to hold small weddings in his lovely Alpine chalet.

Lodging (sidebar)

The Shore House
7170 North Lake Blvd.
Tahoe Vista, CA 96148
530-546-7270 800-207-5160
www.tahoeinn.com

Special Features:
You can enjoy wine and cheese in the afternoons or cookies before bed in the sitting area featuring a river rock fireplace and lots of comfortable log furniture.

The Shore House is a perfect place to plan an outdoor summer wedding. Your guests can stay there and the Cohens will be happy to help you arrange the caterer.

The Shore House

Located on the spectacular North Shore with its own private pier, this bed and breakfast offers all the best of Tahoe. Nine rooms are decorated with modern log furniture and comfortable beds, private baths and lots of knotty pine. One room, the Studio, invites you to use the easel and pastels to recreate the mountain scenery out your window. All rooms come with a journal to record your thoughts. A full mountain breakfast is served in the dining room with a view down the lake.

Your hosts, Marty and Barb Cohen, have lived at Lake Tahoe for more than twenty years and can recommend outdoor adventures to fill your days and dining possibilities for the evening. However, you may choose just to relax and sit on the lawn watching the lake.

Lodging

Black Bear Inn Bed and Breakfast

Lake Tahoe's newest bed and breakfast is a premier property offering luxury accommodations. The new building achieves its rustic mountain charm with high ceilings and log beams. The great room looks out through floor to ceiling windows onto a large wooded yard. Comfortable couches provide seating in front of the beautiful stone fireplace. The main lodge has five rooms featuring king beds, sitting areas and large private baths, all decorated with themes of a fine mountain lodge. Three separate cabins on the property have a fireplace plus kitchenette and bath.

Black Bear Inn
1202 Ski Run Blvd.
South Lake Tahoe, CA 96150
530-544-4451 877-232-7466
www.tahoeblackbear.com

Special Features:
You can enjoy wine and cheese at sunset in front of the fire, or outside on the porch in summer. There is a hot tub for your enjoyment both summer and winter.

You are just a short walk from Café Fiore and Nephele's restaurants. See the descriptions on pages 85 and 88 in "Dining Out."

Courtesy of Black Bear Inn.

The comfortable great room at the Black Bear Inn.

Camp Richardson Resort
P.O. Box 9028
South Lake Tahoe, CA 96158
530-541-1801 800-544-1801
www.camprichardson.com

Directions:
Located on Emerald Bay Road (Highway 89) two miles north of the South Tahoe Y.

Special Features:
The resort operates cross country skiing trails across the highway. Many of South Lake Tahoe's best beaches are just north of the property and numerous summer activities are available just outside the front door at their marina. The moderately priced Beacon Restaurant is right at lakeside. With so many activities close at hand, your family could easily become one of those who wouldn't miss a summer at Camp Richardson.

Camp Richardson Resort

Richardson's Resort has operated continuously since 1921, when Captain Alonzo Richardson leased a large parcel from the Comstock and Lawrence families to set up a stage service between Placerville and Lake Tahoe using his Pierce Arrow touring cars. He built cabins, naming many after automobiles of the day. In 1927, when the neighboring Tallac Hotel was torn down, Alonzo brought the Tallac post office to the site and built a hotel, dining room and many other buildings. He also built a pier so that the steamer *Tahoe* and other vessels could bring passengers, mail and freight to the resort. Present-day operation is under an agreement with the U.S. Forest Service that now owns the land, but the traditions of the Richardson family continue.
The cabins have been renovated and winterized so that winter guests can choose between a hotel room or cabin.

The resort is a popular summer vacation for many families who have continued their annual trek to the property even as children married and grandchildren arrived. Reservations early in the year are recommended.

Lodging

Christiania Inn

The inn is a replica of a fine European hostelry, complete with an elegant gourmet restaurant with fireplaces, cozy bar and six unique rooms and suites. Located just 500 yards from the California Base Lodge of Heavenly, it is as close to ski in, ski out accommodations as possible here. From the moment of your arrival you will be pampered by their attentive staff. The European decor features antiques and wood-burning fireplaces. Each of the four suites has a separate living room. Two suites are two story, with living rooms on the first floor along with wet bar, dry sauna and bath, and second floor bedrooms with king-size beds, sitting room and fireplaces. One other two story suite features a queen sized bed with overhead mirror in the loft. The fourth suite, decorated with a Victorian flavor, comes with king-size bed and a bath/shower steam bath combination. Two rooms have a dinette or dining nooks.

Christiania Inn
3819 Saddle Road
South Lake Tahoe, CA 96150
530-544-7337
www.christianiainn.com

Special Features:
A continental breakfast is brought to you every morning and a decanter of brandy is supplied with each room. In summer the snow gives way to a beautiful garden among the pines. Their advertisement is "all the grace of yesterday, in harmony with the comforts of today." See page 86 in "Dining Out" for a description of the restaurant.

Holly's Place
South Lake Tahoe
800-745-7041
www.hollysplace.com

Special Features:
A separate recreation room has games and a full video library. This is a comfortable place to meet other guests. Wine and cheese is offered on Friday nights and complimentary coffee and muffins are available in the morning. Smoking is permitted only outside.

Spruce Grove
South Lake Tahoe
800-777-0914
www.sprucegrove.com

Special Features:
This is a dog friendly place. The staff will help identify hikes and beaches where dogs are welcome.

Holly's Place

Holly's advertises that they offer a special safe place for all women. Several cabins of varying sizes are grouped on a large property surrounded by a fence. Well-mannered dogs and children are welcome. Each cabin has a fully equipped kitchen and most have comfortable living rooms with TV, VCR and stereo. Cabins sleep from two to six. The Alice Water Guesthouse can accommodate up to ten comfortably in three queen bedrooms, a queen couch and two baths plus an additional unit with queen bed and private bath.

Spruce Grove

Located near to all activities on Spruce Avenue just off Ski Run Blvd., Spruce Grove is a quiet, enclosed compound featuring five separate cabins and two one bedroom suites. All have kitchens, a living room with TV and VCR and stereo and sleeper sofa. One cabin has a private patio. Amenities include an enclosed spa and recreation room. Gourmet coffee and muffins are offered each morning. Barbeques are available outside the units. Comfortable seating under the trees invites a lazy afternoon of reading.

Lodging

The Inn at Heavenly

The longtime owners of a former large motel have created a quiet inn on two acres on Ski Run Boulevard, just a few blocks from the Heavenly Tram. Fourteen tastefully decorated suites offer guests comfortable rooms with fireplaces, private baths, cable televisions and VCRs, plus refrigerators and microwaves. Breakfast is served in the gathering room, where you also will be served wine and hors d'oeuvres in the afternoon. The Inn also features private one to four-bedroom cabins with hot tubs.

Summer guests will revel in the spacious grounds with picnic area, canopies, arbors, barbeques, tables and chairs and even a log swing. They specialize in family reunions and weddings and are happy to help groups coordinate their stay in the area.

The Inn at Heavenly
1261 Ski Run Blvd.
South Lake Tahoe, CA 96150
530-544-4244 800-692-2246
www.inn-at-heavenly.com

Special Features:
Seven rooms have king beds, four have queen beds, and two have two double beds.

There is a private spa and sauna on the grounds.

The Inn at Heavenly is a favorite home away from home for many returning guests.

Sorensen's / Hope Valley Resort
14255 Highway 88
Hope Valley, CA 96120
530-694-2203 800-423-9949
www.sorensensresort.com

Directions:
Just east of the intersection of Hwys. 89 and 88.

Special Features:
You can cross-country ski from your door, or indulge in one of the many workshops offered here. Classes are given in everything from wildflower identification to watercolor painting to fly fishing instruction. There is some kind of workshop every month of the year. So, call for the schedule and plan a special overnight or two in one of their unique cabins. There is a sauna to warm after-ski muscles and a café that serves scrumptious, hearty food. See "Dining Out" on page 90 for restaurant information. You don't need to be an overnight guest to enjoy Sorensen's cuisine.

Sorensen's / Hope Valley Resort

From sheep camp to stopping point for early automobile enthusiasts, Sorensen's Resort was officially opened in 1926. In a beautiful aspen grove beside the West Fork of the Carson River, a group of homey cabins among the trees offers relaxation and all the forms of recreation Hope Valley and Carson Pass have to offer. Now in the capable hands of John and Patty Brissenden, the resort offers romantic cabins for two with wood burning stoves, group cabins that can sleep up to eight, homes on the Carson River and even some cabins where dogs are allowed. Houses for larger groups are located east on Highway 88 at Hope Valley Resort and across the Carson River.

Lodging

Caples Lake Resort

For those who want simple, rustic accommodations for a fishing, hiking or skiing holiday, the setting of Caples Lake Resort in the historic Carson Pass area cannot be matched.

Six redecorated lodge rooms overlooking the lake now have private baths across the hall. Breakfast is included in the price of a lodge room. The simple housekeeping cabins that sleep up to six people are great for a weekend of cross-country skiing or a few days of fishing or hiking in this glorious wilderness. The resort added fireplaces in the cabins.

Caples Lake Resort
Highway 88
Kirkwood, CA 95646
209-258-8888
www.capleslake.com
Closed November to mid December, April to mid May.

Directions:
Four miles west of Carson Pass on Highway 88.

Special Features:
The environs beckon for hikes to Emigrant Pass or Lake Winnemucca. Fishing in Caples Lake or any of the dozen alpine lakes is within a day's hike. You can end your days with a delicious meal in the lodge dining room, then relax in front of the fire or watch the sun cast alpenglow on Round Top Peak from the deck. There are few finer views in all of the Sierra.

© Ellie Huggins

Looking across Caples Lake from the deck of the lodge.

Dining Out

The Lake Tahoe, Truckee and Carson Pass areas have innumerable eating establishments offering every kind of cuisine. Rather than list all the eateries, we have selected establishments where dining out can be a special experience, whether it is brunch at lakeside, dinner in a historic building or a fine restaurant on the top floor of a casino. We have also listed the Casino Hotel Buffets on page 91. Here you can get a good meal for a bargain price. Restaurants are listed alphabetically by regions — Donner Summit to Truckee, Squaw Valley and Alpine Meadows, Tahoe City and West Shore, North Shore and Incline Village, South Lake Tahoe and Carson Pass.

The average cost of dinner is rated according to the following formula:

$ Inexpensive, including soup or salad—under $15

$$ Moderate, including soup or salad—under $22

$$$ Moderately expensive, a la carte—entrées $16 to $22

$$$$ Expensive, a la carte—entrées over $22

These prices do not include alcohol, tax or tips.

It is always advisable to make a reservation for dinner at the height of the summer or winter season. During fall or spring, you can usually drop in and be seated with little or no wait.

During the off seasons of fall and spring, restaurant specials are offered in the free *North Tahoe Truckee Week*. Using these coupons you can often dine at some of the area's finest restaurants for two-for-one or half-off certain entrées.

Dining Out

Ice Lakes Lodge

The dining room and lodge opened for the ski season late in 2000. The Donner summit area has long needed a place to gather and have a good meal. The menu features black angus beef, Ahi tuna plus creative vegetarian soups and entreés. The portions are hearty so that soup and a Caesar salad is almost a full meal. Special appetizers are California roll and beer batter shrimp served with spicy BBQ sauce. The large lounge with two fireplaces back to back next to the bar make it possible to accommodate those without reservations.

Ice Lakes Lodge
$$$ Dinner daily.
1111 Soda Springs Road
Soda Springs
530-426-7660

Directions:
From the I-80 exit at Soda Springs, drive one mile to Soda Springs Rd. Turn right and drive two miles to the lodge. Lodging here is described on page 32.

Rainbow Lodge Engadine Café

The stone and wood tavern was built in the 1880s and expanded when automobile traffic along U.S. 40 began. The main dining room looks out on the Yuba River. There is a second dining room off the bar.

The European/Italian menu is varied with nightly specials prepared by the talented chef. Soup or salad comes with the meal. This is a perfect place for a delicious, leisurely dinner, and it is only twenty miles from Truckee via Interstate 80. For a description of lodging here, see page 33 in "Lodging."

Rainbow Lodge Engadine Café
$$ Dinner, daily.
Sunday brunch.
530-426-3661
Reservations recommended.

Directions:
Take Rainbow Road exit off I-80 about 20 miles west of Truckee. Drive west on Rainbow Road.

Special Features:
The lodge was first called Rainbow Tavern and Trout Farm. Diners caught trout from a stocked pond near the river and brought them to the cook. It is now owned and operated by Royal Gorge Cross Country Ski Resort.

Dining Out

Coburn's Station

Coburn's Station
10007 Bridge St.
$$$ Dinner, daily.
Lunch, daily except Tuesday.
530-587-8318

Special Features:
The bar is a favorite gathering place with Happy Hour from 5:00 to 7:00 pm Sunday to Thursday with $1 off beer and well drinks. Special bar food includes Tacos on Tuesdays and Sushi on Sundays.

Owner-chef Frank Mackey came from a successful Silicon Valley restaurant to take over the former Passage Restaurant in the historic Truckee Hotel. The menu offers plenty of good appetizers such as the prosciuto-wrapped prawns in wine garlic butter sauce. Entrées include veal saltimboca and a great steak au poivre.

Cottonwood Restaurant

Cottonwood Restaurant
$$$ Dinner, daily.
Live music, Friday and Saturday.
530-587-5711

Directions:
In the old Hilltop Lodge off Hwy. 267 just south of the Truckee River bridge.

Special Features:
The windows in the dining room afford a spectacular view of historic downtown Truckee, especially when Christmas lights adorn the buildings. In summer try dining on the terrace overlooking the town.

Cottonwood Restaurant at Hilltop is in a building that dates back to the turn of the century when it served the winter sports area for the town. Photographs of the events through the ages are displayed on the walls of the bar and lounge. The restaurant serves a creative cuisine with a hint of Cajun. The Caesar salad appetizer, enough for two or three, is meant to be eaten with your fingers. Whole pieces of romaine are surrounded by cracker-size croutons drenched in garlic.

Dragonfly

Dragonfly
10118 Donner Pass Road Upstairs
$$$$ Lunch, daily.
Dinner, Thursday through Monday.
530-587-0557
Reservations recommended for dinner.

Bill McCullough, chef-owner, mixes California fresh with Oriental flavors in his inventive menu, which changes as he makes new creations. Appetizers can include such mixtures as sea and

Dining Out

mountain satay of shrimp and chicken with a spicy peanut sauce. For meat lovers there is grilled ribeye steak with caramelized onions and wasabi mashed potatoes. Your tastebuds will be rewarded here.

Special Features:
Dragonfly advertises dining on a higher level, which is true in both senses of the word. Located upstairs with outdoor summer dining on the deck above Main Street, the owners have introduced a high level of cuisine to the Truckee mix.

Java Sushi

Located in the Department of Motor Vehicles shopping center, this little sushi house is fast becoming a favorite with locals. Two chefs work full time to fill orders from their very extensive sushi menu. Aficionados of this Japanese delicacy say that it ranks with the best. The special dishes are very inventive with unusual presentations and sauces.

Java Sushi
11357 Donner Pass Rd.
Truckee
$$$ Lunch and dinner, daily.
530-582-1144

Special Features:
Specials are featured daily on a blackboard, and there is a menu of meat and fish entrées for the less adventurous. No matter what you choose it is very tasty.

O.B.'s Pub and Restaurant

O.B.'s has been a favorite of Truckee residents and visitors for 30 years. The restaurant decor is rustic "Old Truckee" with historic photographs and antique implements decorating the plank walls. The lunch menu is varied and downright tasty, offering delicious salads with a Mexican or Oriental touch as well as pasta and several kinds of hamburgers. Dinners run the gamut from steaks to chicken, as well as seafood and a house smoked seafood sampler appetizer.

O.B.'s Pub and Restaurant
10046 Donner Pass Rd.
Downtown Truckee
$$ Lunch and dinner, daily.
530-587-4164

Special Features:
The newsprint menu will give you a short history of the building and old Truckee, when the red light district was out the back door, and railroadmen, lumbermen and ice cutters filled the local bars.

Dining

Dining Out

Pacific Crest Restaurant
10042 Donner Pass Rd.
Downtown Truckee
$$$ Lunch and dinner, daily.
Reservations recommended for dinner.
530-587-2626

Pacific Crest Restaurant

Ed Coleman has created an immediate hit with his addition to the Truckee dining scene, offering an interesting and novel Mediterranean cuisine. The lunch menu highlights wood-fired pizzas while dinner selections feature fish specialties including a delectable bouillabaisse and the pasta offerings that are always interesting. The elegant but casual atmosphere is very inviting and service is always attentive. The bar, one of Truckee's originals, was rescued from the back room of a store up the street.

Pianeta Cucina Italiana
10096 Donner Pass Rd.
Downtown Truckee
$$$$ Dinner, daily.
Reservations recommended.
530-587-4694

Special Features:
If you're appetite won't let you order both pasta and an entrée, they will split either of these for a small surcharge. As locals will tell you this is one restaurant you will want to try many times.

Pianeta Cucina Italiana

Robyn Sills and Ed Coleman, owner of Pacific Crest, have combined their considerable talents and experience to create an outstanding dining establishment. The antipasti menu is a page long with tempting items such as spicy crab cakes over a bed of wilted spinach or a small plate of pasta of the day. Like any good Italian restaurant, the soup, salad and pasta menus are varied and include such specialties as mushroom and herb dumplings in a mushroom broth and pasta in all configurations. You can't go wrong with anything on the menu, which can be complemented with a wine from their extensive list.

Dining Out

Timbercreek Restaurant

Located in the Northstar Village complex, the restaurant serves hearty entrées, including grilled shrimp with chipotle sauce and three pasta selections. On a cold winter night try the chef's special soup. The signature black and blue caesar salad—a meal by itself—features grilled tri tip steak over bacon and blue cheese dressed lettuce. A wine selection is suggested for each entrée. The bar, located in the front room, serves a café menu.

Timbercreek Restaurant
Northstar Village
Northstar-at-Tahoe
$$$ Winter: Breakfast, lunch and dinner, daily.
Summer: Dinner, daily.
Reservations recommended for dinner.
530-562-2250

Special Features:
If you are staying at Northstar, you needn't drive, for the dial-a-ride will pick you up and deliver you home.

Truckee Trattoria

Ken and Liz Brown invite you into their modern Italian-style trattoria and treat you like family. Ken is the chef who prepares light Italian fare, with antipasti like bruscetta or mussels in wine sauce. All the pastas are prepared with light sauces using fresh ingredients. The wine list includes many Italian offerings, with most available by the glass. With the light fare, you will have room for their excellent tiramisu. The place is small and a favorite with locals, so call ahead for reservations.

Truckee Trattoria
Safeway Shopping Center
Truckee
$$ Dinner, Wednesday through Sunday.
Reservations recommended.
530-582-1266

Dining Out

Alexander's at High Camp

Alexander's at High Camp
Squaw Valley
Fee to ride the cable car.
$$ Summer: 4:00 to 9:00 pm daily.
Winter: 10:00 am to 9:00 pm daily.
Reservations recommended.
530-583-1742

The view from High Camp at 8,200 feet is unmatched and adds to the experience of dinner at Alexander's. There is a café menu from 4:00 to 6:00 p.m. with burgers, salads and desserts. The dinner menu offers many house specials as well as grilled fish and steak with mushroom sauce.

Graham's At Squaw Valley

Graham's At Squaw Valley
1650 Squaw Valley Rd.
Squaw Valley
$$$$ Dinner, Wednesday through Sunday.
Reservations recommended.
530-581-0454

Special Features:
Graham Rock is also the owner of Chambers Landing Restaurant and Bar, a Lake Tahoe favorite (page 68) that is open during the summer.

Graham Rock is your convivial host at this special restaurant in the oldest standing house in Squaw Valley. The menu changes every two weeks with a middle eastern touch to the cuisine, all beautifully presented with exquisite tastes. The extensive wine cellar features French, Italian and Spanish, as well as California wines.

Plumpjack Squaw Valley

Plumpjack Squaw Valley
Squaw Valley Inn, Squaw Valley
$$$ Dinner, daily.
Reservations recommended.
530-583-1576

Special Features:
Plumpjack began life as a wine merchant who sought out lesser known vintners and promoted exciting young wineries. The restaurant reflects this history and features twenty or more wines by the glass at very reasonable prices.

San Francisco's famous Plumpjack has opened a restaurant in Squaw Valley Inn to add luster to the culinary scene in Squaw Valley. The food is beautifully presented in a quiet, elegant dining room. The simple menu changes every two weeks offering a selection of interesting appetizers, salads and entrées, always with a pasta or risotto, a roasted fish and perhaps Grilled Beef Roulade or Roasted Duck Breast Confit.

Dining Out

Resort at Squaw Creek

This hotel and conference center is tucked under the slope of Snow King Mountain at the southeastern end of the valley. **Glissandi** offers elegant dining with a view of Squaw Peak and features continental cuisine. A less expensive alternative with almost the same view, **Cascades** serves an extensive, gourmet buffet with different themes. Friday night's all you can eat fish buffet is a favorite. **Ristorante Montagna**, open for lunch and dinner, serves exceptional Italian cuisine. Their garlic bread can be a meal in itself. If you are looking for a ski-in unhurried lunch, this is a perfect line-free choice and the food is excellent.

Resort at Squaw Creek
Squaw Valley
$$$$ Glissandi
$$$ Cascades
$$$ Ristorante Montagna
Dinner reservations recommended at Glissandi and Ristorante Montagna.
530-583-6300

River Ranch

The bar in the historic River Ranch Lodge is a local gathering place with tables that have a wonderful view of the Truckee River. You can sit here or in the quieter dining room. The menu offers many meat dishes, with wild game specialties such as venison and elk. In summer the patio overlooking the river is a great place for lunch at the end of a pleasant bicycle ride from Tahoe City. A summer concert series is held on the patio.

River Ranch
Highway 89 at Alpine Meadows Road
$$$ Summer: Lunch and dinner, daily.
Winter: Dinner, daily.
Reservations recommended.
530-583-4264

Special Features:
If you want to book a room in this fine old lodge, see page 39 in "Lodging."

Dining Out

Christy Hill
115 Grove Street
$$$$ Dinner, daily except Monday.
Reservations recommended.
530-583-8551

Christy Hill

A magnificent view down the lake from this intimate restaurant complements a unique dining experience. The cuisine is a blend of California and continental and the food presentation equals the exquisite tastes. The appetizer menu offers tantalizing selections that run the gamut from quail to foie gras to Maryland soft shell crab. Entrées are equally diverse, and include two vegetarian specialties — eggplant parmesan or grilled portobello mushrooms and fettuccini. This is a great place for that special occasion.

Fiamma Cucina Rustica
521 N. Lake Blvd.
$$$ Dinner, daily.
Reservations recommended.
530-581-1416

Fiamma Cucina Rustica

Fiamma is in the best tradition of culinary excellence that visitors have come to expect at Lake Tahoe. Now enlarged to include a wine bar, the restaurant offers a wide array of appetizers and inventive pasta and meat dishes that add up to an enjoyable dining experience. The wines are moderately priced and the service attentive. The restaurant is popular, so reservations are important.

Dining Out

Hacienda del Lago

There is excellent Mexican fare in this upstairs restaurant with a spectacular view of the lake. This is a great place to satisfy your craving for fajitas or a taco salad while on a shopping spree at the mall.

Hacienda del Lago
The Boatworks Mall
$$ Summer: Lunch and dinner, daily.
Winter: Dinner, daily.
530-583-0358

Jake's on the Lake

A busy bar and dining with lake views from inside and on the deck make this a favorite of locals and visitors alike. The food is California fresh, with plenty of fish and pasta as well as pizza and hamburgers.

Jake's on the Lake
The Boatworks Mall
$$ Summer: Lunch and dinner, daily.
Winter: Dinner, daily; Lunch, Saturday and Sunday.
Reservations recommended.
530-583-0188

The Pfeifer House

The Pfeifer House has been a restaurant for more than 60 years and has always been popular. Known as Lake Inn during its early years, it was a gambling house until 1947. Purchased by the Giannini family in 1950, it was renovated. When Lois Pfeifer was appointed manager, they named it *The Pfeifer House*. Henry Obermuller and Franz Fassbender bought the business in 1972 and started serving award winning German/continental cuisine in the Alpine-style dining room. If you are hankering for real sauerbraten and potato pancakes washed down with a German Riesling, this is the place to dine.

The Pfeifer House
Highway 89 one quarter mile north of the Tahoe City *Y*.
$$$ Dinner, daily except Tuesday.
Reservations recommended.
530-583-3102

Dining Out

Dining

Sierra Vista Lakefront Dining
Roundhouse Mall
Tahoe City
$$$ Lunch and dinner daily.
Reservations recommended.
530-583-0233

Special Features:
The large heated outdoor deck affords a magnificent view down the lake while you watch the sun set on a summer evening. In winter, the cozy bar has a fireplace to warm you while you sample their cocktails or beer.

Tahoe House Restaurant
Highway 89 one-half mile south of the Tahoe City *Y.*
Lunch, daily.
530-583-1377

Sierra Vista Lakefront Dining

Wayne Smith has taken the former Grazie! Italian bistro, remodelled it with a Tahoe rustic feeling and reworked the menu to offer interesting international cuisine. The unique flavors of the world menu features choices of such items as jambalaya, Hungarian goulash, a Mexican carnitas or perhaps an Australian Outback barbecue. The appetizers are creative flavor sensations, particularly pakora. The menu also features chicken, veal, ahi tuna or grilled salmon and many pastas.

Tahoe House Restaurant and Bäckerei

The Vogts, longtime owners of Tahoe House, have transformed their restaurant into a gourmet deli and grocery store to sell the European baked goods and sauces for which they are famous. Here you can have your bratwurst for lunch and buy their cakes and bread to take home for dinner. Their products are also available at the farmers markets in Truckee on Tuesdays and Dollar Hill on Thursdays during the summer. Tahoe City has long needed a gourmet grocer of this quality.

Dining Out

Truffula

In 1998, the former sous chef from Plumpjack who trained at the New England Culinary Academy opened this restaurant in the best gourmet tradition of North Lake Tahoe. Both the decor and the food presentation are inspired and each of the offerings is a taste sensation. Appetizers are creative and the soups excellent. The house specialty is a three-course vegetarian sampler. The main dishes offer North African braised lamb or filet mignon with wild mushroom sauce with truffle scented mashed potatoes and a nightly fish special.

Truffula
Upstairs at 550 North Lake Blvd.
$$$ Dinner, Thursday through Monday.
Reservations recommended.
530-581-3362

Wolfdale's

Wolfdale's, a North Shore gourmet tradition, features a unique cuisine combining a touch of the Orient with exquisite French cooking. The extensive menu offers special fish each night and there is always a sashimi appetizer as well as an Asian soup. The entrées usually include a risotto and a seared leg of venison with cherry sauce and, if you are a big eater, the turf is offered with a surf addition of king crab. This is our choice for a romantic dinner while watching the light of the setting sun over the lake.

Wolfdale's
540 North Lake Blvd.
$$$$ Dinner, daily.
Reservations recommended.
530-583-5700

Special Features:
In summer the restaurant now features outdoor seating with the same magnificent view.

Dining Out

Chambers Landing
6300 Chambers Lodge Rd.
Tahoma
$$$ Summer only: Dinner,
Tuesday through Sunday.
Lunch, Wednesday through
Sunday.
Reservations recommended.
530-525-7262

Chambers Landing

Come by bicycle, boat or car to dine in an "Old Tahoe" historic lakeside dining establishment overlooking McKinney Bay. Graham Rock of Graham's at Squaw Valley prepares a tempting Mediterranean cuisine with a full menu of vegetarian, fish and meat dishes. Lunch offerings include hamburgers and salads. This is a great bicycling destination on a summer day.

Norfolk Woods Inn
6941 West Lake Blvd.
Tahoma
$$$$ Summer: Dinner, Thursday
through Monday.
Winter: Dinner, Thursday through
Sunday.
Breakfast, lunch daily.
Reservations recommended.
530-525-5000

Norfolk Woods Inn

Another quaint "Old Tahoe" building projects a homey atmosphere but with gourmet fare all the way. Chef Robert Shelton is innovative in creating quality dishes with fresh seasonal produce. For beef eaters there is a filet mignon served on a potato tort with truffles and a red wine demi-glace. If you have room at the end of your meal, the selection of desserts will surely tempt you. The restaurant is part of the Inn, so breakfast and lunch are served daily as well. The lodging at Norfolk Woods Inn is described on page 44 in "Lodging."

Dining Out

Sunnyside Restaurant and Lodge

The restaurant in the Sunnyside resort offers summer lunch and dinner on the deck overlooking their busy harbor. The view from the dining room is almost as good. The cuisine is California fresh with many fish specials. The Seafood Bar Menu and Café Menu offer delectable dishes at a moderate cost. A light meal on the deck watching boats sail by is a great way to end a day of bicycling along the lake. The deep-fried zucchini appetizer is one of the best in town.

Sunnyside Restaurant and Lodge
1850 West Lake Blvd.
Tahoe City
$$ May to September: Lunch and dinner, daily.
October to April: Dinner daily, aprés ski 4:00 pm.
530-583-7200

Special Features:
The beach, within eyeshot of the deck, is a perfect spot for restless children to play while parents relax.

Swiss Lakewood Restaurant

Swiss Lakewood is one of Lake Tahoe's oldest restaurants, in continuous operation since 1919. The current owners remodeled the building in 1971 and brought a little bit of Switzerland to the West Shore. The Swiss decor and hospitality are evident from the moment you enter, with attentive hosts and an extensive wine list to go with a menu of Swiss and Continental dishes. A special appetizer and crunchy, hot rolls arrive as soon as you have been seated. The menu includes veal in the Zurich tradition, Viennese-style Wiener schnitzel, tournedos and daily specials.

Swiss Lakewood Restaurant
5055 West Lake Blvd.
Homewood
$$$$ Dinner, daily except Monday.
May until Memorial Day: Dinner, Friday through Sunday. Closed November 1 to Thanksgiving. Reservations recommended.
530-525-5211

Dining

Dining Out

West Shore Café
5180 West Lake Blvd.
Homewood
$$$$ Summer only: Lunch and
dinner, daily.
Reservations recommended for
dinner.
530-525-5200

West Shore Café

This restaurant directly on the waterfront has tables on the dock as well as the lawn. The food is superb California fresh with a continental flair, beautifully presented to match the timeless view. Appetizers run the gamut from smoked salmon to elegant escargots in phyllo pastry cups.
The rack of lamb is encrusted in macadamia nuts and if you are a pasta lover, try the house specialty Pasta Lobsta, penne with lobster, shrimp and other seafood in a creamy garlic sauce. Dining here is an unforgettable visual and gastronomic experience on a balmy summer night.

©Ellie Huggins

The historic Kirkwood Inn, founded in the 1860s, is described on page 90.

Dining Out

Boulevard Café Trattoria

The extensive wine selection and glasses are in a mahogany sideboard as you enter, giving credence to the fact that you are in for a taste treat at this elegant restaurant. It is hard to decide among the many appetizers or whether to have the special salad creation before one of the entrées or the risotto of the evening or pasta dishes. When you are seated your server brings crunchy Italian bread baked on the premises with spreads of chick pea and garlic and roasted eggplant.

Boulevard Café Trattoria
6731 North Lake Blvd.
Tahoe Vista
$$$$ Dinner, daily.
Reservations recommended.
530-546-7213

Captain Jon's

Enjoy your before-dinner drink in the over-the-water lounge and then dine on French country and seafood specials from this notable lakeside restaurant. Captain Jon's has been voted Lake Tahoe's best seafood restaurant for many years. A sushi bar on the water is open Friday and Saturday nights and there is often a reasonably priced early-bird dinner from 5:30 to 6:30 p.m. with entrée, salad and dessert.

Captain Jon's
7220 North Lake Blvd.
Tahoe Vista
$$$$ Dinner, daily.
Lunch summer only, Wednesday through Sunday.
Reservations recommended for dinner.
530-546-4819

Dining Out

Gar Woods Grill and Pier
5000 North Lake Blvd.
Carnelian Bay
$$ Lunch and dinner, daily.
Sunday brunch.
Reservations recommended for
dinner.
530-546-3366

Special Features:
Boating aficionados will want to walk next door to the marina to view the classic wooden boats for sale or moored there.

Lake Tahoe Brewing Company
Highway 28 and Stateline Road
Crystal Bay
$$ Dinner, daily.
Lunch, Friday through Sunday.
775-831-5822

Gar Woods Grill and Pier

In summer sit on the deck or in winter enjoy the notable views from any table. Tahoe's classic wood boating era is remembered with photos at this classic favorite of locals and visitors. The lunch menu features soups, sandwiches and specials. Try the beer batter prawns for an appetizer before choosing from pork tenderloin, house pastas or seafood specialties for your dinner entrée. No matter what the weather, you can't beat the view.

Lake Tahoe Brewing Company

Recently reopened with many new beers brewed on the premises, the menu has been redone with a full choice of salads, burgers and specials that include a delicious Brats and Mash with caraway kraut that is close to what one would find in a German beer hall. Pub fare is served downstairs in the bar. Dinner can be ordered there, but you might want to go upstairs to the quieter dining room. Desserts to be enjoyed here include a black and tan brownie sundae or the more elegant crème brulee or fresh fruit cobbler. You won't go away hungry from this affordable dining establishment.

Dining Out

Lakeview Room Cal-Neva Resort

At this historic casino, you can dine with an exciting view down the lake. This moderately priced restaurant serves traditional California cuisine including a great prime rib au jus and their special scampi. The wine list is extensive and affordable. After dinner don't miss the Indian Room and its informative Washoe exhibit.

**Lakeview Room
Cal-Neva Resort
24 Stateline Road
Crystal Bay
$$$ Dinner, daily.
775-832-4000**

Le Petit Pier

Dinner in this cozy restaurant directly on the lake features one of the finest French cuisines on the North Shore. Dinner is exquisitely prepared and presented with delicious sauces. The appetizers are varied and a must to complement your dinner entrée. Of particular interest is the lobster ravioli or the escargots. Chef Geno daily prepares a six course complete dinner, or you can choose from the regular entrées. The house specialties are a live Maine lobster steamed to perfection, or the Pheasant Souvaroff for two. The latter must be ordered 24 hours in advance. If you have only one night for a splurge, this is definitely the restaurant to choose.

**Le Petit Pier
7238 North Lake Blvd.
Tahoe Vista
$$$$ Dinner, daily except Tuesday.
Reservations recommended.
530-546-4464**

Special Features:
If you want to be assured a table with a view, come off season and early.

Dining Out

The Moose's Tooth Café
Highway 267 and Highway 28
Kings Beach
$$ Lunch, $$$ Dinner
Summer: Breakfast, lunch and dinner, daily.
Winter: Lunch and dinner daily.
Reservations recommended for dinner.
530-546-9495

The Moose's Tooth Café

The café is part of the new Brockway Golf Course clubhouse. With both inside and outside dining they bill themselves as a Southwest family restaurant. The full selection of tasty appetizers can be a meal with one of their large salads. Dinner entrées include a chef's special fish, St. Louis style baby back ribs and chicken plus hamburgers to please the kids.

The Soule Domain
Crystal Bay
Next to the Tahoe Biltmore.
$$$$ Dinner, daily.
Reservations recommended.
530-546-7529

Special Features:
The Soule Domain is fine dining in a historic log cabin, built by Harry Riley at the same time as the original Cal-Neva Lodge in 1927. The hearth features stones quarried at Crystal Bay and the exposed log beams were cut nearby.

The Soule Domain

The chef-owner, Charles Edward Soule IV, calls his cuisine American, but it is a flavorful combination of California and Italy, plus France and the Orient. Many of the dishes present a mixture of taste sensations that are hard to identify, but add up to a meal with "a high flavor component." This is an excellent choice for a romantic dinner.

Spindleshanks American Bistro and Bar
6873 North Lake Blvd.
Tahoe Vista
$$$ Dinner, daily.
Reservations recommended.
530-546-2191

Special Features:
The wine steward offers "flights" (three different wines for tasting) to accompany your dinner. The dessert menu is old fashioned including a real chocolate sundae or a root beer float.

Spindleshanks American Bistro and Bar

Steve Marks of Boulevard Café and Herman Schuchman, formerly chef at Captain Jon's, have teamed up to give North Tahoe a new and exciting restaurant and wine bar. The food and taste sensations are exceptional. Add all this to attentive service and you have a winning dining experience.

Dining Out

There are two outstanding appetizers to try, light and crisp calamari or the house signature Popo Tito Shrimp cocktail presented in a martini glass with two crab claws. Entrées are equally exceptional and even include Spindleshanks' cheeseburger for the less adventurous in the crowd.

Steamers Beachside Bar and Oven

The clam chowder is among the best there is to complement the salads, sandwiches and, of course, pizza. The old photos on the walls recall the days when steamer ships brought patrons to the door and carried tourists around the lake.

Sunsets on the Lake

The new owner Northstar-at-Tahoe hasn't changed the fine Northern Italian and American cuisine. The antipasti are so tempting you might want to try two for dinner accompanied by one of their special salads. The fried calamari is among the best at the lake and the carpaccio is superb and paper thin. Entreés include a few pastas, fish and meat entrées such as wood fired beef tenderloin.

Steamers Beachside Bar and Oven
8290 North Lake Blvd.
Kings Beach
$ Lunch and dinner, daily.
530-546-2218

Special Features:
Lunch outside on the deck in the summer is a special treat.

Sunsets on the Lake
7360 North Lake Blvd.
Tahoe Vista
$$$ Dinner, daily. Lunch on the lower deck in summer.
Reservations recommended.
530-546-3640

Special Features:
The view down the lake to Freel Peak and Mount Tallac is unmatched along the North Shore. In summer you can dine on the deck warmed by gas heaters when necessary.

Dining

The Big Water Grille at Tahoe
341 Ski Way
$$$$ Dinner, daily.
Reservations recommended.
775-833-0606

The Big Water Grille at Tahoe

The former Spatz with its fabulous views has reopened under the management of a group owning restaurants in Maui. The menu reflects a Hawaiian influence with plenty of fresh fish attractively presented. The appetizers are so enticing that you may just order two and add one of their special desserts featuring Macadamia nuts and Kaanapali estate grown coffee with chocolate truffles. Meat eaters will delight in the selection of duck, pork or venison. The wine list is extensive and you can check it out at the wine rack as you enter.

Café 333
333 Village Blvd.
$$$ Dinner, daily.
Breakfast and lunch, daily.
Reservations recommended.
775-832-7333

Special Features:
The restaurant has won the 1998 and 1999 Wine Spectator award of excellence.

Café 333

Owner Mary Young personally serves dinner in her small dining room behind the breakfast espresso bar and lunch room. Her personal interest in wine is reflected in the most extensive wine list in the area and the dozen wines by the glass, many moderately priced. The entrée menu changes every couple of weeks, but the meat dishes remain, only with different sauces. The black Angus beef and rack of lamb are regulars, along with seared ahi with wasabi.

Dining Out

For starters, try the nightly soup special or the phyllo wrapped wild mushrooms. The dessert menu is a chocoholics dream, with five or six chocolate creations.

Christmas Tree Restaurant

Owners Dana and Lisa Emerson have kept the tradition of this historic restaurant overlooking the Carson Valley on the Mount Rose Highway east of the ski area. Fine mahogany grilled meats, including a petite New York steak grilled to perfection for light eaters, are their stock in trade. However, you can have a lobster and meat combination or opt for one of their fine pastas. Appetizers are many and include everything from crab cakes to a smoked seafood platter.

Christmas Tree Restaurant
20007 Mt. Rose Highway
$$$ Dinner, daily.
Reservations recommended.
775-849-0127

Ciao Mein Trattoria

Located next to the casino in the Hyatt Regency Lake Tahoe, Ciao Mein serves a combination of Oriental dishes with an Italian flare. One would usually expect a coffee shop menu in this location, but the dinner menu is extensive, moderately priced and tasty. This is a great place to satisfy a yen for gourmet oriental cuisine.

Ciao Mein Trattoria
Hyatt Regency Lake Tahoe
$$ Dinner, Wednesday through Sunday.
775-832-1234

Dining Out

Jack Rabbit Moon
907 Tahoe Blvd.
Across from Raley's.
$$$$ Dinner, Wednesday through Saturday.
Reservations recommended.
775-832-3007

Jack Rabbit Moon

The restaurant serves the creations of its two chefs who are graduates of the California Culinary Institute. The taste delights offered here are outstanding. Appetizers range from ginger carrot soup to crispy prawns with an Asian dipping sauce and butternut squash ravioli. The entrées include cider glazed pork chops, goatcheese crusted rack of lamb and fish specials plus pasta dishes.

La Fondue
Country Club Mall
$$$ Dinner, daily except Tuesday.
Reservations required.
775-831-6104

La Fondue

Owner Karin Busch treats diners as her special guests in this intimate Swiss restaurant. The menu features traditional cheese and meat as well as dessert fondues. The schnitzels are mouth-watering, perfectly breaded with a light texture. The restaurant offers a dining treat for those who can't get to Switzerland for their fondue fix or are looking for a dining experience that is a little bit different.

Le Bistro
120 Country Club Mall
$$$$ Dinner, Tuesday through Saturday.
Reservations required.
775-831-0800

Le Bistro

Chef Jean Pierre Doignon, formerly of La Chemineé, offers some of the best French cuisine in the area. The fixed price menu is changed daily and includes soup, salad or appetizer, entrée and the chef's own grand

Dining

Dining Out

dessert. The restaurant features Acme bread from Berkeley that is in the true country French tradition, dark and crusty. Every course has its own taste sensation, beautifully presented with delicious sauces and just the right amount to leave room for dessert.

Lone Eagle Grille

The restaurant is on the site of the former Hugo's Rotisserie and is the Hyatt Regency's star restaurant. The dining room graced by two grand stone fireplaces features fabulous views down the lake from south-facing windows. The menu is hearty American but with some Asian and Hispanic influences. Appetizers feature such specialties as spicy crab cakes. The dining room is large and often full, but the service is excellent.

Lone Eagle Grille
Country Club Drive at Lakeshore Drive
$$$ Lunch and dinner, daily.
775-832-3250

Special Features:
This is a great location for a hearty summer lunch on the deck with its million dollar view down the lake.

Yoshimi Japanese Restaurant

Sushi and sashimi aficionados will find a complete and tempting list of these delicacies at this attractively decorated restaurant. The menu offers a wide selection of combination dinners with nabe, udon or soba.
For the less adventurous, the tempura is light and there are many teriyaki offerings. All come with salad, rice and tea.

Yoshimi Japanese Restaurant
Christmas Tree Village #26
$$$ Lunch and dinner, daily.
775-831-2777

Dining Out

A plethora of dining possibilities exist at the four major casino hotels in Stateline. We have chosen to include several that offer exceptional service and creative food offerings. The Casino Buffets with their value dining are described on page 91.

Caesars Broiler Room and Empress Court
Caesars Tahoe
$$$ Dinner, daily.
Reservations recommended.
775-588-2044

Caesars Broiler Room and Empress Court

You'll find all your favorite steaks and seafood cooked to perfection and served in the quiet, elegant dining room of the **Broiler Room**. This longtime Tahoe favorite has been expanded.

For a fine dining experience with an oriental flair, try the **Empress Court**. Featuring specialties of authentic Mandarin, Cantonese and Szechuan preparations, the selection of dishes will please the most discriminating diners with a desire for gourmet Chinese food.

The Chart House
Highway 207 (Kingsbury Grade)
1.5 miles east of U.S. 50.
$$$ Dinner, daily.
Reservations recommended.
775-588-6276

The Chart House

Dine here for views of the lake from high up on the Kingsbury Grade. The food is traditional American where you know the lobster, prime rib or steaks will be excellent and the service pleasant. Add the view and you have a winning combination. This is a popular dinner house, so make your reservations early and arrive even earlier to assure yourself a window table.

Dining Out

Edgewood Terrace Restaurant

Dine at lake's edge in the imposing Edgewood Golf Course Clubhouse where you feel as though you could reach out and touch the mountain landscape across the lake. This is the place to watch the sun set. Attentive service starts with a complimentary pre-appetizer of pesto, cream cheese and sun dried tomato paste on endive. The dinner menu is varied with and array of unique appetizers such as ostrich medallions sauted with shitake mushrooms on creamy polenta with a cabernet sauce. Entrées are generous and include gourmet preparations of poultry, fish and meats.

Edgewood Terrace Restaurant
Edgewood Golf Course
$$$$ Dinner, Summer, daily;
Winter, Wednesday through
Sunday.
$$$ Lunch, Summer only, Monday
through Friday.
Closed in November.
Reservations recommended for
dinner.
775-588-2787

Special Features:
Affordable lunch choices include a daily special plus unique salads and sandwiches. So if you don't want to spring for dinner, try lunch and watch the summer action on the lake.

© Ellie Huggins

View from the 18th green at Edgewood described on the next page.

Dining Out

Friday's Station
Harrah's Lake Tahoe
$$$ Dinner, daily.
Reservations recommended.
775-588-6611

Friday's Station Steak & Seafood Grill

With panoramic lake views below, you can enjoy the fine menu of steaks grilled to perfection over a custom hardwood grill or delectable seafood plus a salad bar. Friday's Station also offers a Sunday Brunch, and this might be the best time of all to enjoy the view from the 18th floor.

Josh's
Horizon Casino Resort
$$ Dinner, daily.
775-588-6211

Josh's at the Horizon Casino Resort

If you're looking for an elegant dining experience that is a bargain, this is an excellent choice. The dinner menu features beef, seafood and pasta entrées served with soup or salad at a very reasonable price.

Llewellyn's
The Penthouse
Harvey's Resort Hotel
$$$$ Dinner, daily.
Reservations required.
$$$ Lunch, daily.
775-588-2411

Special Features:
This is the place to choose for that special evening or, if you want the view but not the expense, try lunch with a menu that features sandwiches such as a salmon pancetta club.

Llewellyn's

The restaurant on the top floor offers a superb dining experience with one of the best views in town. Every table looks across the lake with Mount Tallac providing the backdrop. The international cuisine with a California flair is beautifully presented, and the attentive service makes dining an enjoyable experience. The appetizers are tantalizingly different. Dinner entrées run the gamut from venison medallions to range chicken and all with unusual sauces.

Dining

Dining Out

Mirabelle

Camille Schwartz from Alsace by way of New York, Los Angeles and Santa Barbara has brought elegant French cuisine to the South Shore. The food is exceptional with many Alsace specialties such as Alsatian onion tart, and a particularly unusual presentation of escargots sauteed in garlic butter, tomatoes, parsley and white wine. The decor is simple French with pale yellow walls and pottery on the mantel. The service is attentive and the wine list reasonable with offerings from France and California. It is hard to save room for dessert but this would be one place where you should.

Mirabelle
290 Kingsbury Grade
775-586-1007
$$$$ Dinner, Tuesday through Sunday.
Reservations recommended.

Special Features:
The restaurant serves cocktails and cordials as well as wine and the tables are nicely spaced.

The Ridge Club

Located on the top floor of the timeshare hotel, the restaurant is open to the public. The view from the dining room is spectacular, especially at sunset. Their hearty menu is varied, featuring specialty steaks, poultry and seafood plus several pasta dishes. Dinner entrées come with fresh bread, a family style salad, seasonal vegetables and choice of baked potato, steak fries or rice, and portions are generous. Luckily there is a light eaters menu. This is a place where you can take the whole family.

The Ridge Club
400 Ridge Club Dr.
775-588-3553
$$$ Dinner, Wednesday through Saturday.
Sunday brunch.
Reservations required to get through the gate.

Dining

Dining Out

Dining

Sage Room
Harvey's Resort Hotel
$$$$ Dinner, daily.
Reservations recommended.
775-588-2411

Sage Room at Harvey's

Guests at Harvey's have been dining in the Sage Room since 1947. If you're looking for great beef and traditional western food and hospitality, you can't go wrong here. The Black Angus beef is one-inch thick and is topped with their special onion rings. Other specialties of the house include a mixed grill of venison medallions. You can finish your meal with a chocolate port cake and their Viennese coffee for two.

The Summit
Harrah's Casino Hotel
$$$$ Dinner, daily.
Reservations required.
775-588-5611

Special Features:
There is a chef's special selection offered each night that includes appetizer, salad, choice of entrée and dessert. This fixed price meal is a great way to enjoy several menu items economically, and you can always share with your dinner partner.

The Summit at Harrah's Casino Hotel

The Summit has won numerous awards for its cuisine. Although very expensive, the taste delights that await you are worth the price. Your meal begins with a complimentary appetizer. The appetizers are varied, and each is served with an interesting sauce. Entrées include a delicious rack of lamb and a tender Beef Wellington. Save room for desserts, for along with the double chocolate delights, the soufflé Grand Marnier can be ordered to put the final touch to your five star dinner.

Dining Out

Beacon Bar and Grill

This is a fine place to take the family for dining on the lake with moderate prices for lunch and plenty of burger choices as well as sandwiches and pastas. Since you can walk along the beach to Valhalla, this would be an excellent dinner spot before or after the performance. The dinner menu includes daily fish specials and cioppino as well as homemade soups, meat or pasta.

The Beacon Restaurant
Camp Richardson Resort
1900 Jameson Beach Rd.
$$ Lunch and dinner, daily.
530-541-0630

Café Fiore

Café Fiore is an intimate restaurant serving a complete Italian menu. Antipasto may be followed by insalata or pasta or one of the traditional entrées of veal scaloppine or bistecca alla Fiore. The dinner entrées are served with salad, fresh vegetable and pasta of the day, and the portions are large. The restaurant is very small, but in summer you can dine on the patio when weather permits.

Café Fiore
1169 Ski Run Blvd. at Tamarack
$$$$ Dinner, daily.
Reservations recommended.
530-541-2908

Dining

Dining Out

The Cantina
Emerald Bay Rd. at 10th Street
$$$ Lunch and dinner, daily.
Reservations recommended.
530-544-1233

The Cantina

Evan Williams has transformed the former Cantina Los Tres Hombres into a gourmet Sante Fe style restaurant. He still serves the usual burritos, enchiladas, fajitas and tacos, but he has added his own gourmet touches to Southwestern cuisine. This is not your traditional Mexican fare. You can choose from Texas crab cakes or smoked chicken polenta or an astounding array of nightly specials which your waiter will explain to you.

Christiania Inn
3819 Saddle Road
$$$$ Dinner, Tuesday through Sunday.
Reservations recommended.
530-544-7337

Special Features:
If a full a-la-carte dinner is beyond your pocket book, try the "Sunset Specials" between 5:30 and 6:30 p.m. that include choice of three entrées, soup and salad for a very reasonable price. During ski season ask for the "Apres Ski Specials." If you are looking for a unique bed and breakfast at the slopes, Christiania Inn is described on page 51 in "Lodging."

Christiania Inn

Christiania Inn was built in 1965 to replicate a fine European country inn. The dining room exudes elegant, old-world charm. From the moment your waiter brings your hot, freshly baked bread to the last cup of coffee, service is attentive. The menu features exciting appetizer choices, including a house-cured salmon carpaccio and beluga caviar. The Caesar salad is prepared at the table. The entrées cover the spectrum of veal, beef and poultry with a daily fresh catch, all presented with an eclectic selection of sauces. If you have room, cherries jubilee or any of a number of delicious desserts are available.

Dining

Dining Out

Evan's American Gourmet Café

Evan's, named for chef and owner Evan Williams, is possibly the finest dining experience in the Tahoe Basin. Attentive service complements an extensive menu including a long list of nightly gourmet specials. Evan has named his cuisine "Gourmet American," but his sauces and presentation speak of continental training mixed with a unique California touch. Appetizers include a daily pasta or one-person pizza. It is difficult to choose from the long list of entrées, but each meat dish features a special sauce. The wine list is as extensive as the menu. Save room for one of the delectable desserts that Evan's wife, Candice, bakes to test your will power.

Evan's American Gourmet Café
536 Emerald Bay Road
$$$$ Dinner, daily.
Reservations required.
530-542-1990

Fresh Ketch

Dine among the yachts at Fresh Ketch where fresh seafood is the fare of the day. Lunch offerings include traditional clam chowder along with fish specials, burgers and salads. Pastas and meat entrées are included in the dinner menu. The bar features beers from around the world as well as from many micro breweries in the west. The wine list includes offerings from France and California.

Fresh Ketch
2435 Venice Drive
Tahoe Keys Marina
$$ Lunch and dinner, daily.
Reservations recommended.
530-541-5683

Nephele's
1169 Ski Run Blvd.
$$$ Dinner, daily.
Reservations recommended.
530-544-8130

Dining

Nephele's

This small restaurant features creative California cuisine. The flavorful food is beautifully presented by the chef of many years. You can start your meal with a tasty treat from an extensive appetizer menu before choosing from entrées that run the gamut from salmon poached in chardonnay then baked and served with a camembert cheese sauce to filet mignon with grilled onions and bacon, served with champagne cognac sauce. If you still have room at the end of the meal, the scrumptious desserts are baked daily.

Riva Grill on the Lake
900 Ski Run Blvd.
$$$ Lunch and dinner, daily.
Sunday brunch.
Reservations recommended.
530-542-2600

Special Features:
Along with an extensive California wine list they also serve their famous Wet Woody drink of three rums in a fruit slush. You will be able to sit on the deck in the summer and watch the Tahoe Queen and other boating action. South Shore has long needed this fine dining experience with a lake view.

Riva Grill on the Lake

As part of the Ski Run Marina redevelopment, Tom Turner of Gar Woods Grill and Pier has opened a sister South Shore restaurant. The ambiance of course is boating, with beautiful paintings of Italian Riva runabouts for which the restaurant is named. The fare is Italian with a Mediterranean touch including many Gar Woods favorites such as conchiglie with grilled chicken, smoked Gouda, pancetta and artichoke hearts.

Dining Out

Scusa! on Ski Run

Enticing smells of Italian cooking waft from the front door. The menu offers something for every taste. Appetizer selections include oysters Scusa and mozzarella and Italian plum tomato salad. There is a large selection of pastas plus entrées such as calamari, veal and chicken. The house specialties include a flavorful sea scallops Mediterranean (artichoke hearts, button mushrooms, sun-dried tomatoes and capers) as well as a classic lasagna.

Scusa! on Ski Run
1142 Ski Run Blvd.
530-542-0100
$$$ Dinner, daily.
Reservations recommended.

Dining

Swiss Chalet Restaurant

Kurt and Ruth Baumann came to Lake Tahoe in 1957 to bring a little bit of Switzerland to the South Shore. With four generations of restaurant experience in the family, they offer gourmet Swiss cuisine with impeccable service. A collection of beer steins and huge cow bells hang from the ceiling, creating a decor that transports you to Zurich or Zermatt. Here you can indulge in fondue for two or any number of traditional Swiss dishes, such as bratwurst with spaetzli, or delectable, tender sauerbraten served with red cabbage. The menu also includes daily fish and pasta specials as well as house-baked Swiss pastries to finish your meal.

Swiss Chalet Restaurant
2544 Lake Tahoe Blvd.
$$$ Dinner, daily except Monday.
Reservations recommended.
530-544-3304

Dining Out

Kirkwood Inn
Five miles west of Carson Pass on Highway 88, just east of the entrance to Kirkwood Resort.
$$
Summer: Breakfast, lunch and dinner, daily.
Winter: Lunch and dinner daily.
209-258-7304

Kirkwood Inn

The Inn has been in continuous operation feeding locals and travelers over Carson Pass since the late 1800s. The hand hewn beams that support the ceiling are originals, installed in the 1860s by the Kirkwood and Taylor families. Great hamburger lunches are the daily fare, but dinner offerings include pastas, fish specials and baby back ribs or steak.

Sorensen's / Hope Valley Resort
1425 Highway 88, Hope Valley
Breakfast and lunch, daily.
$$$ Dinner, daily.
Reservations recommended.
530-694-2203

Special Features:
Some evenings a guitarist may accompany your dinner. If they are busy, you may be asked to share your table with others, a great opportunity to meet new folks.

Sorensen's / Hope Valley Resort

Sorensen's has been providing food and accommodations for weary travelers since 1926. The lodge and cabins are a full-scale resort with year-round activities for wilderness-loving tourists. See page 54 in "Lodging." A fine wine list complements an array of hearty stews and nightly fish specials, and you can get the recipe for items you enjoyed from the front desk.

Caples Lake Resort
Highway 88
Kirkwood
$$$ Dinner, Wednesday through Saturday.
Closed November to mid December, April to mid May.
Reservations recommended.
209-258-8888

Caples Lake Resort

The dining room is open to the public with tasty meals of fish, steak and pastas. The wine list is excellent, and there is no finer place to watch the setting sun on this beautiful lake while enjoying a gourmet dinner. For lodging see page 55 in "Lodging."

Dining Out

If you have a hungry crowd, and you want lots of good food, the casino hotel buffets offer the best dining bargain on the South Shore.

Caesars Roman Feast Buffet

The selections at this buffet are fit for a Roman emperor, with such offerings as rotisserie prime rib, pasta and brick oven pizzas plus a salad bar and desserts galore.

Caesars Casino
Stateline, Nevada
775-588-3515

Special Features:
A 24-hour menu is available.

Le Grande Buffet at the Horizon Casino Resort

Every night Le Grande Buffet at the Horizon Casino Resort puts on a complete, all-you-can-eat buffet dinner that includes prime rib for less than $10 per person.

Le Grande Buffet at Horizon
Casino Resort
Stateline, Nevada
775-588-6211

Special Features:
Brunch with many specialties is served on weekends.

Harvey's Garden Buffet

Breakfast and brunch buffets are offered daily. Dinner menus include Mexican, Basta Pasta, BBQ, German and Seafood themes plus salad bar, fresh fruit, dessert, and yogurt.

Harvey's Garden Buffet
Harvey's Resort Hotel
Stateline, Nevada.
775-588-2411

Special Features:
Weekend buffets feature prime rib, steak and fish entrées plus the salad, fruit, dessert and yogurt bars.

Harrah's Forest Buffet

On the 18th Floor with a view of the mountains, brunch or dinner buffets include a complete salad bar and a wide choice of meat, pasta and fish entrées. A fabulous seafood buffet is served every Friday from 4:30 to 10:00 p.m.

Harrah's Forest Buffet
Harrah's Casino Hotel
Stateline, Nevada
775-588-6606

Kayaking in Emerald Bay.

The lady worked hard to land this big one in 1890.

SUMMER ACTIVITIES

Lake Tahoe is world-renowned for the azure color of the water and the beauty of its setting. There are dozens of beaches for sunning and picnics. Although the average summer water temperatures seldom reach 68°F, some beaches feature shallow water that warms enough for swimming. Lake Tahoe is a boater's paradise. You can paddle along the shore in a kayak or canoe, take a high speed run in a powerboat, sail, or enjoy a cocktail cruise on a sternwheeler to Emerald Bay.

Donner Lake near Truckee is favored for watersports and fishing. Being a smaller lake, the water temperatures can climb above 70°F.

Carson Pass and Hope Valley offer a true wilderness experience where you can hike trails to high mountain lakes and meadows where wildflowers abound or along rushing streams. The West Fork of the Carson River, Caples Lake and Blue Lakes are well-stocked with trout. For those with an interest in history, you can walk along traces of the Emigrant Trail or stop at a Pony Express station.

Watersports are not the only Lake Tahoe attraction. Trails into the surrounding mountains take you to wildflower gardens of incredible beauty and to peaks with 360-degree views. If you seek adventure, you can take a glider ride out of the Truckee Tahoe Airport, ride high above the lake in a balloon, try parasailing or take a rock climbing class. Summer visitors will also find championship golf courses, tennis courts, and riding stables offering horseback tours into the mountains.

Simply said, there are activities to please every member of the family during the day, and music, fine dining or gambling in the evening.

Special events are held throughout the year: concerts, a Shakespeare festival, summer music at the Tallac Historic Site, art shows, boat shows and the Truckee rodeo. These are all listed in the "Special Events" section. You will want to check the free *North Tahoe Truckee Week* magazine or the entertainment sections of the *Sierra Sun, Tahoe World, The Bonanza* and the *Tahoe Daily Tribune* for exact dates and times.

Adventures

This section tells of activities for the adventurous. From balloon rides to challenge ropes courses, from rock climbing to parasailing there is something for everyone in the family who wants to try something new. The activities are not cheap.

Parasailing

Kings Beach Aqua Sports
Kings Beach State Beach
530-546-2782

Kings Beach Aqua Sports offers stay-dry flights from their parasail boat. They also have a water ski school, and while some of your party parasails, the rest of the family can enjoy the beach.

Action Watersports of Tahoe
Reservations:
South Lake Tahoe - 530-541-7245

Action Watersports of Tahoe offers parasailing adventures from their facility at Timber Cove Marina. All flights are from a boat so you won't even get your feet wet.

Zephyr Cove Jet Ski and
Parasailing
Zephyr Cove Marina, Nevada
Reservations recommended.
775-588-3833

Zephyr Cove Jet Ski and Parasailing rents you a jet ski or launches you off the boat or dry land to parasail high above the lake and take in the incredible views. With the many activities at Zephyr Cove, the whole family can come, rent boats, swim or just lie on the beach.

Ski Run Boat Company
900 Ski Run Blvd.
South Lake Tahoe
530-544-0200

Ski Run Boat Company not only rents everything for a day on the water, but they have parasailing rides from their facility at the end of Ski Run Blvd.

Adventures

Glider Rides

Soar Truckee offers glider rides for a unique view of the Truckee and Tahoe Basins. Soar high above Martis Valley and view Lake Tahoe to the south.

Soar Truckee
Truckee Tahoe Airport
Off Martis Lake Rd. Follow the signs.
530-587-6702

Balloon Rides

Mountain High Balloons rise above the Truckee area providing passengers with a thrilling and memorable view. Flights lasting several hours leave early in the morning . Meeting time is at 7:00 a.m. and some evenings. Each ride will take two to five people. Lift-off location varies.

Mountain High Balloons
Reservations required.
530-587-6922
888-462-2683

Balloons Over Lake Tahoe will pick you up anywhere in the South Lake Tahoe area and bring you to your flight that begins before sunrise and ends about three hours later with a tour over the lake. Your adventure ends with a champagne and orange juice toast along with pastries and fruit.

Balloons Over Lake Tahoe
South Lake Tahoe
Reservations required.
530-544-7008
www.balloonsoverlaketahoe.com

Lake Tahoe Balloons' pilot and owner has more than 15 years experience in the business and offers flights year-round. You lift off from an aircraft carrier at Tahoe Keys and fly high above the lake with close-up views of Emerald Bay and Cascade Lake. Flights last one hour ending with a champagne brunch.

Lake Tahoe Balloons
South Lake Tahoe
Reservations required.
530-544-1221
800-872-9294

Summer

Adventures

Scenic Flights

Todd Aero
Truckee Tahoe Airport
Truckee
Reservations required.
530-587-4465

Todd Aero offers instructional flights over the Lake Tahoe Basin, leaving from the Truckee Tahoe Airport. Regular hours are Wednesday through Sunday but flights can be arranged for any day.

Alpine Lake Aviation
South Lake Tahoe Airport
Reservations required.
775-588-4748
800-251-4748

Alpine Lake Aviation owner Jerry Capps operates charter flights and tours out of South Lake Tahoe Airport. The 45-minute to one-hour flight around Lake Tahoe includes commentary about the history, tall tales and Indian legends through individual head sets as you fly around the lake.

Rock Climbing and other Challenges

Alpine Skills International
P.O. Box 8
Norden, CA 95724
530-426-9108
800-916-7325
www.alpineskills.com

Alpine Skills International at Donner Summit offers weekend rock climbing instruction for all levels. If you want to watch a class in session, check out the cliffs along Donner Pass Road west of Donner Lake.

Squaw Valley
Tram Building
530-583-7673

Squaw Valley Climbing Wall is located in the cable car building and operates year-round. You can practice the art on this interesting wall before trying the real thing. Experienced trainers lead you through the steps.

Adventures

Squaw Valley Adventure Center has a challenge ropes course dominated by high elements — 50-foot towers, rope extension bridges and treehouses. Participants choose their level of challenge. Waist harnesses and mountaineering helmets are provided.

Squaw Valley Tram Building
530-583-7673

Northstar-at-Tahoe offers adventure challenge courses for all ages. The ropes course combines ropes, cables and tall trees in a beautiful setting. For the truly adventurous, the high elements are 30 to 60 feet above ground, including climbing a perch and jumping for the trapeze, or riding a 300-foot zip line. A 24-foot climbing wall is open daily with rental shoes available to those who want to try this challenge for the first time.

Northstar-at-Tahoe
Summer only.
Reservations required.
530-562-2285
www.skinorthstar.com

Sierra Mountain Guides offer introductory, intermediate and advanced rock climbing courses out of Kirkwood Resort. The climbing wall for practice sessions is located adjacent to the ski school building.

Sierra Mountain Guides and Doug Robinson are both booked with Kirkwood Resort.
209-258-6000
www.skikirkwood.com

Doug Robinson is one of the most respected professional mountaineers. His "Moving Over Stone" classes share his expertise with students of all levels, starting on Kirkwood Resort granite and moving into the El Dorado National Forest with experienced climbers.

Summer

Adventures

Bungee Jumping

Bungee Squaw Valley
High Camp, Squaw Valley
Fee to ride the cable car.
530-583-4000

Bungee Squaw Valley is right at the edge of High Camp Bath and Tennis Club. Operating all year, here's your chance to say you've done it from 8,200 feet in summer shorts or your ski clothes.

Guided Hikes

Tahoe Trips and Trails
Tahoe City
530-583-4506

Special Features:
They offer mountain biking tours and multi sport samplers with hiking, biking, rafting, kayaking and horseback riding. August trips usually feature one night at the Shakespeare Festival at Sand Harbor. Special family trips are listed on page 211 in "Just For Kids."

Tahoe Trips and Trails takes groups of 10 to 16 into the Lake Tahoe area mountains on hikes for all abilities. With two guides for each trip, you can choose a faster or slower pace. Their guides have a broad knowledge of local flora, fauna and geology as well as stories of the old timers. Lunch and healthy snacks are provided.

Adventure Companies

Swayback Adventure Services
Reservations: 1-800-swayback
(1-800-792-2225)
www.swayback.com

Swayback Adventure Services offers custom adventures for families and small groups. Owner Dave Rintala is a class five river guide and helicopter ski guide who will take you mountain biking, kayaking, rock climbing or backpacking anywhere you want to go. Check the website for all the possible packages and plan a special trip.

Rock climbing lesson near Donner Pass.

Spooner Lake Outdoor Company
Spooner Lake Nevada State Park
775-749-5349 888-858-8844
www.flumetrail.com

Spooner Lake Outdoor Company offers mountain bike tours for groups of six people and will rent you a mountain bike. They also have kayak rentals and give fly fishing instruction. Their overnight wilderness cabins for rent are described in Cross Country Skiing on page 241. You can also arrange a bus shuttle from the state park parking lot for hikers, bikers and runners from the Mount Rose Highway to trailheads along the Tahoe Rim Trail.

Gallagher's Flying Trapeze
3225 North Lake Blvd.
Next to The Watermelon Patch
Tahoe City
530-308-6452
Tuesday through Sunday
10:00 am - 6:00 pm.

Gallagher's Flying Trapeze will let you experience the thrill of the flying trapeze with the aid of safety harness rigging. Experienced instructors take you to the top of the 25-foot-high trapeze where you swing out over a safety net from bar to bar with the help of a professional catcher. All ages, no experience necessary.

Skydiving

Skydive Lake Tahoe
530-832-1474
www.skydivelaketahoe.com

Skydive Lake Tahoe operates out of the Nervino airport in Beckworth, a 25-mile drive north of Truckee. Licensed and certified instruction for all abilities is supplied for jumps from 13,000 feet. You must be over 18 and under 220 pounds.

Adventures

Hummer and ATV Tours

Lake Tahoe Adventures offers ATV, Jeep and Hummer high mountain scenic tours on the Rubicon Trail, Carson Valley and Genoa Peak.

Lake Tahoe Adventures
Meeks Bay
530-577-2940
www.laketahoeadventure.com

Northstar-at-Tahoe has guided ATV tours for two hours, three times daily through the rugged terrain to Sawmill Lake and along ridges with views of the Martis Valley. Helmets, gloves and goggles are provided. Riders must wear closed-toe sturdy shoes.

Northstar-at-Tahoe
Reservations: 530-562-2267
Daily, mid June to Labor Day
weather permitting.
Tours leave 9:30 am, noon, and
2:30 pm.

Adventures for the Disabled

Disabled Sports USA offers year-round recreational instruction for those with physical handicaps. Summer offerings include water-skiing, hiking, rafting, kayaking, cycling and camping. Their longtime winter program includes all snowsport instruction.

DSUSA
Alpine Meadows
530-581-4161
www.bsusafw.org

In-Line Skating Instruction

All ages and abilities can benefit from group or private instruction in starting, stopping and negotiating obstacles and hills. Skates and gear is available to rent. After learning you can then take the West Shore Bike Trail.

In-Line Skating
530-412-1928
gnorgren@extreme.net

Summer

Excursions

If you have had too much sun, or the kids want a change of scenery, there are many interesting places to go for a special day-long excursion. You can visit Nevada's oldest town, go to the National Automobile Museum or visit one of the many hot springs on the east side of the Sierra. These excursions need a whole day, so pack a picnic, bathing suit, map of Nevada and pile into your car, for there are adventures over the hill. This section also lists three companies that will do the driving for you and tell you about the area's interesting history along the way.

Squaw Valley High Camp
Fee to ride the cable car.

Squaw Valley High Camp

Ride the cable car to High Camp at 8,200 feet above sea level to hike around the plateau, or, if you are feeling energetic, you can take the Pioneer Trail and climb to Emigrant Pass in order to see over into the North Fork of the American River. The views of the Lake Tahoe Basin are spectacular from the decks. Restaurants at High Camp include Alexander's for a sit-down dinner, the Poolside Café and a deli. This is an excellent way for families with small children to "climb" a mountain and get the views. For those who are sports-minded, facilities include a skating rink, spa, and heated swimming lagoon, all open to the public for additional fees. The skating rink is covered and you may rent skates or bring your own for a one-hour session. You can bungee jump here too. See "Adventures" on page 98 for information.

Excursions

Ponderosa Ranch

You'll step back into time when you visit the site used in the famous 1970s TV series, "Bonanza." You can search the town for memorabilia of the Old West, order barbeque food, and taste real sarsaparilla. There are gun fights to watch and you can pan for gold. A petting farm awaits the youngsters, and you can take a guided tour of the Cartwright's ranch house. Hayride breakfasts are held every day for only $2 above the price of admission to the park. The stables offer guided mountain trail rides and breakfast rides.

Ponderosa Ranch
Just south of Incline Village on Highway 28.
Admission fee.
Daily, mid April through October, 10:00 am to 6:00 pm.
775-831-0691
Stables: 775-831-2154

Special Features:
The 1871 chapel is available for weddings.

Grover Hot Springs State Park

Grover Hot Springs State Park is outside Markleeville on the eastern slope of the Sierra Nevada under Hawkins and Markleeville Peaks. The park is best known for two concrete pools that are fed from the runoff of six mineral springs and are regulated at 102°F to 104°F, just the right temperature to soak out tired muscles after hiking or cross-country skiing on the miles of trails through the 519-acre park.

Grover Hot Springs State Park
Fee per vehicle.
Fee per person for hot pools.
530-694-2248

Directions:
Take Highway 88 to Woodfords and south on Highway 89 to Markleeville. Follow signs to the park.

Bowers Mansion
Off U.S. 395 on Hwy. 429 north of Carson City.
Fee to tour mansion and use the pool.
775-849-1829

Historic Bowers Mansion and Hot Spring

This is a nice place to spend the day with the family, to picnic on the green lawns of Bowers Mansion Park, dip in the pool and tour the mansion. The pool is kept at about 80°F with a wading pool for toddlers. The fancy mansion was built by Sandy and Eilley Bowers who made their fortunes from the Comstock mines.

Nevada State Railroad Museum
Fee to visit museum.
Wednesday through Sunday year-round.
Train rides on weekends Memorial Day through Labor Day, some weekends in October.
775-687-6953

Directions:
Fairway Drive off U.S. 395 one mile south of Carson City.

Nevada State Railroad Museum

The museum is a tribute to Nevada's Virginia and Truckee Railroad that served Virginia City in its glory days. Not far from the museum millions of logs from the mills in Glenbrook on the east shore of Lake Tahoe ended their flume ride from Spooner Summit and were loaded onto the trains. The logs were used to shore up the tunnels of the Virginia City silver mines. Two engines and cars from the V&T have been lovingly restored by state employees. Volunteers drive a steam train and a 1920s motorcar for those who wish to step back in time on these grand machines. Times vary, so check with the museum for days and hours. There is something for every train buff in the museum gift shop.

Summer

Excursions

Nevada State Museum

The museum was formerly a U.S. Mint with its nineteenth-century machinery still intact. The 100-year-old coin machine stamped out 118 million quarters, dimes and pennies in its last three years of life when it was loaned to the Denver Mint to alleviate a coin shortage.

The exit is through a recreated silver mine where you walk along the mine rails and stand in the cage that took miners deep into the earth.

Genoa and the Mormon Station

Genoa was the first permanent town in the state of Nevada. Because the site was an ideal resting place for thirsty emigrants before they tackled the Sierra Nevada, a trading post was established in 1850 by six Mormons from Salt Lake City. In 1851 a new proprietor built a two-story log cabin in an "L" shape that formed two sides of a five-sided stockade.

Because Mormon Station was still a part of the Utah Territory, Brigham Young appointed Mormon apostle Orson Hyde to serve as probate judge and spiritual head of the community. Judge Hyde named the town Genoa because the area reminded him of the mountains near Genoa, Italy.

Nevada State Museum
U.S. 395 in Carson City across from the Nugget Casino.
Admission fee.
Daily, 10:00 am to 4:00 pm.
775-687-4811

Special Features:
Extensive natural history dioramas let you see the animals and birds of the region in their natural habitat. Don't miss the skeleton of the giant mammoth that lived in Nevada only 17,000 years ago, as well as fossils of creatures from dinosaur times.

Genoa and the Mormon Station

Directions:
From South Shore take Hwy. 207 east over the pass (Kingsbury Grade) to Hwy. 206 (Foothill Rd.) and drive north 2.5 miles to Genoa. From Carson Pass take Hwy. 88 east to junction with Hwy. 206 and drive north about 12 miles to Genoa.

Special Features:
You can wander around the now sleepy town and visit the recreated Mormon Station. The Genoa Country Store is in the rebuilt former Pony Express Station. Across Main Street you can peek in Nevada's first bar which has hosted many gun-toting cowboys and even an outlaw or two. The building has been used for Hollywood films, including John Wayne's last picture.

Excursions

The Story of John "Snowshoe" Thompson.

The grave of "Snowshoe" Thompson in the Genoa cemetery
Walk up Mill or Nixon Street to the cemetery. Here you will be able to find the grave of one of the Sierra's most colorful characters.

On a cold winter day in January 1856, a stranger schussed down out of the mountains on 10-foot skis with a canvas sack full of mail. No resident of the town ever expected to see outsiders once the snow had fallen on the mountain passes, much less to receive mail from home via California. On that day "Snowshoe" Thompson, an immigrant from Telemark, Norway, began a 20-year career carrying the winter mail twice a month between Placerville, California, and Genoa, Nevada. It took him an average of five days to cross the Carson Pass on the general route of the Emigrant Trail, and he seldom missed a delivery. "Snowshoe" Thompson was never paid by the U.S. Government for his services but he bought a homestead in Diamond Valley, near Markleeville. You can see a "Snowshoe" Thompson exhibit in the Courthouse Museum.

Summer

Excursions

National Automobile Museum

We all have the citizens of Reno to thank for creating a foundation to keep the fabulous automobile collection of William Fisk Harrah in town after he died. Old and young, men and women, all will find something of fascination at this spit and polish museum of automobiles and related history from the 1880s to the present. You can't miss this museum on the banks of the Truckee River painted the 1957 Chevrolet color known as Heather Fire Mist which looks like mauve to us. Four halls house 200 autos of every description, from carriages cum auto of the late 1800s to the corvette designed for John Wayne.

**National Automobile Museum
Corner of Lake Street South and Mill Street
Reno, Nevada
Monday through Saturday, 9:30 am to 5:30 pm.
Sunday, 10:00 am to 4:00 pm.
775-333-9300**

Special Features:
Appropriate gowns, hats and jewels worn by automobilists at the turn of the century are in cases along the walls. Walk down a 1930s street or remember the fins of the 1950s in the hall devoted to this era. Docent-led tours follow a 22-minute, high-tech, multi-media show chronicling the impact of the auto on our society. The museum store stocks a marvelous collection of auto memorabilia and the best book collection anywhere.

Summer

Courtesy of the National Automobile Museum

1938 Packard 1607 Convertible Coupe featured on the 1930s period street scene in the National Automobile Museum.

Excursions

Nevada Historical Society
1650 No. Virginia Street
Reno, Nevada
Wednesday through Sunday,
10:00 am to 5:00 pm.
Open all year.

Nevada Historical Society

The museum has well-documented dioramas of Nevada history, including debris from the pioneer trails across the hot Nevada desert. There are wall-size maps of the emigrant routes across the state, and the bookstore sells books about Nevada's colorful history including pamphlets for rock hounds and lovers of ghost towns.

Tour Companies

Tahoe Tours
Departures daily, 10:30 am.
Reservations required.
530-544-8687 800-458-9743
www.tahoe-tours.com

Tahoe Tours offers daily narrated tours around the rim of the lake, with plenty of stops at the best places for photographs. They also stop in Squaw Valley for a ride on the cable car to High Camp, or for shopping and lunch at the Boatworks Mall in Tahoe City, or they may stop to tour the Ehrman Mansion at Sugar Pine Point. This is any easy and relaxing way to see the best of Tahoe and let someone else do the driving.

Adventures Unlimited
Reservations required.
775-588-4772

Adventures Unlimited has been operating for many years. Julie and Rick Wright take people on narrated tours of many special places in the area. Their 30-passenger vans are specially equipped with televisions and headsets. There are gambling tours to the North Shore casinos, mansion tours or trips to Virginia City. In the

Excursions

fall you can go on an Apple Hill Winery Tour, a great way to have your own designated driver for a wine tasting adventure.

Eco Adventures

Owner Bob Anderson loves to tell people about the natural and human history of the region. Scheduled tours typically include two to 13 people with an experienced guide, lunch at one of his favorite restaurants and all admissions where applicable. One tour explores the natural history of Lake Tahoe with illuminating information about the geology, plants, animals and history. A Virginia City tour stops at Carson City's Capitol Building and the Nevada State Museum. Bob also leads rafting trips on the East Carson and Truckee Rivers, as well as guided hikes in Spooner State Park. You can even plan a private tour to any local destination.

Eco Adventures
Zephyr Cove
Reservations required.
775-588-6142

Summer

Beaches

More than thirty public beaches ring the shores of Lake Tahoe inviting you to loll on a blanket to soak up the sun, help the kids build sand castles or take long walks. Those along the North and East Shores are mostly sandy with shallow water, making them ideal choices for families. Along the West Shore most beaches tend to be rocky until you reach Meeks Bay. The beaches west of the South Tahoe *Y* are operated by the U.S. Forest Service, and some are free. These beaches can all be accessed via the bike path. The Nifty Fifty Trolley also stops at certain beaches in South Lake Tahoe. For those seeking warmer water and a more intimate view, Donner Lake west of Truckee has two beaches to offer.

Donner Memorial State Park
Fee per vehicle. Dogs on leash.

Directions:
Donner Pass Road just west of I-80 exit to Donner State Park.

Special Features:
There is no lifeguard on duty, and this beach can be windy in the afternoon.

Donner Lake West End Beach
Fee per person. No dogs allowed.

Directions:
Corner of South Shore Drive and Donner Pass Road.

Special Features:
An added attraction is the beautiful view of the Carson Range to the east. This is a favorite beach of locals and Nevadans, especially on weekends, so come early to find parking close to the beach.

Donner Memorial State Park

The beach at China Cove in the southwest corner of the park has a magnificent view of Donner Pass. Picnic tables and barbeque grills in a secluded forest setting make this an excellent choice for a day's outing that can include a visit to the museum and a walk in the woods.

Donner Lake West End Beach

Run by the Truckee Donner Recreation and Parks District, the beach and lawn area has facilities for every member of the family. There are a volleyball net and one tennis court, picnic tables and barbeque grills, jungle gym and swings, horseshoe pits and pedalboats for rent. With a lifeguard on duty, this is probably one of the best choices for families with small children.

Beaches

Tahoe City Commons Beach

A playground and large grassy area complement this beach in the heart of town, a great place to spend the afternoon when you first arrive. The views are spectacular as well.

Tahoe City Commons Beach
Tahoe City

Tahoe State Recreation Area

The beach is open daybreak to sunset. Operated by California State Parks, it offers camping, picnic facilities, barbeques and restrooms as well as a beach with shallow water.

Tahoe State Recreation Area
Fee per vehicle. No dogs allowed.

Directions:
One half mile east of the Tahoe City *Y*.

Lake Forest Beach, Skylandia Park and Beach, Pomin Beach and Lake Tahoe Public Access and Boat Launch

A wealth of possibilities are located in the Lake Forest area near Dollar Point. Some of the better-kept secrets are the trails through Skylandia Park woods. For those who want to mix boating with a day at the beach, this is a good choice.

Lake Forest Beach complex
Fee per vehicle. No dogs allowed.

Directions:
Lake Forest Road off Highway 28 one mile east of Tahoe City.

Summer

Patton Beach
Highway 28 in Carnelian Bay

Patton Beach

This small rocky beach has picnic facilities and barbeque grills and beautiful views of the blue waters of Carnelian and Agate Bays.

National Avenue Beach
End of National Avenue
Tahoe Vista

National Avenue Beach

A small grassy area for picnicking is close to the beach. It may look private, but it is open to the public free of charge.

Near Piño Grande Avenue
Tahoe Vista

Moondunes Beach

This small sunbathing and swimming beach has shallow water suitable for small children, but there are no picnic facilities or restrooms.

Agatam Beach
Across from Agatam Street
Tahoe Vista
No dogs allowed.

Agatam Beach

The beautiful sandy beach has shallow water that makes swimming enjoyable. With picnic tables, barbeques and restrooms, this is a great place to spend the day with a view down the lake toward South Shore. Best of all, it is free.

Secline Beach
End of Secline Street
Kings Beach

Secline Beach

This small, undeveloped beach has fantastic views down the lake and it is free.

Summer

Beaches

North Tahoe Beach Center

The sandy beach next to the community center is open to the public free of charge. However, there are fees to use the clubhouse, sauna, showers or large hot tub and picnic facilities.

North Tahoe Beach Center
Free parking for the beach.
Fees for facilities. No dogs allowed.

Directions:
Just west of Highway 267 on Highway 28 in Kings Beach.

Kings Beach State Recreation Area

This state-operated, sandy beach has shallow water and views the length of the lake. Facilities include a children's playground, picnic tables, barbeques and restrooms.

Kings Beach State Recreation Area
Fee per vehicle. No dogs allowed.

Directions:
A quarter-mile east of the intersection of Highway 28 and Highway 267.

Coon Street Picnic Area and Park

A quiet beach at the end of Coon Street is next to the brand new park near the State Recreation Area parking lot. There are benches, grass and picnic facilities and basketball hoops. It is next to a boat launch with boat rentals. There are restrooms.

Coon Street Park
Coon Street, Kings Beach

Incline Village Beaches

The beaches along Lakeshore Drive are not open to the public, but, if you are renting, you may obtain a permit from the Incline Village General Improvement District (IVGID) that operates all the recreational facilities in Incline Village.

IVGID Recreation Center
980 Incline Way
Incline Village
775-832-1310
No dogs allowed.

Special Features:
Renters must have a form signed by the owner or rental agent and pay a small fee. Passes are purchased at the IVGID Recreation Center.

Summer

Beaches

William Kent Campground
Fee per vehicle to enter park.

Directions:
Two miles south of the Tahoe City Y on Highway 89.

William Kent Campground

This rocky beach is operated by the U.S. Forest Service and has picnic tables, barbeques and restrooms. It's a good sunbathing spot with expansive views across the lake to the Nevada mountains, although not necessarily a comfortable place to swim.

Sunnyside Beach
On the north side of Sunnyside Resort.

Sunnyside Beach

The pebbles on this beach are perfect for skimming across the lake. It is a good place to amuse the children before or after dining at Sunnyside Resort.

Sugar Pine Point State Park
Entrance fee per vehicle.
No dogs allowed.

Directions:
Ten miles south of the Tahoe City Y on Highway 89.

Sugar Pine Point State Park

The pier and boat launch are part of the original summer haven of the Ehrmans who donated their beautiful corner of Lake Tahoe to the State of California. The lawns sloping down to the water make a perfect picnic spot and it is a great destination for a boat trip or bike ride along the West Shore. After your picnic on the lawn or pier, be sure to tour the mansion.

Meeks Bay Resort
Entrance fee per vehicle.
No dogs allowed.

Directions:
On Hwy. 89, eleven miles south of the Tahoe City Y.

Meeks Bay Resort

The resort is located near a wide sandy beach with boat launching, picnic facilities and restrooms. It has been a favorite with campers for many years.

Summer

Beaches

D.L. Bliss State Park

Beautiful beaches line the lakeshore just north of Rubicon Point. This is often a launching site for those with kayaks and canoes who wish to explore the coves and beaches south of the point on down to Emerald Bay. For those who tire of sitting in the sun, take the Rubicon Trail to Emerald Bay. (See page 194 in "Special Hikes" for a description.)

D.L. Bliss State Park
Entrance fee per vehicle.
No dogs allowed.

Directions:
Ten miles north of the South Lake Tahoe Y, 16.5 miles south of the Tahoe City Y.

Emerald Bay Beach

One mile down the trail from the overlook is a beautiful white beach. This a great place for a picnic, but don't feed the begging Canada geese or they will continue to pester you. The Vikingsholm is there to tour. With a car shuttle arranged you might want to consider hiking from Bliss Park on the Rubicon Trail to Emerald Bay, or you can come early and hike to Eagle Falls or on the new trail to Eagle Point. (See pages 195 and 197 in "Special Hikes.")

Emerald Bay Beach
Parking at Emerald Bay Overlook.
Fee to tour Vikingsholm.
Hike one mile from Emerald Bay Overlook. No dogs allowed.

Directions:
Overlook parking is 9.2 miles north of the Tahoe City Y.

Summer

Baldwin Beach
Fee per car.
No dogs allowed.
Directions:
Four miles north of the South Tahoe *Y* off Highway 89.

Baldwin Beach

The beach is managed by the U.S. Forest Service. With ample parking and views across the lake to Heavenly Ski Resort and a long wide beach, this is a good place to take the kids for the day. Restrooms and picnic facilities are available.

Kiva Beach, Tallac Historic Site
No fee. Dogs on leash are allowed on the shoreline up to Tallac Point. You may not take them farther onto the sand spit in front of Taylor Creek. This is a wildlife area.

Directions:
Three miles north of the South Tahoe *Y* off Highway 89.

Tallac Historic Site

This long beach is seldom crowded and stretches from Richardson's Resort to the Tallac Point Picnic Area. If you want to mix a little history with a day at the beach, park in the parking lot and walk along the paths of the Tallac Historic Site before your picnic and day at the beach. This is good beach for those who prefer to bike in and stop at the Historic Site beforehand.

Camp Richardson Resort Beach
Fee per vehicle. No dogs allowed.

Directions:
Located 2.6 miles north of the South Tahoe *Y* off Highway 89.

Camp Richardson's Resort Beach

The beach at Richardson's Resort is under concession from the U.S. Forest Service. All kinds of water-related activities are offered here, including kayak tours, parasailing, boat rentals and cruises to Emerald Bay. Guests at the resort and campground favor this beach, so it may be crowded on weekends.

Summer

Beaches

Pope Beach

This is a very popular U.S. Forest Service beach. Beautiful views and a gently sloping swimming area create an ideal location for a day of sunning and swimming. Dogs are not allowed at any designated swimming areas. You can avoid the traffic by taking the trolley or riding bicycles here. See "Area Bus Service" on page 2 for information and phone numbers.

Thomas Reagan Memorial Beach

This South Lake Tahoe Recreation Department beach has a snack bar and a playground for the children. Views to the north are spectacular. The water is shallow and therefore often warm.

El Dorado Beach

Operated by the South Lake Tahoe Recreation Department, this beach offers at least a mile of walking with views to the North Shore. There are picnic facilities with barbeques and restrooms.

Pope Beach
Fee per vehicle. No dogs allowed.

Directions:
Two miles north of the South Tahoe *Y* off Highway 89.

Thomas Reagan Memorial Beach
No dogs allowed.

Directions:
Take Lakeview Dr. off U.S. 50 to Sacramento St.

El Dorado Beach
No dogs allowed.

Directions:
Along U.S. 50 between Rufus Allen Blvd. and Lakeview Dr. in South Lake Tahoe.

Summer

Beaches

Connolly Beach
Limited parking. No dogs allowed.

Directions:
On U.S. 50 east of El Dorado Beach behind Timber Cove Lodge.

Connolly Beach

This small beach is operated by the South Lake Tahoe Recreation Department. It is shallow with warm water, making this a good place for toddlers. There are restrooms and picnic facilities.

Round Hill Pines Beach
Fee to park and fee per person.

Directions:
About 1.5 miles north of Stateline off U.S. 50. Look for the sign and drive down to the beach.

Special Features:
A protected sun deck next to the snack bar has tables and barbeques for sandless picnics. The barbeque and beach facilities are rented to large groups throughout the summer, but the beach remains open to the public at all times.

Round Hill Pines Beach

This is a private concession beach on U.S. Forest Service land. It is great for families because of its protected location and the variety of activities available. A heated pool allows swimming even when the lake's water temperatures are cold. There are two volleyball courts as well as horseshoe pits and a tennis court that is not for a championship game but is fine for practicing.

Nevada Beach
Fee per vehicle. No dogs allowed.

Directions:
Drive 1.5 miles north of Stateline on U.S. 50 to Elk Point Road. Turn left and drive .8 miles west to parking.

Nevada Beach

This beautiful beach next to the campground is also for day visitors. There is a special boaters' area if you want to rent a boat at Zephyr Cove and cruise in. The views from this beach across to Mount Tallac are some of the best.

Summer

Beaches

Zephyr Cove

There is a U.S. Forest Service beach at the cove as well as a commercial beach. Cruise lines that leave from the cove and all manner of water toys can be rented. This makes Zephyr Cove an excellent choice for families that want a variety of activities.

Secret Harbor Beaches

A series of secluded coves surrounded by shining granite boulders can be reached with a moderate hike along an access road that winds gently downhill. Take the first trail to the right after the parking lot to access the most northerly beach called Chimney Beach. Secret Harbor beach is in a cove at the end of the road. Some of these beaches are clothing optional.

Sand Harbor

The beach is part of the Lake Tahoe Nevada State Park. It has one of the most spectacular views anywhere in the Tahoe Basin. There are walking paths onto rocky promontories and acres of shallow water for swimming. Facilities at the park include picnic areas, barbeques and restrooms. A boat launch is at the northernmost entrance to the park.

Zephyr Cove
Fee per vehicle.

Directions:
At Zephyr Cove, 4 miles north of Stateline on U.S. 50.

Special Features:
Picnic facilities, restrooms and barbeques along with a snack bar provide everything you need.

Secret Harbor Beaches
Chemical Toilets. Dogs allowed.

Directions:
The parking lot is on Highway 28, five miles north of U.S. 50. Parking along the road is limited.

Special Note:
As of the time of publication, plans were being discussed to restrict parking on Highway 28. If you do park on the highway, please use designated trails in order to protect the lake from erosion caused by going cross country down to the beaches.

Sand Harbor
Fee per vehicle. No dogs allowed.

Directions:
On Highway 28, five miles south of Incline Village or 8 miles north of U.S. 50.

Special Features:
Sand Harbor is the site for Shakespeare performances in August. In midsummer the parking lots fill early.

Summer

Boating

With its crystal-clear water and spectacular scenery, Lake Tahoe is a boater's paradise. Whether you want to paddle along the shore, try your hand at windsurfing, charter a boat for fishing, or explore the lakeshore with a powerboat, all is possible. There are lovely coves where you can put in to a beach for a picnic. However, storms with high winds can come up at any time and Lake Tahoe can froth up with ocean-size waves, so be sure to check the weather forecast with the launch facility before casting off on your own.

Several beaches are favorite destinations for boaters. They include the beach and campground on the north side of Emerald Bay, although many just cruise in to the sandy beaches at the west end to take a tour of Vikingsholm or have a picnic. Nevada Beach, Round Hill Pines Beach and Zephyr Cove are on the East Shore. North along the East Shore are Skunk Harbor, Secret Harbor and, of course, Sand Harbor.

© Ellie Huggins

Moored for the day at Skunk Harbor.

Boating

Water craft rentals of all kinds are available at many locations at Donner Lake and Lake Tahoe. Some public launch ramps charge only for parking. Marinas charge for use of their launch facilities. Marinas and public launch ramps at Lake Tahoe are at the following locations, listed in the following order: West Shore, Tahoe City, North Shore, along the East Shore, around the South Shore and north to Camp Richardson.

Meeks Bay Resort: 530-525-7242

Homewood Marina: 530-525-5966

Obexer's, Homewood: 530-525-7962

Sunnyside Marina: 530-583-720

Tahoe Boat Company in Tahoe City:
530-583-5567

Lake Forest Beach Area public ramp:
530-581-4017

Sierra Boat Company, Carnelian Bay:
530-546-2551

North Tahoe Marina, Tahoe Vista:
530-546-8248, 546-4889

Coon Street public launch ramp,
Kings Beach: 530-546-7248

Sand Harbor Boat Launch:
775-831-0494

Cave Rock on U.S. 50: 775-831-0494

Zephyr Cove Marina, boat mooring only:
775-588-6644

Lakeside Marina, So. Lake Tahoe:
530-541-6626

Ski Run Marina, So. Lake Tahoe:
530-544-0200

El Dorado Boat Ramp, Hwy. 50,
So. Lake Tahoe

Timber Cove Marina, So. Lake Tahoe:
530-544-2942

Tahoe Keys Marina, So. Lake Tahoe:
530-541-2155

Anchorage Marina, Camp Richardson:
530-541-1777

There are special regulations in effect on Lake Tahoe and Fallen Leaf Lake regarding two-stroke engines. Personal watercraft must have electronic or Rotax fuel injections engines. No carbureted two stroke engines greater than 10 horsepower are allowed. All rentals meet the requirements.

Other locations for boating are Echo Lakes and Fallen Leaf Lake. Lower Echo Lake and Fallen Leaf Lake have boat rentals and a launch site for your own boat. Echo Lakes is particularly nice for canoes or kayaks as you can paddle from Lower Lake into Upper Echo Lake. In the Carson Pass area, boat rentals and a launch site are available at Caples Lake Resort. See Caples Lake under "Fishing" on page 137.

Boating

Donner Lake
Public docks are located along Donner Pass Road along the lake.

Special Features:
The lake is augmented by a dam and releases usually begin the day after Labor Day.

Donner Lake Boat Launch
Donner Pass Road at the west end of the lake.
Fee to launch.

Prosser Creek, Boca, Stampede

Directions:
Drive north from the Boca I-80 exit to Stampede Dam Rd. Prosser Creek Reservoir is on Prosser Dam Rd. off Highway 89 North.

Special Features:
The water level drops during the summer so that some launching ramps become inaccessible.

Donner Lake

Donner Lake is a favorite place for all kinds of boating. Morning, when the lake is calm, is the perfect time to canoe or water-ski. Anglers will be found on the lake at all times of day and in all seasons.

Truckee Donner Recreation and Parks Boat Launch

The Truckee Donner Recreation and Parks District operates a public boat launch on Donner Pass Road not far from the West End Beach.

Prosser Creek, Boca and Stampede Reservoirs

Water-skiing is permitted on Boca and Stampede Reservoirs. Prosser Creek Reservoir is open to sailing and fishing. Boat launching ramps are available at each lake.

© Ellie Huggins

Boating on Donner Lake.

Summer

Boating

Water Ski Instruction

Goldcrest Water Ski School

Children as young as four years old have taken lessons from this school. The instructors will hold on to beginners to make sure that they get up and ski next to them if they wish. After your lessons, you can use the heated pool and jacuzzi at the resort the rest of the day, and they'll even serve you continental breakfast if you have an early lesson.

Goldcrest Water Ski School
8194 North Lake Blvd.
Kings Beach
530-546-7412

Kings Beach Aqua Sports

The guaranteed learn-to-ski program will take children four years old and up including their parents and teach you all to water-ski.

Kings Beach Aqua Sports
Kings Beach State Recreation Area
530-546-2782

Directions:
On Highway 28, one quarter-mile east of Highway 267.

Lake Tahoe Water Ski School

This ski school gives lessons at two locations and will pick you up at any waterfront location upon request. They give lessons for skiers of all abilities and supply wet suits.

Lake Tahoe Water Ski School
Camp Richardson Resort
South Lake Tahoe
530-544-7747

Don Borges Water Ski School

The school is located at Round Hill Pines Beach and Marina, where you can rent everything you need to take a lesson or charter a boat to ski on your own.

Don Borges Water Ski School
Round Hill Pines Marina
Round Hill, Nevada
530-541-1351

Kayaking

Tahoe Whitewater Tours
Reservations recommended.
Tours leave from the Regional
Park just south of the Tahoe
City *Y*.
530-581-2441 800-581-2441

Tahoe Whitewater Tours

Tahoe Whitewater Tours takes up to
12 people on the tour of a lifetime.
They transport you to their starting
point at Eagle Point and lead you in
one and two-person kayaks around
Emerald Bay. You don't need to have
kayaked before, as their experienced
guides teach you how to paddle.
Picnics are provided at the boat camp
in Emerald Bay or on Fannette Island.
The leaders also conduct trips for
handicapped or wheelchair sports
enthusiasts.

Kayak Tahoe
Timber Cove Marina
South Lake Tahoe
Reservations recommended.
530-544-2011

Kayak Tahoe

No need for special experience to go
out on the lake with Kayak Tahoe.
The Llanoys offer special tours, give
you lessons or rent kayaks, and lead
Emerald Bay tours throughout the
summer.

From their Hope Valley Outdoor
Center they rent kayaks so you can try
the East Fork of the Carson River and
open deck kayaks for float trips on the
West Fork of the Carson River and
Red Lake.

Cruising Lake Tahoe

There is no better way to experience the beauty of the Lake Tahoe basin than to cruise to the middle of the lake or to fabled Emerald Bay. You can pick a sailing yacht, catamaran, luxury yacht or one of three large paddlewheelers that operate from the North Shore or South Shore. All require reservations. In addition, a number of fishing charter boats offer cruises of Emerald Bay for small groups. See "Fishing Charters" on page 138 for details.

Hornblower's Tahoe Queen

Hornblower Cruises-Lake Tahoe operates the glass-bottomed paddlewheeler *Tahoe Queen* for year-round cruises along the shore to Emerald Bay. A richly appointed interior enhances the dining experience of a sunset dinner-dance cruise. A special family Emerald Bay cruise includes a scavenger hunt for the kids and meeting Tahoe Tessie. Best of all, the kids ride free.

Hornblower Cruises
Ski Run Marina Village
South Lake Tahoe
530-541-3364 800-238-2463
www.hornblower.com

Special Features:
The company has introduced *The Meteor*, a 125-passenger motorboat that can accommodate all your adventure toys. It will stop at Ski Run Marina, Tahoe City Marina and Sand Harbor. There will be packages that include transportation for raft trips, golf or skiing. It will be used for the Squaw Valley ski shuttle as well.

Summer

The *M.S. Dixie II* in Emerald Bay.

© Ellie Huggins

M.S. Dixie II
Zephyr Cove, Nevada
775-588-3508
www.tahoedixie2.com

Special Features:
Free shuttle service for individuals can be reserved throughout the South Shore Casino area.

North Tahoe Cruises
Lighthouse Marina behind
Safeway in Tahoe City.
530-583-0141

M.S. Dixie II

The original paddlewheeler company has been Cruisin' the Lake since 1949. The *M.S. Dixie II*, a new Mississippi sternwheeler, sails to Emerald Bay year-round. With heated decks they can offer comfortable winter cruises. Their dinner-dance cruise to Emerald Bay is a favorite year-round – dining with complimentary wine and dancing to tunes of Tahoe's "Phoenix." From April to November you can cruise along the South Shore and enjoy a champagne brunch. A special two-hour dinner cruise that is just right for families and with special senior rates leaves daily in the summer at 5:00 p.m. Breakfast cruises to historic Glenbrook take place in summer only.

North Tahoe Cruises

The *Tahoe Gal*, a Mississippi paddlewheeler, sails daily to Emerald Bay. With restaurant and bar service on board, you can sit on the deck or inside and see the beautiful homes, beaches and parks along the West Shore. The captain spins stories of Tahoe's human and natural history on the trip south. Weather permitting, they operate all year. There are daily dinner cruises, and private parties may hire the boat for a dinner-dance.

Cruising Lake Tahoe

GO'N BOAT'N

The high-end water limo service specializes in day, around-the-lake and sunset cruises, as well as weddings and special occasions. The 32-foot power boat is powered by an 830 horsepower motor and reaches 70 mph.

GO'N BOAT'N
Sunnyside: 530-583-7417
Homewood: 530-525-1214
Home Office: 530-581-3962
www.gonboatn.com

Special Features:
They pick up and drop off anywhere your sense of adventure might take you.

The Party Boat of Tahoe Keys Yacht Charters

You may rent their party boat for a group or for a perfect wedding on Lake Tahoe.

The Party Boat
Tahoe Keys Yacht Charters
530-542-2111 888-542-2111

Special Features:
They will provide all food for your wedding or party by High Altitude Catering Company.

Sailing Ventures

You can either charter one of their yachts for a day on the lake, or join their sailing classes and then rent one on your own.

Sailing Ventures
2435 Venice Drive East
South Lake Tahoe
530-542-1691
www.sailtahoe.com

Action Watersports Catamaran Cruises

Sail the lake on a 55-foot catamaran to Cal-Neva Bay on the north shore. Libations and appetizers are included.

Action Watersports
Sierra Cloud Catamaran Cruises
Hyatt Regency Lake Tahoe
Daily, 1:30 pm, 4:00 pm, 6:30 pm.
775-831-4386

Action Watersports "Windsong"

The 65-foot Mac Gregor "Windsong" leaves three times daily. The can take up to 24 people. Chips, sodas and water are available and brown bagging is allowed.

Action Watersports "Windsong"
Timber Cove Marina
Daily, 12:00 pm, 3:00 pm, 6:00 pm.
530-544-2942

Summer

Cruising Lake Tahoe

Tahoe Para-dice Charters
Summer: Camp Richardson
Resort
Winter: Tahoe Keys
530-541-7499

Tahoe Para-dice Private Charters

The 70-foot *Tahoe Para-dice* takes up to 49 passengers every day on a cruise to Emerald Bay for a close-up view of Vikingsholm. They offer party cruises and weddings with live entertainment or a hot tub for a memorable event.

Tahoe Sailing Charters
Captain Mike Pavel
Tahoe City Marina
Daily, 1:00 pm, 3:00 pm, 5:30 pm.
Reservations: 530-583-6200

Tahoe Sailing Charters

The company offers skippered sailing cruises, yacht charters, sailing lessons and even regatta racing on their 33-foot sloop *Avalanche*. Cruises last two hours and are for up to six people. If you wish you can plan a special sunset sail or Emerald Bay trip.

Tahoe Schooner Co.
Tahoe Keys Marina
South Lake Tahoe
530-542-2217 775 423-4399
888-550-4575
tahoeschooner@webtv.net

Tahoe Schooner Co.

Experience the thrill of sailing in a 1931 schooner. They will give instruction or take you for a sail to Emerald By, for wildlife viewing or for a very special wedding. You can even charter the boat to go to dinner at a restaurant on the water.

Tahoe Thunder at Action
Watersports of Tahoe
3411 Lake Tahoe Blvd.
South Lake Tahoe
530-544-5387
www.action-watersports.com

Tahoe Thunder at Action Watersports of Tahoe

Ride on Tahoe's fastest speedboat for the thrill of wind in your face. There are daily tours of Emerald Bay, or you can plan a group charter of this special boat.

Cruising Lake Tahoe

Woodwind Lake Tahoe

Captain Steve Dunham offers you a special opportunity to feel the wind in your face sailing Lake Tahoe on a catamaran or trimaran with glass-bottom views. Four times a day the *Woodwind II* departs from Zephyr Cove with up to 50 passengers on board. Brisk winds take you up the Nevada shore. A romantic sunset champagne cruise departs every evening, a special way to see the sun set behind the western mountains ringing the lake. Beverages are included in the ticket price. The 30-passenger trimaran sails out of Camp Richardson on the South Shore to Emerald Bay with unparalleled views of Mt. Tallac and the Desolation Wilderness. You might also be lucky and see one of the bald eagles that nest at Eagle Point.

Woodwind Lake Tahoe
Zephyr Cove, Nevada
Reservations: 775-588-3000
"Woody" charter: 775-588-1855
Camp Richardson Resort
South Lake Tahoe
Reservations: 530-542-2212
888-867-6394
www.sailwood.com

Special Features:
Woodwind now offers a restored 15-passenger "woody" power boat for private charter out of Zephyr Cove. Experience the wind in your face while racing over the waters in a famous Tahoe "woody."

Summer

Fishing

Boca, Stampede and Prosser Creek reservoirs near Truckee offer good fishing. Many streams off Highway 89 north of Truckee are also good places to cast a fly. Donner Lake's north shore docks are easily accessible and many good-sized trout have been landed from these locations. Near South Lake Tahoe you will find excellent fishing at Fallen Leaf Lake and the Echo Lakes. In the Carson Pass area, Caples Lake and the Blue Lakes are favorites. All lakes are regularly stocked with rainbow trout in summer.

Lake Tahoe is open to fishing all year. However, upstream to the first lake of any tributaries, and the banks of Lake Tahoe within 300 feet of the mouth of a tributary, are only open to anglers from July 1 to September 30. If you don't mind hiking, the lakes in Desolation Wilderness beckon with excellent fishing possibilities. Don't forget that along with your fishing license you will need a wilderness permit and your favorite mosquito repellant.

For those who want to catch one of Lake Tahoe's famous Mackinaw or kokanee salmon, there are numerous charter services and fly-fishing guides listed in the next section, "Fishing Charters," on page 138.

Hardy anglers can try ice fishing at Caples Lake or one of the reservoirs when they are frozen. It would be a good idea, however, to check on the condition of the ice with the local stores that sell fishing licenses.

Remember a fishing license is necessary for all anglers 16 years and older. These may be purchased at most sporting goods and hardware stores.

The daily limit for Lake Tahoe is five trout, but no more than two Mackinaw. Fishing in Lake Tahoe is legal one hour before sunrise to two hours after sunset. In all other bodies of water you may fish from one hour before sunrise to only one hour after sunset.

Fishing

Donner Lake

Troll all year for those famous Mackinaw trout. Bank fishing brings in rainbow and brown trout. The north shore docks and boat launch area are favorite spots for casting a line to catch the planted rainbows. Kokanee salmon are also found here.

Donner Lake

Directions:
Along Donner Pass Rd. west of Truckee.

Martis Creek Lake

This is a catch-and-release lake where cutthroat trout are caught. Only barbless artificial lures or flies are allowed.

Martis Creek Lake

Directions:
Off Highway 267 between Truckee and Northstar.

Prosser Creek Reservoir

You can bank fish and troll for rainbow and brown trout in this local reservoir.

Prosser Creek Reservoir

Directions:
Take Prosser Dam Road off Highway 89 North.

Summer

© Ellie Huggins

Waiting for the rainbows to bite.

Fishing

Boca Reservoir

Directions:
Take the Boca Exit off I-80 and drive 2 miles north on Stampede Dam Road. A special wheelchair access ramp is located at the dam.

Stampede Reservoir

Directions:
Take the Boca exit off I-80 and drive 7-8 miles north on Stampede Dam Road.

Little Truckee River between Stampede and Boca Reservoirs

Directions:
Follow directions to Stampede.

Truckee River between Tahoe City and Truckee

Directions:
Park along Highway 89 or in the U.S. Forest Service campgrounds.

Boca Reservoir

Both bank fishing and trolling for rainbow and brown trout are good on this local reservoir, and fly fishing is worthwhile near the inlet of the Little Truckee River.

Stampede Reservoir

Fish from the bank or troll here for rainbow and brown trout. This is one of the best spots for kokanee salmon. The water level is drawn down during the summer.

Little Truckee River between Stampede and Boca Reservoirs

Fly fishing for both rainbow and brook trout is good in this stream below the Stampede Dam. However, due to extremely high releases of water in 1994, the habitat in this part of the river was changed. Check with local sporting goods stores about the status of this section of the Little Truckee.

Truckee River between Tahoe City and Truckee

The river was planted with rainbow trout below River Ranch at the entrance to Alpine Meadows. Habitat restoration along this section of the river has improved spawning areas.

Fishing

Truckee River between Truckee and Nevada State Line

This is a wild trout river. No live bait or barbed hooks are allowed and there are size limits. A two-mile stretch of the river is marked private and is off-limits. A Truckee River Access Map is available at most stores that sell bait and equipment.

Sagehen Creek

Sagehen Creek is catch and release only and is a favorite for fly fishing. The wildflowers are spectacular on the trails along the creek, which makes this an excellent place to take a companion who may not want to fish.

Lake Tahoe Bank Fishing

You can find rainbow trout along the North Shore at Dollar Point, Crystal Bay Point, or along the West Shore south of Tahoe City. Sand Harbor and Cave Rock are listed separately below. The tributaries into the lake are closed to fishing except for certain months in the summer. See page 130 for details.

Truckee River East of Truckee

Directions:
Access is off Glenshire Drive and Hirshdale Road.

Sagehen Creek

Directions:
Take Highway 89 north 7.5 miles from the I-80 Sierraville exit.

Lake Tahoe Fishing

Directions:
Along Highway 89 south from Tahoe City or Highway 28 around the lake.

Summer

Fallen Leaf Lake

Directions:
Take Fallen Leaf Road from Highway 89 to the lodge.

Special Features:
The new lodge rents boats, operates the launch and a store with gifts and groceries. A hamburger stand satisfies hungry anglers after a morning on the water.

Fallen Leaf Lake

This beautiful alpine lake, created by a glacier that scooped out a long bowl, is deep enough for Mackinaw. You will need a boat and spinners to reel in this trophy fish. Otherwise, try using worms from the bank near the lodge for rainbow trout.

Taylor Creek

Directions:
Park at the U.S. Forest Service Interpretive Center 3.2 miles north of the South Tahoe *Y*.

Special Features:
See page 198 for information about the Rainbow Trail to the Stream Profile Chamber.

Taylor Creek

Taylor Creek drains Fallen Leaf Lake and is a principal spawning stream for the kokanee salmon of Lake Tahoe. The fishing season starts July 1. You will need worms, eggs or flies to catch the resident brown and rainbow trout.

Trout Creek and the Upper Truckee River

Directions:
Can be reached off U.S. 50 between Al Tahoe Blvd. and Tahoe Keys Blvd. in South Lake Tahoe.

Trout Creek and the Upper Truckee River

The season starts on July 1 on these tributaries where only native fish are found. Hike along the stream and bring your fly rod or regular tackle with small spinners, salmon eggs or worms.

Cave Rock
Fee per vehicle.

Directions:
Drive north from Stateline 6 miles on U.S. 50 to the Cave Rock Boat Launch parking lot.

Cave Rock

The boat launch is operated by the Nevada State Parks Department. The rocks along the shore are a favorite place for catching rainbow or brown trout. Bring spinners, worms, salmon eggs or even marshmallows for bait.

Fishing

Sawmill Pond

The pond is operated by the U.S. Forest Service for anglers 15 years old and under, although adults may help children fish.

Sawmill Pond
530-573-2600

Directions:
On Lake Tahoe Blvd. 3 mile south of the U.S. 50 intersection.

Spooner Lake

Spooner Lake is the only catch-and-release lake in Nevada. Float tubes are recommended as the fishing is best in the middle of the lake.

Spooner Lake
Fee per vehicle

Directions:
In Lake Tahoe Nevada State Park on Highway 28 just north of U.S. 50.

Sand Harbor

There is no more beautiful place at Lake Tahoe to sit on the shore and cast for the trout that inhabit the waters around the rocky shoreline here. You'll be able to catch rainbow and brown trout, and, if not all members of the family want to fish, the rest can enjoy the beach and swimming.

Sand Harbor
Fee per vehicle

Directions:
On Highway 28 about 5 miles south of Incline Village and 8 miles north of U.S. 50.

Echo Lakes

The Echo Lakes have long been favorite fishing lakes. Favorite shore fishing spots are near the dam and along the north shore of Lower Echo Lake. Rainbows, brook trout and an occasional kokanee salmon can be caught on lures, salmon eggs and power bait.

Echo Lakes

Directions
Drive 9 miles west on U.S. 50 from the South Tahoe Y to Echo Lake Rd. Drive north to the Sno-Park and turn left following signs to Echo Lake.

Special Features:
The Echo Chalet rents fishing boats and canoes. Since water-skiing is not allowed on Upper Echo Lake, trolling is good here.

Summer

Fishing

Tahoe Trout Farm
1023 Blue Lake Ave.
South Lake Tahoe
Memorial Day through Labor Day.
530-541-1491

Tahoe Trout Farm

Here's a chance for everyone in the family to catch the limit. However, you will need to have a large group over for dinner if you do. Admission, bait and tackle are free. You only pay for what you catch.

Carson Pass Area

Anyone willing to hike several miles can reach scores of back country lakes from the Carson Pass area. All you need is one of the excellent hiking guidebooks of the region for descriptions of the trails to alpine lakes that are regularly stocked. A few easy ones are in the "Special Hikes" section starting on page 208. Suggestions follow for places that you can reach by car.

The Carson River

Directions:
Access points can be reached easily at Picketts Junction or from Hope Valley Campground on Blue Lakes Road.

The Carson River

The Carson River meanders through Hope, Faith and Charity Valleys and anglers have been known to catch cutthroats right off the bridge at Picketts Junction, or you can try your favorite fly or bait anywhere you can get to the bank. The river is stocked with rainbow. Below Picketts Junction the river runs swiftly downhill. The best access points are at the various U.S. Forest Service Campgrounds east of Sorensen's Resort.

Fishing

Blue Lakes

The Upper and Lower Blue Lakes can be reached easily with any automobile. However, to reach other lakes in the area, you will want a four-wheel-drive car. The lakes offer some of the best fishing in the region and are stocked with rainbow. Power bait, worms or your favorite fly will probably catch the daily limit.

Blue Lakes

Directions:
Drive east on Highway 88 to Blue Lakes Road. Drive south about 10 miles to Lower Blue Lakes Campground.

Caples Lake

Caples Lake is inhabited by six species of trout: Mackinaw, brown, rainbow, cutthroat, eastern brook and cutbow. Boat rentals are available at the Caples Resort Marina. You will want to take a boat onto the lake for those feisty Mackinaw, but casting a line from the bank can bring in many of the other species. The lodge offers boat rides to the far shores for those who want to hike into back country lakes or streams for rainbow or brown trout. Anglers may want to bring along their companions, for this is spectacular country for gazers, photographers or flower lovers to spend a quiet day while others are fishing.

Caples Lake Resort Marina
209-258-8888

Directions:
Four miles west of Carson Pass on Highway 88. Boat rentals available.

Fishing Charters

Trolling for Mackinaw trout and kokanee salmon that live deep in Lake Tahoe, casting for wild trout or learning techniques to fish in local creeks and alpine lakes are best done with a local guide. This section lists the Lake Tahoe and Donner Lake charter services and fly fishing guides. Most boat trips start either before dawn or late in the afternoon. All charter companies supply tackle, and one-day licences, if necessary. Some also provide sightseeing tours as well. The fly fishing guides offer half-day, all-day or longer trips to special lakes and streams. Reservations are necessary.

Clearwater Guides
Truckee
530-587-9302
800-354-0958

Clearwater Guides

Chris Turner will take you out on Donner Lake, Stampede Reservoir or Lake Tahoe to find trophy-size browns, kokanee or Mackinaw. Groups of one to six persons can choose between 4 and 7-hour trips on Donner Lake and Stampede Reservoir, or 4 and 5-hour trips on Lake Tahoe.

Kingfish
Homewood
530-525-5360

Special Features:
Kingfish offers daily tours of Emerald Bay.

Kingfish

The *Kingfish* is a 43-foot boat specially designed and built for Lake Tahoe. This charter service operates all year. Trips leave early in the morning with snacks, coffee and cold drinks provided, and they'll even clean the fish for you.

Reel Deal Sportfishing and Lake Tours
Tahoe City
530-581-0924

Special Features:
You can arrange a tour of the lake as well.

Reel Deal Sportfishing and Lake Tours

Fish year-round with Captain Big Pete on his comfortable cabin cruiser with fully loaded galley. He supplies all tackle.

Fishing Charters

Mickey's Big Mack Charters

Mickey operates 48-foot and 32-foot boats out of Sierra Boat Company in Carnelian Bay. His more than 30 years of experience assures that he will find the fish. You can select a full trip and take four people for the price of three. All you need is a fishing license and your own food and drink.

**Mickey's Big Mack Charters
Sierra Boat Company
Carnelian Bay
530-546-4444**

Reel Magic Sport Fishing

Early morning sportfishing trips leave daily. Bring your own food and drink.

**Reel Magic Sport Fishing
Tahoe City
530-587-6027**

Mac-A-Tac Fishing Charters

Mac-A-Tac specializes in groups of three to six people. Charters leave early in the morning or late afternoon. Sightseeing charters are also available. Bring your own food and drink.

**Mac-A-Tac Fishing Charters
North Tahoe Marina
Tahoe Vista
530-546-2500**

Dennis' Eagle Point Fishing Charter

Dennis Mitchell has a special offer to make. He'll take you out morning or afternoon and, if you catch the biggest fish for the week, he'll take you out free the next time. Charters go any month of the year, so bundle up and try fishing one day of your ski vacation.

**Dennis' Eagle Point Fishing Charter
Anchorage Marina
Camp Richardson
530-577-6834**

Summer

Fishing Charters

Captain Bruce Hernandez
Tahoe Paradise
530-577-2246

Captain Bruce Hernandez Guide Service

Bruce Hernandez offers his expert guide service to take you on the lake and catch the big ones. He supplies all tackle and bait aboard his 25-foot Taira Cutty.

Tahoe Sports Fishing
Ski Run Marina
South Lake Tahoe
530-541-5448
530-577-4147

Tahoe Sports Fishing

Captain Dean and Captain John have six boats and over 30 years experience. The boats go out three times daily and furnish all the gear.

Mile High Fishing Charters
Tahoe Keys Marina
530-541-5312
www.Fishtahoe.com

Special Features:
Homemade light breakfast snack and fruit are provided. Lunches can be arranged for all day trips.

Mile High Fishing Charters

Captain Joby Cefalu is a Lake Tahoe native with 15 years experience fishing on Lake Tahoe. He provides light tackle and bait on his state of the art fishing boat.

O'Malley's Fishing Charters
Zephyr Cove, Nevada
775-588-4102

O'Malley's Fishing Charters
O'Malley offers private charters with all tackle provided. His 22-foot Radon craft has all the latest equipment to help you find the big ones.

Summer

Fly Fishing Guides

If you want to learn more about fly fishing from the experts or want a guide to help you find golden trout in an alpine lake, there are experienced guides to take you to their special places for wild trout or teach you new skills.

Thy Rod and Staff

Thy Rod and Staff
Truckee
530-587-7333

Frank Pisciotta, a licensed guide endorsed by Orvis, teaches catch and release with barbless hooks. He specializes in finding the rare wild trout in the area. He'll take you and the kids to those special creeks where you can try your new art and probably catch a few. Nothing comes home for dinner, however. He teaches in the best tradition of Norman McClean from *A River Runs Through It*.

California School of Flyfishing

California School of Flyfishing
Truckee
530-587-7005

Ralph and Lisa Cutter's California School of Flyfishing has been honored by *Rod and Reel* magazine. Together they published *Sierra Trout Guide*, a best-selling guide to fishing in the Sierra. Operating since 1981 out of Truckee, Lisa takes novices and experienced alike to the Truckee River, Martis Lake and other North Sierra waters. Your day with her includes instruction in the skills of flycasting, mastering knots and reading the water.

Fly Fishing Guides

Truckee River Outfitters
10200 Donner Pass Rd.
Truckee
530-582-0900
www.renoflyshop.com

Truckee River Outfitters

Andy Burk operates his fly fishing guide service out of Dave's Ski Shop in downtown Truckee. He offers one day and half-day trips to local streams. His full-service shop can supply all your needs.

Johnson Tackle and Guide
Service
Tahoma
530-525-6575
www.flyfishingtahoe.com

Johnson Tackle and Guide Service

This service specializes in "nymph" fishing on the Truckee River. They also give lessons and guided trips to local lakes and streams. You can also arrange an overnight into the back country.

A-Action High Sierra Fishing
Adventures
South Lake Tahoe
530-541-3254

A-Action High Sierra Fishing Adventures

Captain George has over 30 years experience and will take you out for a five-hour guided fishing tour. All bait and tackle are provided.

Alpine Fly Fishing Service
South Lake Tahoe
530-542-0759

Alpine Fly Fishing Service

Jim Crouse guides to lakes in the Carson Pass or to alpine fishing country as far south as Mono County. He knows all the best places to cast your fly. He is a regular instructor at Kirkwood Resort.

Fly Fishing Guides

Trout Creek Flies and Tackle

With over 20 years experience fly fishing in the area, Geoff Beer has opened his own shop where you can get advice and purchase everything needed to try your hand in local streams and lakes. He gives special guided trips to areas near Markleeville in Alpine County. He also offers clinics through Kirkwood Resort.

Trout Creek Flies and Tackle
775-588-3310
530-541-1589

Summer

Lisa Cutter of the California School of Flyfishing shows her catch before release.

Rafting

Mountain Air Sports
530-583-7238

Truckee River Raft Rentals
530-583-0123

Fanny Bridge Raft Rentals
530-583-3021

Summer

Tahoe Whitewater Tours
Tahoe City
Information and reservations:
530-581-2441

Rafting on the Truckee River

Three companies offer self-guided family raft trips on the Truckee River between Tahoe City and River Ranch at Alpine Meadows Rd. These trips are a safe, leisurely float on the river for about four miles downstream. Bring bathing suit, hat and plenty of sun screen, and if you must stop along the way, please use the restrooms provided by the companies and respect the private property along the river. The companies provide return buses to Tahoe City after you disembark.

Tahoe Whitewater Tours

Leaving in vans from Tahoe City at 8:00 a.m., this group takes you on one-day rafting trips on the South Fork of the American River or the East Fork of the Carson River. Both are considered beginner runs, but the American River will provide more thrills. They also offer a challenging ride on the Truckee River from Boca to Floristan and Emerald Bay kayak tours. See "Boating" on page 124 for a complete description. The owner of Tahoe Whitewater Tours is an experienced guide for handicapped or wheelchair sports enthusiasts.

Rafting

Truckee Whitewater Adventures and IRIE Rafting Company

The perfect way to start is a trip on the Lower Truckee from Boca to Floristan for six miles through a canyon with sagebrush and soaring eagles. This trip is suitable for families. Or, you can elect a Class III-IV paddle on the Middle or North Fork of the American River. Their equipment is state of the art and their guides are dedicated to guest service and familiar with the flora, fauna and history of the area.

**Truckee Whitewater Adventures
IRIE Rafting Company
Truckee
530-587-1184 888-969-4743
irierafting.com**

Tahoe Whitewater Tours guide, Dan Zemple, with Boy Scouts on the Truckee River.

Courtesy of Tahoe Whitewater Tours

Father and child along the Pope-Baldwin bike path.

© Ellie Huggins

Bicycling

There are marked bicycle paths in several locations in the North Tahoe-Truckee area, and the Tahoe National Forest is a mountain biker's dream. U.S. Forest Service roads abound in almost every wilderness area. A Tahoe National Forest map is for sale at the Truckee U.S. Forest Service headquarters. The map shows all the roads in the Tahoe National Forest. Mountain bikes are not allowed on the Pacific Crest Trail or into Desolation Wilderness. Bike shops also sell recreation maps and books with good descriptions of the trails. The best map for the region is the *Recreation Map of Lake Tahoe* by Tom Harrison. Trails and their designations are shown, as well as mileages.

Bicycle Paths

Donner Memorial State Park

There are three miles of flat roads in Donner Memorial State Park. The camping areas in the southeast corner lead to the road into Coldstream Valley.

Coldstream Valley

At the southeast corner of the park there is a road that leads into the valley. After a fairly steep climb the road flattens out and continues on the north side of two large ponds. You can continue on this fairly level road until you reach the railroad tracks.

Donner Memorial State Park

Directions:
Donner Pass Road just west of the I-80 Donner Lake exit.

Special Features:
You can bike all the way to Donner Summit. After crossing the tracks, take the first right turn up a hill. This road leads to Emigrant Creek which you must cross to continue to the summit.

Bicycling

Truckee cyclists may wish to start at the Albertson Market parking lot, just south of I-80 on Hwy. 89.

Truckee River Public Access Trailhead is just south of the Tahoe City Y.

Truckee to Squaw Valley

Cyclists from Truckee will find a marked bicycle route on Highway 89 between Interstate 80 in Truckee and Squaw Valley, a distance of 8.4 miles. A bike path that parallels the Squaw Valley meadow and golf course begins one mile up Squaw Valley Road. Once there you can ride the cable car to High Camp and zoom down one of the trails in the mountain bike park. The views are spectacular. See the description of the park on page 153.

Tahoe City to Squaw Valley

This trail starts across the bridge over the Truckee River and leads to an easy four-mile ride to River Ranch where you can stop for lunch on the patio. Or you can take a picnic for any good riverside spot along the way. The trail continues along the Truckee River and crosses it on a new bridge which accesses Squaw Valley Road.

West Shore Bike Path from the Tahoe City Y to Sugar Pine Point State Park

This trail is also accessed from the Truckee River Public Access Trailhead. It follows Highway 89 along the West Shore. It is easily broken up into sections with picnicking or dining

Bicycling

opportunities along the way. From the *Y* to Sunnyside makes an excellent lunch or brunch ride, or you can go farther south to Kaspian Picnic Area, where the beach and U.S. Forest Service Campground offers good picnic sites. From Tahoe City to Sugar Pine Point State Park and back is an all-day ride.

Note:
The bicycle path crosses Highway 89 several times, and riders should cross each intersection with care.

Tahoe City to Dollar Point

The trail is along the south side of Highway 28 between Tahoe City and Dollar Point. It is not necessarily a good trail for an outing because of the traffic on the highway.

North Tahoe Regional Park in Tahoe Vista

A marked trail goes steeply up National Avenue to Pinedrop Street and into the park where there are miles of mountain biking trails to explore.

Lakeshore Boulevard in Incline Village

This trail runs from one end of Lakeshore Boulevard to the other, offering great views of the million-dollar real estate along the way. The trail is used by walkers and runners, so ride carefully.

Bicycling

Bicycle Paths and Routes - South Lake Tahoe

The city of South Lake Tahoe maintains a nearly flat 14.4-mile bike trail system. The trail starts in the Stateline area (see map) where it meanders through the town on separate paths and bike routes by the side of the road. One mile north of the South Tahoe *Y* next to Highway 89 (Emerald Bay Road) the Pope-Baldwin Bike Path will take you to Spring Creek Road with access to the beaches from Pope to Baldwin, as well as the Tallac Historic Site and the U.S. Forest Service Visitor Center. Another bike trail is on the south side of U.S. 50 between Meyers and Pioneer Trail which allows access to Upper Truckee Road in Lake Valley. Mountain bike enthusiasts will find much challenging terrain in the area, and expert riders who really want to be tested can try the Flume Trail from Spooner Lake. Wherever you ride, it's smart and safe always to wear a helmet.

Summer

Pope-Baldwin Bike Path
Plans are in the works for an extension of the bike path that connects at the end of Eloise Ave. so that riders may start at Rufus Allen Ave. This would be a perfect all day family ride with a stop at one of the beaches for a picnic lunch.

Pope-Baldwin Bike Path

This off-the-highway bike path starts about one mile north of the South Tahoe *Y* on Highway 89. It is an easy four-mile ride to Spring Creek. The U.S. Forest Service maintains an almost flat bike path that is parallel to Highway 89. It winds through the forest to connect with roads or trails down to the beaches. You can also use your bike in the Tallac Historic Site to visit the various buildings. This is the perfect trail for families who want to bike to the beach for a day, or try a longer trip to the U.S. Forest Service Visitor Center.

Bicycling

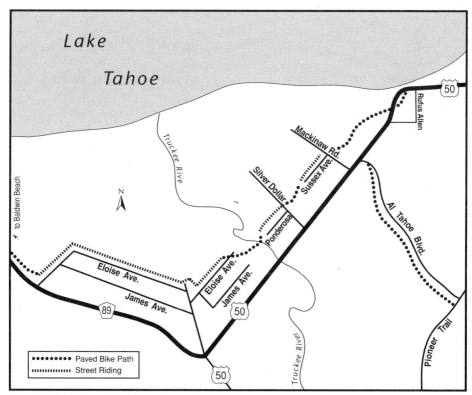

South Lake Tahoe bicycle paths and routes.

Bicycling

Pioneer Trail to Highway 89

There is paved trail on the east side of Highway 50 between Pioneer Trail and Highway 89. A bike lane is provided along Al Tahoe Boulevard and Pioneer Trail. It is possible to ride the several miles from Heavenly all the way to Highway 89 on either a bike lane or paved trail.

Mountain Bike Parks

Eagle Mountain Bike Resort

Eagle Mountain Bike Resort
530-389-2254 800-391-2254

Directions:
Take the Yuba Gap exit off I-80 and drive south one mile to the resort.

Eagle Mountain Resort suffered a major forest fire the summer of 2001. However, they think that their bike trails will be better than ever in 2002. During the week they are mostly open for organized groups or private parties. Individuals may use the park weekends and holidays, but you may want to call ahead for a schedule of their many specialized races and events.

Northstar-at-Tahoe

Northstar-at-Tahoe
Directions:
Six miles south of Truckee on Highway 267.

The resort offers challenging mountain bike routes on Mount Pluto. You can ride two of the ski area lifts with your bike to access miles of trails for all skill levels. Clinics are offered each morning for those interested in perfecting their mountain climbing techniques.

Summer

Bicycling

Squaw Valley Mountain Bike Park

An extensive park has single track and roads for an exciting biking experience and fabulous views of Lake Tahoe. You can start below and huff and puff to the top, or ride the cable car for a thrilling downhill adventure. There are trails for all abilities, with 15 percent that are suitable for beginners. You can purchase a swim with your tram ticket and enjoy biking the upper mountain before plunging in the pool to cool off. When new ski lifts are under construction, some access roads may be closed to bikers.

Squaw Valley

Directions:
At the end of Squaw Valley Road 8.4 miles south of I-80 in Truckee.

Lake Tahoe Cross Country Ski Area

Most of the trail system of the Lake Tahoe Cross-Country Ski Area is open and perfect for mountain bikes of all abilities. The Fiberboard Freeway, the route for the Great Cross Country Ski Race, allows a full day ride to Truckee and back. If you are not up to the return trip, arrange a car shuttle at either end. In Truckee the road takes off from Thelin Drive.

Lake Tahoe Cross Country Ski Area

Directions:
From the Tahoe City *Y* drive north on Hwy. 28 to Fabian Way. Turn left, follow signs via Village Rd. and Country Club Dr.

Kirkwood Resort
West of Carson Pass on Highway 88.
209-258-6000 800-967-7500
www.skikirkwood.com

Kirkwood Resort

Two chair lifts access many trails for all abilities that lead to the top of the park. Trails then descend to the base facilities, with unsurpassed views of the mountain scenery and many places to stop for a picnic or to look at the wildflower display. Lessons and guided tours are available with advance reservations. For more adventurous riders the Adventure Center staff will supply you with maps to the many bike trails in the Carson Pass area.

Mountain Bike Roads

Prosser Creek, Stampede and Boca Reservoir Tour.
Moderate. Twenty-seven miles with minimal elevation gain.

Prosser Creek, Stampede and Boca Reservoir Tour.

A good dirt road leads north to Stampede Reservoir with eight miles of easy riding. The scenery alternates between deep woods and open sagebrush meadows. The generally rolling terrain is interrupted by only one climb of any consequence. Stampede Reservoir is about halfway through the ride and a good place to stop for lunch. There are picnic sites and a vista point alongside the roadway over Stampede's spillway. The road surface reverts to asphalt at Stampede, and once you've crossed the dam and climbed a short steep grade,

Bicycling

the road turns to the south and heads for Boca. Nearing Boca, there is a final, relatively flat section which crosses through great open meadows. At Boca Reservoir Dam, the route back to Prosser is clearly marked.

Commemorative Overland Emigrant Trail

A single track trail traverses the meadows and forest between Donner Camp on Highway 89 North and Stampede Reservoir. The well-marked trail ends at a parking lot just southwest of Logger campground. You will cross old logging roads many times.

Commemorative Overland Emigrant Trail
For experienced, single track riders. Twelve miles each way.

Many riders start at the bridge crossing Prosser Creek on Highway 89 North, skipping the first part of the trail from Donner Camp.

Marlette Lake in Spooner Lake Park.

Start in Spooner Lake State Park riding downhill out of the park toward the dam. The dirt road begins and heads along North Canyon Creek to road 15NO4A that intersects to the right. Continue straight to Marlette Lake. The creek will be on your right during the last mile which is a strenuous climb. This is a spectacular ride in the fall when the aspens along Canyon Creek turn the hillsides gold. (This is not a suitable ride for young children.)

Marlette Lake in Spooner Lake Park.
Moderate to strenuous with 1,140 feet elevation gain, 270 feet loss. 4.8 miles to the lake's edge, 6.2 miles to the dam.

Experienced riders may continue on the famous Flume Trail that leaves from Marlette Lake and exits on Tunnel Creek Road in Incline Village. This trail is not for beginners. You may want a car shuttle for this one or you can return to Highway 28 and ride south to Spooner Lake Park.

Summer

Bicycling

Blue Lakes and Beyond.
Easy. Six miles one way with 100 feet elevation gain. Bring fishing rod, camera and mosquito repellant.

Mountain bikes are not allowed in wilderness areas. If you didn't detour into the lakes area riding in, do so on the way back.

Hope Valley Outdoor Center just east of Pickett's Junction on Highway 88.
The folks who operated the Hope Valley Cross Country trail system in winter rent mountain bikes. They provide a map to the trails as well as expert advice about the best terrain in the area.

Burnside Lake
Moderate. 6.2 miles one way with 1100 feet elevation gain.

Blue Lakes and Beyond

This easy riding dirt road meanders through a valley with spectacular scenery, especially in the fall. Begin riding at Lower Blue Lake Campground. Turn left onto Blue Lakes Road. At 1.2 miles turn right towards Tamarack Lake. You will pass the road to Upper and Lower Sunset Lakes at 4.3 miles. Either detour to the lakes or continue straight. At 4.5 miles go right into Indian Valley. This is a small valley with a meandering creek. The road continues for 1.5 miles to the Wilderness Boundary.

Burnside Lake

The ride on Burnside Road starts in Hope Valley at Pickett's Junction, the intersection of Highway 89 and Highway 88. A dirt road heads south and climbs gradually to Burnside Lake offering many views of Hope and Faith Valleys to the west. Traffic should be relatively light and the ride is suitable for novice riders and children with some experience.

Horseback Riding

Tahoe Donner Equestrian Center

Tahoe Donner Equestrian Center is in the Tahoe Donner development. This large stable has one and two-hour trail rides as well as all day and full moon rides at night. Half-hour pony rides and lessons are also available. Saturday nights at 5 p.m. there is a 90-minute ride followed by a barbeque. They also offer a Horsemanship Camp (see "Just for Kids" on page 211 for details) and boarding for your steed if you reserve early in the season.

Tahoe Donner Equestrian Center
Alder Creek Drive
Tahoe Donner
Reservations recommended.
530-587-9470

Northstar Stables

Northstar Stables offers year-round, family trail rides and barbeque rides on trails throughout the forest on the resort. There are pony rides for children and lessons.

Northstar Stables
Northstar-at-Tahoe
Reservations recommended.
530-562-1230

Directions:
Six miles south of Truckee on Highway 267.

Receiving instructions before a ride at Tahoe Donner.

© Ellie Huggins

Summer

Horseback Riding

Squaw Valley Stables
Squaw Valley
Reservations not required.
530-583-7433

Squaw Valley Stables

Squaw Valley Stables offers one, two and three-hour rides that leave hourly on a route around the edge of the valley. Six-year-olds may take the two-hour valley rides and pony rides are available for tots. Special breakfast and group rides can be arranged.

Alpine Meadows Stables
Alpine Meadows Road
Alpine Meadows
Reservations recommended.
530-583-3905

Alpine Meadows Stables

Alpine Meadows Stables offers one and two-hour rides across Bear Creek and through the forest. Children as young as five years old are welcomed. Half-day rides require reservations.

Camp Richardson's Corral
Reservations required.
530-541-3113

Directions:
On Highway 89 at Fallen Leaf Road 2.6 miles north of the South Tahoe Y.

Camp Richardson's Corral

Ride along the Aspen, Meadow and Fallen Leaf Lake trails for a one-hour ride, or take a two-hour or half-day trail ride through mountain meadows and forest. Other offerings include a morning ride to a hearty cowboy breakfast or an easy evening ride that ends with a steak barbeque. There are wagon rides for families with little ones. On overnight or extended pack trips into the wilderness with a guide, they provide you with everything but a fishing license.

Horseback Riding

Cascade Stables

The stable near Cascade Lake offers everything from one-hour scenic rides to all-day trips into Desolation Wilderness, plus fishing and extended pack trips. Breakfast and steak dinner rides go to Cascade Lake.

Zephyr Cove Stables

Zephyr Cove Stables will take you into the High Sierra wilderness with fabulous views of Lake Tahoe. All rides are guided by courteous cowboys who will help you. One and two-hour rides, as well as breakfast, lunch and dinner rides are available. Bus service from the casinos will bring you out to Zephyr Cove.

Kirkwood Stables

The Lazy K Pack Station operates the Kirkwood Stables offering guided trail rides around the resort as well as into the surrounding U.S. National Forest lands. Rides last from one hour to all day and pony rides are available for young children. Catered lunches can be arranged and groups can request horse-drawn wagon rides for special occasions.

Cascade Stables
Reservations recommended.
530-541-2055

Directions:
Six miles north of the South Tahoe Y off Highway 89.

Special Features:
Children must be at least 8 years old and there is a 200-pound weight limit.

Zephyr Cove Stables
Zephyr Cove, Nevada
Reservations advised, required for meal rides.
775-588-5664

Kirkwood Stables
Reservations recommended.
209-258-7433

Directions:
Five miles west of Carson Pass on Highway 88 next to the Kirkwood Inn.

Summer

Tennis

Many tennis courts are open to the public in various locations in Truckee and at Lake Tahoe. Most require reservations and have fees per person per hour. The free courts are in parks or at schools, although some are of dubious quality.

Donner Lake West End Beach
South Shore Dr. and Donner Pass Rd., Truckee
Fee to enter beach.

Truckee Regional Park
Highway 267 just south of Truckee.

Granlibakken Resort
Granlibakken Rd., Tahoe City
Fee to use courts.
530-583-4242

Kilner Park
Ward Ave. and Highway 89
Tahoe City

Sugar Pine Point State Park
Ten miles south of the Tahoe City Y on Highway 89.
Fee for car to enter park, but free to bicyclists.

Donner Lake West End Beach

There is one court that is fine for a casual game or for practicing with the children.

Truckee Regional Park

The two courts have been resurfaced. They are located below the ball fields.

Granlibakken Resort

Six courts at this resort are open to the public.

Kilner Park

Two tennis courts are nestled in the woods with a courtside reservation system and coin lighted at night. They are not available some hours due to tennis lessons. However, you can take a walk in the park or sit by the lake while you wait to play.

Sugar Pine Point State Park
There is one court near the Ehrman mansion. Pack a picnic lunch, take your tennis racket, and spend the day in the park.

Tennis

Tahoe Marina Lodge

This lodge near the *Y* in Tahoe City has courts open to the public.

**Tahoe Marina Lodge
270 No. Lake Blvd.
Tahoe City
Fee to use courts.
530-583-2365**

North Tahoe High School

The four courts at the school are open to the public free of charge.

**North Tahoe High School
2945 Polaris Rd.
Tahoe City**

North Tahoe Regional Park

Five courts in the park are open to the public and are lighted at night.

**North Tahoe Regional Park
Donner Rd. and Estates Dr.
Tahoe Vista
Fee to use lighted courts.**

Kings Beach Elementary School

The school has two courts that are open to the public.

**Kings Beach Elementary School
Steelhead Ave. and Wolf St.
Kings Beach**

Incline High School

Two newly-surfaced courts are open to the public free of charge.

**Incline High School
Incline Blvd.
Incline Village**

Incline Village Tennis Complex

Seven new courts are open to the public. Lessons are also available.

**Incline Village Tennis Complex
Incline Way
Incline Village
Fee per person per hour.
775-832-1235**

Lakeside Tennis Club

The club has resurfaced its nine courts, three of which are lighted. You must call ahead to reserve a court.

**Lakeside Tennis Club
987 Tahoe Blvd.
Incline Village
Fee per person.
775-831-5258**

South Tahoe Middle School
2940 Lake Tahoe Blvd.
South Lake Tahoe
530-542-6055

South Tahoe Middle School

The courts here are free on a first-come first served basis. All four courts are operated by the South Lake Tahoe Parks and Recreation Department. The courts at this complex are lighted for night games.

South Lake Tahoe High School
1735 Lake Tahoe Blvd.
South Lake Tahoe
530-542-6055

South Tahoe High School

There are six courts that are free on a first-come, first served basis. Three of the courts have lights for night games.

Zephyr Cove County Park
Warrior Way off Highway 50
Zephyr Cove, Nevada
775-588-7230

Zephyr Cove County Park

Four public courts, all with lights, are open 24 hours at this local park. Here's your chance to play a midnight game.

Whittel High School
Warrior Way
Zephyr Cove, Nevada
775-588-7230

Whittel High School

Three courts have coin operated lights 24 hours. First come, first served.

Summer

Golf

Your golf skills will be tested on any of the 13 Lake Tahoe-Truckee links. Three are resort courses, while the newest, Coyote Moon opened in 2001. Because the golf season is relatively short, the courses are crowded and require reservations.

A note about high altitude golf: the ball flies straighter and longer in the thinner air of Lake Tahoe. Remember to adjust your club selection accordingly. That usually means playing one club less on many shots.

The Resort Courses

Resort at Squaw Creek is a true test of target golf. A premium is placed on shot selection not length. Squaw Creek meanders throughout the course and comes into play on all but six holes. The course's signature hole is the par-5 13th that plays close to 500 yards and requires a 200-yard carry over marshland off the tee.

Resort at Squaw Creek
Squaw Valley
Reservations required.
530-583-6300

Special Features:
Driving range: yes; Course rating: 70.9; Length: 6,931 yards (gold tees).

Northstar is really two courses. The front side is links-style golf where big hitters can let it rip. But from No. 10 on, finesse and shot selection to postage-stamp greens are a must. No. 16 is Northstar's signature hole. It is a par-4, 450-yard tester with water waiting for those with chronic fades.

Northstar-at-Tahoe
Six miles south of Truckee of Highway 267.
Reservations required.
530-562-2490

Special Features:
Driving range: yes; Course rating: 70.5; Length: 6,897 yards (gold tees).

Summer

Golf

Coyote Moon
10685 Northwoods Blvd.
Truckee
Reservations required.
530-587-0886

Special Features:
Driving range: no; Course rating: 71.1 from the blue tees.
Length 7,177 yards.

Coyote Moon, the area's newest, covers 250 secluded acres of rolling hills with pines and stunning rock outcroppings. It is owned by East West Partners of Northstar. The course is picturesque and forgiving, with trees lining every fairway. The signature hole, No. 13, is par 3 with a 110 foot downhill fairway across Trout Creek.

Tahoe Donner Golf Course
11531 Northwoods Blvd.
Truckee
Reservations required.
530-587-9440

Special Features:
Driving range: yes; Course rating: 73.1; Length: 6,914 yds.

Tahoe Donner plays tight and long, period. Not surprisingly, it is the toughest of Lake Tahoe's golf courses, and one of the hardest to get on so reservations are an absolute must. The signature hole is the par-4 18th that plays downhill with water in front of an extremely well-bunkered green. It is not the hardest hole on the course, but it certainly typifies high Sierra golf.

Incline Village Championship Course
955 Fairway Blvd.
Incline Village
Reservations required.
775-832-1144

Special Features:
Driving range: yes; Course rating: 72.6; Length: 6,910 yards.

Incline Village Championship Course combines tree-lined fairways and water on 13 of the 18 holes. There isn't a flat green to be found and the key to sinking putts is to remember that every putt breaks toward Lake Tahoe. The monstrous 600-yard, par-5 No. 4 is Incline's signature hole. Not enough that the fairway is flanked on both sides by out-of-bounds markers, normal landing areas are bordered by bunkers.

Golf

Nine-holers and Executive Courses

Ponderosa Golf Course only has nine holes, but each offers a test to golfers. Ponderosa greens and fairways are always in tip-top condition. No. 9 is a dogleg right with tall pines blocking a direct second shot to the green.

Tahoe City is a favorite hangout for longtime locals, both on and off the course. The entrance is hidden behind commercial development, but well worth the search. It is the shortest course on the North Shore in total yardage.

Old Brockway touts itself as one of the region's oldest and receives the heaviest play throughout the summer. The par-5 7th is 553 yards long and demands a strong drive and a sound short game.

Incline Executive has one of the lake's shortest holes, the 113-yard 3rd, yet is the longest course of the nine holers. It is a fun course to tune up the short game and you'll still have energy for an afternoon of other activities.

Ponderosa Golf Course
Highway 267 at Reynold Way
Truckee
530-587-3501

Special Features:
Driving range: no; Course rating: 67; Length 3,018 yards.

Tahoe City Golf Course
Behind Albertsons in Tahoe City.
530-583-1516

Special Features:
Driving range: no; Course rating: 64.3; Length: 2,696 yards.

Old Brockway Golf Course
Corner of Highways 267 and 28
Kings Beach
530-546-9922

Special Features:
Driving range: yes; Course rating: 69.5; Length 3,202 yards

Incline Executive Golf Course
Golfers Pass off Mt. Rose
Highway
Incline Village
775-832-1150

Special Features:
Driving range: yes; Course rating: 55; Length 3,513 yards.

Summer

Golf

The Resort Course

Edgewood Golf Course
Tahoe Parkway
Stateline
Reservations required.
775-588-3566

Special Features:
Driving range: yes; Course rating: 75.1; Length: 7,491 yards.

Edgewood has long been considered Lake Tahoe's premier resort course, with the lake coming into play on several of the holes. Indeed, the par-3 17th is reminiscent of fabled Pebble Beach, for when the prevailing winds come off the lake, golfers are forced to hit the ball over the lake in order to hit the green. Certainly, the last four holes demand the most from the golfer, but the par-5 16th, at 545 yards from the blues, is the course's signature hole. Not only is it the most picturesque, but everyone who plays it has to decide whether they have the skills necessary to go for a minuscule green on the second shot.

Nine-holers and Executive Courses

Bijou Municipal Course
Corner of Fairway and Johnson Blvd. off U.S. 50.
South Lake Tahoe
530-542-6097

Special Features:
Driving range: yes; Course rating: NR; Length: 2,016 yards.

Bijou Municipal Course is a favorite local's course as well as being the lake's shortest in overall length. Golfers tee off on the par-4, 300-yard No. 1 with the Sierra Nevada as a backdrop. The sixth hole, a 342-yard par 4, is the course's lone water hole.

Summer

Golf

Tahoe Paradise Golf Course underwent a face lift in 1994, with bunkers added on many holes and greens getting a well-deserved reworking. The improvements, when coupled with the tight landing areas and tilted fairways, makes the course a golfing challenge. The 15th, a dogleg par 4 that measures 254 yards, is a good example of the changes in the course. Instead of hitting to a small green, players now face a two-tier green that demands pinpoint placement. The par-3 14th is the signature hole. A player has to carry the entire 130-yard length in order to avoid putting the ball in the water.

Lake Tahoe Golf Course is for players who like to live dangerously: the Upper Truckee River crisscrosses like a coiled snake and other water hazards lie in wait along many of the holes. That said, Lake Tahoe GC has its own version of Augusta's Amen Corner, with holes 10 through 14 serious challenges for any golfer. The 16th, a par-4 357-yard dogleg left, is the course's signature hole, with everything that Lake Tahoe offers coming into play: water, trees and spectacular scenery.

Tahoe Paradise Golf Course
On U.S. 50 at Meyers
530-577-2121

Special Features:
Driving range: yes; Course rating: 59.9; Length: 4,021 yards.

Lake Tahoe Golf Course
On the north side of U.S. 50 just west of the Lake Tahoe Airport.
530-577-0788

Special Features:
Driving range: yes; Course rating: 70.9 Length: 6,718 yards

Summer

Golf

Miniature Golf

Magic Carpet
5167 No. Lake Blvd.
Carnelian Bay
530-546-8693

Magic Carpet Golf

Two courses, a 19-hole castle and 28-hole dinosaur course, offer hours of fun for the whole family.

Bobergs Kings Beach Mini Golf
8693 No. Lake Blvd.
Kings Beach
530-546-3196

Boberg's Kings Beach Mini Golf

This small course is for the whole family. It is great for an evening game or for a few hours when you have tired of the beach.

Magic Carpet Golf
2455 Lake Tahoe Blvd.
South Lake Tahoe
530-541-3787

Magic Carpet Golf

There is a discount for those who want to try the 19-hole castle course and 28-hole dinosaur course together. A video arcade and kiddie rides add to the fun.

Fantasy Kingdom
4045 Highway 50
South Lake Tahoe
530-544-3833

Fantasy Kingdom

Located not far from the casinos, this 23-hole course is perfect for an afternoon or evening of outdoor fun for the family.

Summer

Historical Walks

The Emigrant Trail at Big Bend

Look north from the easternmost end of the parking lot and you will see a brown steel Emigrant Trail marker. Pick your way down to the marker which was placed here by Trails West and marks the route of the trail at this point.

For a sleuthing adventure start walking east from the marker keeping to the lowest and flattest places. Do not drop down toward the river. Round, green Emigrant Trail signs with white lettering are tacked on the east side of many lodgepole trees. The forest of the emigrant period had large old trees spaced quite far apart, and much of the brush you see today would not have been growing here then.

See if you can determine the route the emigrants would have picked. You will eventually come to the river about a quarter mile to the east. The bank is quite flat and you will see why wagon masters chose this place to cross the Yuba River.

The Emigrant Trail at Big Bend

Directions:
Take I-80 west 16 miles to the Rainbow Rd. exit. Drive west on Rainbow Rd. past the Rainbow Lodge to the U.S. Forest Service parking lot on the north side of the road.

Special Features:
Retracing your steps to the parking lot will be much simpler, for the signs will guide you. Back at the Trails West sign look northwest across the granite to find another trail marker. You will notice that the wagons had to wind north downhill across the granite to reach a good route along the river. If you have very sharp eyes, you will be able to find two places where the wagon wheels slid across the granite leaving telltale rust marks. Run your hand over the marks to notice how the wheels polished the granite as smooth as glass.

Historical Walks

Donner Summit Emigrant Trail and First Highways

Directions:
From Truckee take Donner Pass Rd. west to Donner Summit. From I-80 take the Soda Springs exit and drive east on Donner Pass Rd. to Donner Summit. Turn south on the road at the Alpine Skills International. Drive about 200 yards until you see the sign on the left for the Pacific Crest Trail. Park along the side of the road.

Special Features:
Follow the roadbed until it curves down and goes through the tunnel under the railroad. As you walk along the road as it curves to the left, you can see a 1920s advertisement painted on the rock proclaiming "Whitney Hotel Truckee."

Recent research has raised the possibility that the first emigrants used a route just north of the Rainbow Bridge. By the fall of 1846, a route up Coldstream Valley and over Roller Pass below Mount Lincoln (Sugar Bowl) had been opened.

Donner Summit Emigrant Trail and First Highways

The route of the Emigrant Trail is to the left of the Pacific Crest Trail. The traces are buried in a roadbed that was excavated for the intercontinental fiber optics cable. Climb over the rocks and follow the path. In summer the cliff to your left will be filled with clumps of blue or scarlet trumpet-shaped flowers called penstemons. The scarlet one was named "mountain pride" by John Muir. After walking about one-quarter mile down the trail, look carefully to the right for a large rock with a bronze plaque. This monument marks the trail of the wagon train led by Elisha Stephens that passed this way in November of 1844. They found this route over the pass in two feet of snow. In some places they had been forced to unload their wagons and haul them piece by piece up the cliffs. These pioneers were the first to bring their wagons over the forbidding Sierra Nevada, thus opening the trail to California. "The Emigrant Trail at Big Bend" walk on page 169 traverses another portion of the journey taken by this group.

Continue through the willow corridor down the road until you've gone under the railroad. At this point you are

Summer (sidebar)

Historical Walks

standing on a portion of State Highway 37, built in 1915 for the new automobile traffic. The roadbed was abandoned in 1928 when the current alignment of U.S. 40 was finished. After passing through the tunnel, look back at the wall supporting the railroad tracks. This mortarless wall of rocks was built by the Chinese workers who labored here in 1867 and 1868 for the Central Pacific Railroad to build the western portion of the country's first transcontinental railroad.

© Ellie Huggins

A section of old Highway 37 as it curves down the hill after passing through the Chinese wall.

Historical Walks

Historic Downtown Truckee

Special Features:
Follow the map on the next page for your tour of Truckee's fine old buildings. You might also wish to hike up to the rocking stone with its great vista of the town. To learn more about the Paiute legend of the rocking stone see "History" on page 10.

Two books, available locally, recite detailed information about the area's history. *Truckee, an Illustrated History of the Town and its Surroundings* is by local author, Joanne Meschery. The other, *Fire and Ice, A Portrait of Truckee*, is published by the Truckee Donner Historical Society.

The jail now houses some exhibits gathered by the Truckee Donner Historical Society. Volunteers open the jail many weekends in the summer.

Historic Downtown Truckee

Truckee is the oldest High Sierra town in California, and much of the original town, as well as its first building, has been preserved. You can walk around downtown in less than an hour and end your tour with a meal or a snack at one of the many eateries on Commercial Row.

Start your walking tour at The Truckee Hotel at the corner of Highway 267 and Bridge Street. This hostelry began life as the American Hotel in 1868. Later it was known as Whitney House, New Whitney House, Alpine Riverside, and now The Truckee Hotel. Currently it is a bed and breakfast inn that has been renovated and decorated to reflect its nineteenth-century past. See page 37 in "Lodging" for a description of this hostelry.

Walk north to Church Street where Gray's Log Cabin, Truckee's first building, is on the left a few hundred feet from the intersection. Now return to Bridge Street and continue walking north to the stone building on the site of Truckee's original Gray's Toll Station. Walk west along Jibboom Street to the Old Jail, the last building on the right. The jail was in use continuously from 1875 until 1964.

Summer

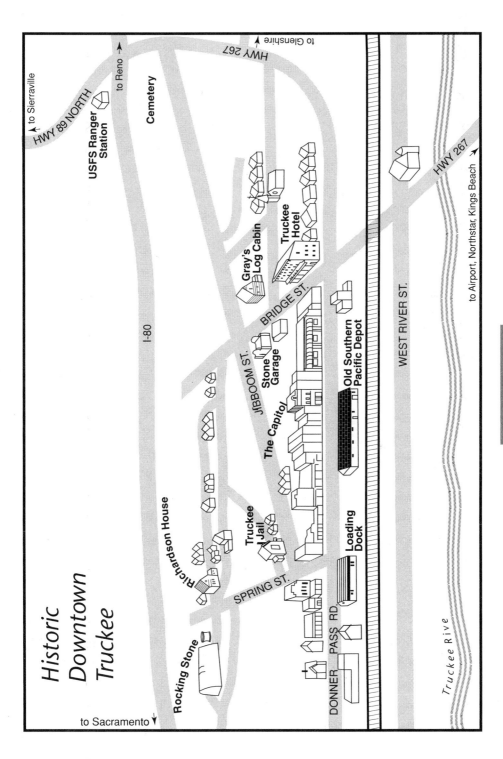

Historic Downtown Truckee

Boca Historic Town Site

Directions:
Drive 6 miles east of Hwy. 89 North on I-80 to the Boca Reservoir and Hirschdale Rd. exit. Turn left, driving under the freeway and shortly after crossing the railroad tracks turn right up a gravel road to parking for the trail.

Boca Historic Town Site

The United State Forest Service has opened this walk into Truckee's past with a quarter-mile trail on a hillside above the confluence of the Truckee River and the Little Truckee River as it exits the Boca Dam. Interpretive signs along the way point out the sites of the Boca Mill and Ice Company whose operations supported a town of more than two hundred during the latter decades of the 19th century. The lumber was cut to help build the Central Pacific Railroad and then the tunnels of the Comstock silver mines at Virginia City. The company dammed the river to create ponds which were harvested of their ice in winter, thus ensuring year-round employment for the men of the mill. The ice was used in railroad cars to preserve fruit shipments and to cool the tunnels of the mines. A prize-winning beer was made in the nearby Boca Brewery.

However, the town's life was destined to be short. Having cut down all the trees in the area, the lumber mill closed. The closing of the silver mines and introduction of refrigerated railroad cars spelled doom for the ice

Historical Walks

industry. When a fire destroyed the brewery, the town went into decline. It was finally dismantled in 1927.

As you hike up the trail, the base of the schoolhouse flagpole, old rusted iron gates and other metal detritus of civilization is everywhere along the path. The most poignant reminder of the past, however, is the tiny cemetery. A lonely Iceland poppy planted by a grieving relative still blooms each spring, and three tiny headstones for deceased infants bear testimony to the harsh frontier life. When you return to your car, walk over to the site of the hotel where a lilac bush still blooms amid the trees.

Courtesy of Donner Memorial State Park

Winter life was not all work. Ladies still enjoyed days on the slopes.

Historical Walks

Tallac Historic Site

Tallac Historic Site
Fee and reservations for Pope Estate Tours.
Summer: museum daily, 10:00 am to 4:00 pm through Labor Day.
530-541-5227

Directions:
From the South Tahoe Y, drive 3.1 miles north on Hwy. 89 to the Kiva Beach and Tallac Historic Site parking lot.

Start your walk heading east along the bike path. The first group of buildings houses art workshops and galleries operated by the Tahoe Tallac Association. The galleries and artists studios are open to the public from 11:00 am to 3:00 pm every day except Thursday. Artists in residence have openings on Sunday afternoons from 1:00 to 3:00 pm. The U.S. Forest Service leads tours of the Pope Estate daily during the summer.

Walk on the path to the Baldwin House Museum and then take the paved path to Valhalla and the Arts Store of the Tahoe Tallac Association. The store features work of local artists and many other interesting items. To return to your car, walk along the path that hugs the shore and be sure to visit the gazebo and pond with its carefully planted gardens.

Valhalla is the site of regular concerts and outdoor musical events as well as art workshops throughout the summer. Be sure to check the schedule posted on the boards near the grand hall. Regular concerts are listed in the "Special Events" section on page 289.

Tallac Historic Site

The Tallac Historic Site is on 74 acres of the Pope, Heller and Baldwin/McGonagle family estates that were transferred to the U.S. Forest Service in the 1960s and 1970s. Because it was necessary to restore many of the buildings on the site, the Tahoe Tallac Association, a bi-state non-profit organization, was formed to help raise money for restoration and to promote the area as a cultural center to increase community and visitor involvement.

Settlement of this beautiful part of the Lake Tahoe shoreline began when Yank Clement bought eight acres at Tallac Point in 1873. He foresaw the tourist potential of the area and built a hotel he named Tallac Point House. By 1875 his hotel was quite popular, but financial difficulties forced him to sell the property to E. J. "Lucky" Baldwin, a San Francisco Realtor and stock speculator who turned Tallac Point House into a first-class, nineteenth-century destination resort of giant proportions. He claimed that it rivaled Saratoga Springs in New York. He piped water down from Fallen Leaf Lake, built bridle paths and promenade walks and installed electricity to light the paths at night. A steam plant supplied heat for the

Historical Walks

hotel rooms and dining room that seated 100. He constructed the first casino on the lake and added bowling alleys, sun parlors, ballroom, theatrical stage and more. This was surely the place in which to be seen and represented an era of high living at the lake.

When "Lucky" died in 1909, his daughter Anita took control and operated the resort into the 1920s. However, in 1927 she removed all the buildings because she wanted no more commercial activity on her property. The Tallac Hotel disappeared. When Anita Baldwin died, one-half of her considerable estate passed to her daughter, Dextra Baldwin McGonagle, who built a summer home on the shores of the lake.

Neighboring land was the summer retreat for the Pope family, prominent in San Francisco Bay Area society. Next door to the Pope estate, another San Francisco financier, Walter Heller, built a summer house on 200 feet of shoreline along with two small cottages with a common veranda and, finally, the main house called Valhalla, with 40-foot high ceilings and grand fireplace (now the site of Valhalla Concerts).

The Baldwin House
The home is now a museum operated by the U.S. Forest Service and is open to the public in summer. Here you can get a taste of the refined living of this prominent family, as well as learn about "Lucky" Baldwin's exploits as miner, financier and hotel proprietor. In one of the rooms you'll also find an excellent exhibit prepared by the Washoe Tribal Council to acquaint visitors with the culture of Lake Tahoe's native peoples.

Summer

Historical Walks

Emigrant Trail over Carson Pass

Directions:
Carson Pass is on Hwy. 88 west of Pickett's Junction. Just east of the pass there is an old road heading east. It is easiest to see driving east. This is old Highway 88. Drive down the road one-quarter mile to the old vista point.

A diary entry:
In 1853, William Brown wrote in his diary about this portion of his trip: "Started early, traveled over good roads, came to Red Lake. Here we begin to see the Elephant, the High Mountain was before us to ascend. We got up a short distance and camped on a level on the mountain side. . . . Teams here had to double as there was a part of the road over a smooth steep rock and cattle could not stand on it. They had to haul the waggons to the rock, take the teams around and haul over by long ropes tied to the tongues of the waggons."

Emigrant Trail over Carson Pass

The route over Carson Pass was opened by Mormons returning to Salt Lake City from California in 1848. The next year, as thousands rushed to the California mines, this trail became a favorite for those seeking the most direct route to Hangtown (Placerville) and its nearby gold. It is estimated that at least 4,000 wagons passed this way in 1849, and by 1850 this became the preferred route to the California gold sites.

Start walking downhill on the former highway just east of the parking area. In about 100 feet take the easiest route down (left) off the road into a grove of large fir trees. You will see a metal arrow on one of the trees. Continue steeply downhill as far as you wish, guided by more trail markers on the trees. Notice how each tree has a groove near its base left by the chains emigrants used to winch their wagons up this hill. As you huff and puff back up toward the road, you will understand the task that the emigrants faced to haul their wagons up this first pass over the Sierra.

When you reach the road, look uphill and you will find another marker on a tree. Follow these markers uphill along

Historical Walks

the south side of the road until you reach a rock with what at first glance looks like modern graffiti. The plaque on the rock will explain that a group of Odd Fellows paused in their toil up this slope "to paint on this and adjacent boulders their names and links of the great order they so dearly loved."

Odd Fellows' nineteenth century graffiti. Whitewash has been used to enhance the emigrant carvings in the rock

© *Ellie Huggins*

Historical Walks

Carson Pass

Directions:
Take Highway 88 east from Pickett's Junction.

If you would like to see Lake Tahoe as Frémont might have spied it, take the hike on page 207 that takes you up the Pacific Crest Trail to Meiss Pass.

Farther west in the parking lot is a monolith with a broken top. It was placed here by the Nevada chapter of E. Clampus Vitus to commemorate "Snowshoe" Thompson who carried the mail every winter over this pass between Hangtown (Placerville), California, and Genoa, Nevada.

Carson Pass

Carson Pass is the location of an Emigrant Museum that opened in 1994 and is staffed by volunteers in the summer. Here you can get information about trails in the area and buy books and maps as well as see the interpretive panels about the emigrants who passed this way.

After visiting the museum, be sure to check out the monument to Kit Carson. It memorializes the tree where Kit was supposed to have carved his name in 1844 when he and John Charles Frémont were trying to cross the Sierra Nevada to California after a year of mapping the Pacific Northwest and Nevada. On this expedition they stopped at Pyramid Lake northeast of Reno, giving the lake its name because of the pyramid-shaped rock near the southeastern shore. By the time they reached this spot, they were weary and practically snowbound. Carson and Frémont climbed Red Lake Peak to the north, and were the first to see Lake Tahoe and note its location on maps. Frémont called the mountain lake he saw "Lake Bonpland" after a French botanist of the period.

Tom Fiene enjoying the view south from the Rubicon Trail. The special hike on this trail is described on page 194.

Special Hikes

We have selected special hikes that take several hours and are best planned to include a picnic along the way. Most have some elevation gain, and hiking boots are recommended but not required. Each hike is graded (easy, moderate or strenuous) according to the total miles and elevation gain.

Hikes at Donner Summit are listed first and from west to east around Lake Tahoe. Carson Pass area hikes are listed in the last section. We have chosen only a few of many possible trails into Desolation Wilderness or along the Tahoe Rim Trail. We list some of the most popular and least difficult hikes, as well as one or two lesser known trails into lakes nestled in granite bowls, or across open ridges with spectacular views of the mountains surrounding Lake Tahoe. One of the treats awaiting hikers in the Tahoe Basin is the opportunity to view the "gem of the Sierra" from a variety of vantage points above the lake.

The Donner Lake Rim Trail

Under the guidance of the Truckee Donner Land Trust, volunteers have been building several miles of trail on the north side of Donner Lake. Planned land acquisitions will connect a 22-mile, multi-use trail around the ridges above Donner Lake. In the summer of 2002 the trail between Summit Lake and the Tahoe Donner trail system north of I-80 will be complete. For information about the trail call 530-582-4711 or write: Truckee Donner Land Trust P.O. Box 8816 Truckee, CA 96162. www.tdlandtrust.org.

The Tahoe Rim Trail

The volunteer effort to establish and build the Tahoe Rim Trail, a 150-mile hiking and equestrian trail which follows the ridge tops of the Lake Tahoe Basin, was completed in 2001. Distances between trailheads with parking require a car shuttle to hike the entire way. We have described two segments of the trail in the South Lake Tahoe area, one with a car shuttle for the complete trip and one with a loop possibility. For more information and a trail brochure, call 775-588-0686, or write: The Tahoe Rim Trail P.O. Box 11551 South Lake Tahoe, CA 96155.

Special Hikes

For those who seek an overnight experience or who want to try more strenuous hiking, we suggest that you buy one or more of the following books available in bookstores. Michael Scialfa has produced a small booklet with 13 hikes entitled *Trail Guide to the Lake Tahoe Basin.* Jeffrey P. Schaffer has compiled two trail guides to the area. *The Tahoe Sierra, A Natural History Guide to 100 Hikes in the Northern Sierra* has detailed descriptions of hikes off Highways 49, 80 and 50. The section on trails off Highway 50 applies to the South Tahoe region. His other title, *Desolation Wilderness and the South Lake Tahoe Region,* includes a map of the Fallen Leaf Lake quadrangle which can be most helpful for planning your own forays into the wilderness. For those interested in finding the best wildflower gardens in the entire area, *Hiking Tahoe's Wildflower Trails* by Julie Stauffer Carville is a wonderful guide, complete with drawings and descriptions of the flowers to be found.

The best all-round map of the area is the *Lake Tahoe Recreation Map* produced by Tom Harrison Maps.

Wilderness Permits:
A wilderness permit is required to hike in Desolation Wilderness. Day hikers can fill out a permit at the trailhead, but overnight campers must obtain a permit from the El Dorado National Forest, Camino Unit. The telephone number is 530-644-6048. Overnight reservations are limited to 1500 between Memorial Day and Labor Day and there is a maximum fee of $10.00 per person. Permits are 50% by reservation and 50% first-come-first-served.

Dogs in Desolation Wilderness:
The U.S. Forest Service is becoming strict about dogs. You may take your animal into the wilderness, but it must be under control at all times.

More tips:
Mosquitoes abound in the first weeks after the snow melts, so pack the repellant.

Giardia, a tiny, microscopic organism, is in all the lakes and streams of the Sierra Nevada. Unless you own an approved filter, carry your own water. The intestinal disturbance from this bug is very unpleasant and can last a long time. Don't take chances.

Thieves, unfortunately, prey on cars in many parking lots. Take your valuables with you or leave them at home.

Summer

Pacific Crest Trail between Donner Pass and Castle Peak Trailhead.
Dogs allowed.

Moderate. Hike starts at 7,200 feet. Four miles one way with about 200 feet elevation gain.

Hiking north from Donner Pass Road.

Drive west on Donner Pass Road from Donner Lake to just west of the pass. Park along the south side of the highway. The trail starts from the north side of the highway.

This is our recommendation for a car shuttle trip one way. You can leave a car on I-80 at the Pacific Crest Trail parking lot and take the second car to Donner Summit. Drive west on I-80 to the Soda Springs exit then east six miles to the pass.

Hiking south from I-80.

Take the Castle Peak/Boreal exit and follow signs to the Pacific Crest Trail on the south side of the freeway. This is the best direction with children as the climbs are more moderate and you can stop at the summit before dropping down to Donner Pass Road.

Pacific Crest Trail between Donner Pass and Castle Peak Trailhead

This trail may be hiked in either direction. From Donner Pass Road, the trail starts on the north side of the highway. The hike features moderate ascents and descents through lodgepole forests and across granite ridges with magnificent vistas of Castle Peak to the north and Donner Lake and the Carson Range to the east. Wildflower gardens of red and blue penstemon, Indian paintbrush and many other species adorn either side of the trail in summer. This is an easy hike for children. Many fine picnic spots atop rocky promontories have magnificent views. Because the hike begins at 7,200 feet, you feel as though you are on top of the world.

Hiking south from the trailhead off I-80, the trail meanders through forests of white fir and Jeffrey pine, climbing gradually until you reach the crest with views toward Donner Lake and east. The mountain above you is the newly christened Mount Stephens, named for the leader of the first wagons to cross the Sierra Nevada in 1844. The scramble to the top of this peak affords expansive views of the region.

Special Hikes

Pacific Crest Trail from Donner Pass to Mount Lincoln and Anderson Peak

The trail climbs the granite ridge south of Donner Pass with excellent vistas in all directions. Penstemon, tiger lilies, lupine and many other species abound, especially on the first mile of the trip over rocky ledges and under red firs. The trail crosses a road and continues in a moderate climb to the saddle between Mount Lincoln and Mount Judah. Be sure to go out to the ledge at Roller Pass near the sign for the Emigrant Trail. Those intrepid pioneers actually winched their wagons up this cliff from the Coldstream Valley below. It is only 2.5 miles to this point, and Roller Pass is an excellent picnic spot. Ambitious hikers can follow the trail across the ridge toward Anderson Peak. From this vantage point you can look south into the headwaters of the North Fork of the American River. The trail climbs around the shoulder to Anderson Peak before continuing to Tinker Knob, too far to go for most hikers. From here you will want to return the way you came.

Pacific Crest Trail from Donner Pass to Mount Lincoln and Anderson Peak.
Dogs allowed.
Moderate to strenuous. Five miles round trip to Mount Lincoln; 12 miles round trip to Anderson Peak, with 1,500 feet elevation gain.

Directions:
Drive west on Donner Pass Road from Donner Lake to the road just west of the pass and drive downhill to the Pacific Crest Trailhead on your left. Park along the road.

Special Features:
Portions of the trail have been impacted by the lifts and trails of Sugar Bowl Ski Resort. The mitigation measure for this construction is the trail listed on the next page that crosses the summit of Mount Judah and descends to join the trail you are on, making a wonderful loop across the crest of the Sierra.

Summer

Mount Judah Loop Trail
Dogs allowed.
Moderate to strenuous. Six-mile loop with 2,000 feet elevation gain.

Directions:
Start at the Pacific Crest Trailhead at Donner Summit. Directions are on the previous page.

Special Features:
The Roller Pass was discovered in 1846 by Joseph Aram who had decided it took too long to get over Donner Pass up from the lake. He scouted the creek in Coldstream Valley and found a longer but easier route to the bottom of this cliff. As described in one diary, "We made a roller (log) and fastened chains together and pivoted the wagons up with 12 yoke of oxen on the top, and the same at the bottom." Later, other wagon trains found a way to zigzag up the slope just to the north of the pass.

We recommend doing the loop in a counterclockwise direction. Continue straight when you come to the first Judah Loop trail sign in the first ski run.

Mount Judah Loop Trail

Take the Pacific Crest Trail (PCT) described on the previous page to the saddle between Mount Lincoln and Mount Judah. This is the famous Roller Pass, used by emigrant wagon trains from 1846-1856. Walk over to the edge and imagine the work necessary to get the wagons up this fearsome cliff.

Retrace your steps around the first bend to find the loop trail over the summit of Mt. Judah. The hike takes you past spectacular wildflower displays in early summer. After descending from Mount Judah you arrive at a pass between Mt. Judah and Donner Peak. This old road is currently marked as an emigrant trail from Coldstream Valley. Recent research of diaries has been unable to substantiate that this historic road is a branch of the California Emigrant Trail. Diary accounts only mention the Roller Pass route. It is possible that this road was built during railroad construction in 1864-1866. Follow the road west and downhill about a quarter mile to a trail connection back to the PCT where you turn right back to your car.

Special Hikes

Donner Peak

From the same Pacific Crest Trailhead at Donner Pass, take the Pacific Crest Trail for about a mile until it reaches the Mount Judah Loop Trail in the first ski run. Turn left up the trail until you come to a road that leads to a saddle just below Donner Peak to the left. The trail to the summit leads to a group of granite outcroppings a short scramble away. Views in all directions make this a superior picnic spot.

Summit Lake

The trail leads north to a tunnel under Interstate 80 then enters a forest and shortly after the underpass there is a sign to Summit Lake. The trail is clearly marked. This easy hike is a perfect family outing to picnic on the shores of a beautiful alpine lake.

Summit Lake is the end point of the new Donner Lake Rim Trail that connects to the Tahoe Donner trail system. Ambitious hikers might like to arrange a car shuttle at the bottom of Negro Canyon. Call the Truckee Donner Land Trust for directions.

Donner Peak
Dogs allowed.
Easy. Three miles round trip with 1,000 feet elevation gain.

Directions:
Follow directions on page 185 for parking at the Pacific Crest Trail.

Summit Lake
Dogs allowed.
Easy. Four miles round trip with 200 feet elevation gain.

Directions:
Take the Castle Peak/Boreal exit off I-80 from east or west. Drive to the frontage road on the south side of the freeway, then east about one-quarter mile to the Pacific Crest Trailhead.

Truckee Donner Land Trust
530-582-4711

Summer

Donner Memorial State Park
Easy. About 1.5 miles with no elevation gain.

Directions:
The park is on Donner Pass Rd. just west of the Donner State Park exit off I-80. The entrance to the park is marked with a state historic marker, and parking for the museum is to the left as you enter.

Special Features:
The Museum at the park explains the emigrant and railroad history of the region. A special slide show tells the story of the Donner Party and the bookstore features books about emigrant history. See "Museums" on page 279 for show times.

Around Donner Memorial State Park

This is a perfect afternoon walk with ample opportunity to swim at the park's beach. After visiting the museum, take the road past the entrance kiosk and continue to the right. When you reach the outflow creek, there is a trail through the woods that is close to the water. Interpretive signs along this trail will increase your knowledge of history and ecology of the region. Near the beach in a cove at the southwest corner of the park, a trail leaves the main road and follows the perimeter of the park toward the campground. Entering the first set of campsites, keep to the right. Turn left where the road leads to Coldstream Valley. When you reach a *Y,* turn right to return to your car. Bring your bathing suits and a picnic. The beach is an excellent place for children to play in the shallow water, and picnic tables are close by in the trees. The long drought of the 1990s killed many of the lodgepole pines. Some have been cut down, leaving a very sparse forest in many areas.

There is also a short nature trail that leaves from the museum and crosses the outlet creek a few times.

Summer

Special Hikes

Mt. Lola

Mt. Lola, at 9,143 feet, affords unmatched 360° views of the Sierra and Carson Range. After about an hour of steady climbing the trail exits onto a logging road for a few hundred yards and crosses Cold Stream. Look for white arrows on a brown background indicating where the trail leaves the road. From this point you climb gently through the forest until entering a broad meadow with many old beaver ponds. An abandoned beaver house is clearly visible in one pond. If more climbing is not for you, coming this far makes a perfect outing.

After the beaver ponds, one mile of climbing brings you to a ridge with your first views south and north. The trail crosses a plateau with bent and wind-sculpted hemlocks and western white pine. Notice the drooping form of hemlocks that John Muir called "the most graceful, pliant and sensitive" of Sierra trees. Western white pines have five needles in a bunch and the cones dangle in threes from the highest branches. Also present are two-needle lodgepole pines. The last half mile of trail is very steep, but the view from the top is well worth the effort.

Mt. Lola
Strenuous. Five to six hours for nine miles round trip with 2,600 feet elevation gain.

Directions:
From I-80 drive 20 miles north on Highway 89 to Henness Pass Road. Drive west toward Jackson Meadow 1.5 miles. Turn left driving 0.8 mile toward Independence Lake crossing the Little Truckee River and turn right onto Old Henness Pass Road. The Mt. Lola Trailhead is 3.2 miles west. Park here to start the 4.5 mile hike. The trail is marked with white diamonds on trees as well as old T-shaped blazes.

Special Features:
The hike up Mt. Lola offers an opportunity to study conifers of our region. The first part of the trail passes through colorful aspen and willow groves lining seasonal drainages. The forest becomes predominantly white fir and Jeffrey pine with its deeply furrowed, reddish bark smelling of vanilla. Pick up a cone. The saying is, "Gentle Jeffrey, prickly ponderosa." This is one way to determine if you are near a Jeffrey or ponderosa pine. To identify a white fir, notice that the needles are 1 to 2 inches long arranged in two rows almost at right angles with the branch. The cones in summer are 3 to 5 inches high standing upright on the topmost branches.

Unfortunately the trail passes through a private forest which has been extensively logged in the past few years. You can only grin and bear it through this section which is less than a mile.

Summer

Special Hikes

Five Lakes Basin

Five Lakes Basin
Dogs allowed.
Moderate. Five miles round trip with 980 feet elevation gain.

Directions:
Take Alpine Meadows Rd. off Hwy. 89. The trailhead is 2.1 miles west on the right-hand side across from the Deer Park entrance road.

This well-marked, popular trail climbs, sometimes steeply, for two miles then flattens before descending through red fir forest to the most northern of the five lakes. The lakes are clustered within a square-mile area, making this a great place to explore. The first mile of the hike is exposed as you climb along a south-facing slope, so be sure to bring plenty of water.

Eagle Rock

Eagle Rock
Dogs allowed.
Easy. One and a half miles round trip with 240 feet elevation gain.

Directions:
Drive 4 miles south from the Tahoe City Y on Hwy. 89 to the Kaspian Sno Park on Blackwood Canyon Rd. or 4.5 miles to a small parking area on the west side of the road.

This is a perfect late afternoon or early evening photo hike to one of the high points above the lake. There are two trails up Eagle Rock. The easiest when there is no water starts a quarter of a mile up Blackwood Canyon Road. A trail ascends a ridge along a power line to the south. At the top, near a power line pole, an unofficial trail turns east up to the volcanic promontory that is Eagle Rock. Head out across the rocks to several tall Jeffrey pines. Be sure to bring your camera to record the expanse of the "Lake of the Sky."

The other approach is from the parking area half a mile south of the Kaspian Recreation Parking. A broad trail follows Blackwood Creek for about a quarter-mile.

Special Hikes

Take the first unofficial trail that heads uphill steeply through the brush. You will intersect the power line and find the trail heading east from the power line trail. This is a steep but quick way to reach the peak. You can return by following the power line trail down to Blackwood Canyon Road then out to Highway 89, returning south along the bike path to your car.

Crag Lake

The first mile of the trip is along a dirt road on the north side of Meeks Creek. There are many wildflower gardens to admire here. Look for tiger lilies and columbine. The trail into the wilderness area begins at the far end of the valley and climbs quickly through the forest. Suddenly you will emerge onto the shining granite terrain that symbolizes the Desolation Wilderness. After a few miles climbing through the open forest of giant Jeffrey pine, you will come upon Lake Genevieve. You may be tempted to stop here, but it is only a short hike to Crag Lake, much larger and more scenic. Here the many rocky ledges beckon you to sunbathe, picnic and swim to cool off after the climb. This hike is a perfect all-day family outing.

Crag Lake
Wilderness Permit required.
Dogs allowed under control.
Moderately strenuous. Ten miles round trip with 2,000 feet elevation gain.

Directions:
From the Tahoe City Y, drive 11 miles south on Hwy. 89 to the trailhead parking at Meeks Bay. From the South Tahoe Y drive 16 miles north on Hwy. 89.

Special Features:
Adventurous hikers may want to continue at least as far as Stony Ridge Lake which will give you a good workout, climbing another 1,000 feet.

Summer

Barker Pass
Dogs allowed.
Moderate to strenuous. Five miles round trip.

Directions:
Drive four miles south on Highway 89 to the road up Blackwood Canyon. Drive 6.5 miles up the paved road to Barker Pass. The road turns to dirt at this point. Drive downhill a quarter mile to the trailhead on the right. There is parking and a restroom here.

Special Features:
Adventurous hikers can climb Twin Peaks via a trail that forks east off the Pacific Crest Trail about a quarter mile along the ridge.

Barker Pass

Here is a chance to drive up to the Pacific Crest and Tahoe Rim Trail for a hike that leads to panoramic views of both Lake Tahoe and the American River gorges west of the range. In early summer the trail passes through some of the best flower shows in the basin.

The trail climbs gradually for the first mile through open meadows and high forests of lodgepole and fir. When you reach a volcanic outcropping with a magnificent view of the lake, the trail begins to descend and crosses several drainages where stream ecosystems produce abundant wildflower displays. You must then climb back to the saddle below Twin Peaks. Here you can see both Lake Tahoe and north along the Pacific Crest. You can also see much of Desolation Wilderness to the south.

Special Hikes

Looking south from the trail toward Desolation Wilderness.

One of the many magnificent views of Lake Tahoe from the trail to
Twin Peaks.

Rubicon Trail
No dogs.
Fee per vehicle at Bliss Park.
Easy. Nine miles round trip with 200 feet elevation gain.

Directions:
Drive 10 miles north of the South Tahoe Y on Highway 89 or 16 miles south of the Tahoe City Y. Drive into the park to the Calawee Cove parking lot at the edge of the lake.

Special Features:
The Rubicon Trail is easiest from D. L. Bliss State Park to Vikingsholm in Emerald Bay and back. You can shorten the walk and stop anywhere up to Emerald Point for a picnic on the beach before returning to your car.

Vikingsholm from Emerald Bay Overlook
No dogs.
Fee for the tour. Tours daily June through Labor Day.
Easy. One mile downhill to the beach.

Directions:
The overlook is on Hwy. 89 about 8 miles north of the South Tahoe Y and 18 miles south of the Tahoe City Y.

Rubicon Trail from D.L. Bliss State Park to Emerald Bay

The trail starts at the south end of Calawee Cove parking lot and climbs up the ridge to the site of the Old Lighthouse. From there it is a gentle downhill trek to Emerald Point where the trail hugs the beach all the way to Vikingsholm. The views from this trail are the most spectacular anywhere in the area, each curve bringing into view another cove or another rock formation. In early summer, ospreys may be seen nesting on the top of trees, some at eye level from the trail.

Vikingsholm from Emerald Bay Overlook

The trail winds down an old road to Vikingsholm and the Emerald Bay Beach where you can watch the sternwheelers circle the bay.

Vikingsholm was built by Mrs. Lora J. Knight in 1929. She planned an exact reproduction of a Norse fortress from A.D. 800. Since much of the furniture she tried to buy in Scandinavia was so valuable that it could not be exported, she had the designs meticulously copied to complete her Viking castle.

Special Hikes

Emerald Bay and Fannette Island from the overlook. Mrs. Knight was rowed daily to her small house on the island where she had her afternoon tea.

Eagle Falls and Eagle Lake

You will need a wilderness permit for this hike. This is one of the easiest yet most spectacular hikes in the area. Start up the trail to Eagle Falls, a simple one-eighth mile climb to cross above the falls. Proceed through a red fir forest as you climb toward Eagle Lake. Before reaching the lake you will cross expanses of granite rock with beautiful specimens of old Jeffrey pines. It is only one mile to Eagle Lake in its granite bowl. The first shoreline you reach offers many wonderful picnic spots.

Eagle Falls and Eagle Lake
Dogs allowed under control.
Fee to park at the trailhead.
Wilderness permit required.
Easy. Two miles round trip with 400 feet elevation gain.

Directions:
The parking lot is just south of the Emerald Bay Overlook. There is a fee to park in the lot.

Special Features:
If you wish to continue, the trail climbs the ridge on the east side of the lake and continues for several miles toward the three Velma Lakes. The views at the top of the first ridge are worth the climb, and the photo opportunities of Emerald Bay and Lake Tahoe from this elevation are superb.

Cascade Falls
Dogs allowed.

Easy. One and a half miles round trip, some up and down, but little elevation gain. No wilderness permit required.

Granite Lake
Wilderness Permit required.
Dogs allowed under control.

Moderate. Two miles round trip with 800 feet elevation gain. Wilderness permit required.

Directions:

Drive 18 miles south from the Tahoe City *Y* or 10 miles north of the South Tahoe *Y* on Hwy. 89 to the Bayview Campground and Trailhead, opposite Emerald Bay Inspiration Point.

Cascade Falls and Granite Lake

The trail starts behind the wilderness permit sign-up board. Take the left fork which climbs gently until you are on a beautiful granite ledge above Cascade Lake. The trail dips then climbs again until Lake Tahoe and Cascade Lake are both visible. The top of the falls is best viewed early in the summer when snowmelt fills the creek. Be careful with small children when descending across the granite slabs to look at the top of the falls.

It's possible to follow the creek upstream where you will find picnic sites beside deep pools. Because it is so easy, this is a perfect hike for young children while parents will enjoy the views and photo opportunities.

More ambitious hikers may elect to take the trail to Granite Lake in Desolation Wilderness. You will need a permit for this one. It is a steep climb of about 800 feet in one mile. However, the views of Emerald Bay reward the effort, and a swim in this relatively warm lake will help cool you off before the return hike.

Special Hikes

Vikingsholm to Eagle Point

A brand new trail has been built by California State Parks which lets you hike around Emerald Bay. Start at Vikingsholm parking lot hiking down the road to the bay. The trail circles Emerald Bay from Vikingsholm to Eagle Point Campground. The last quarter mile is on the road down to the campground. Part way down the hill is a short trail to a promontory with views of both Emerald Bay and Lake Tahoe.

A trail to Cascade Creek starts across from Tent Site #53. It was only partially complete as we went to press.

Vikingsholm to Eagle Point
No dogs.
Moderate. Three miles one way to Eagle Point Campground.

Directions:
Follow directions to Emerald Bay Overlook on page 194.

Special Features:
At the point where the trail crosses Eagle Creek, you can also hike a quarter mile up to view lower Eagle Falls, a worthwhile side trip.

The beautiful pink shooting star is found in moist meadows in early summer.

© Ellie Huggins

Special Hikes

Summer

Mount Tallac
Wilderness Permit required.
Dogs allowed under control.
Strenuous. Ten miles round trip with 3,300 feet elevation gain. This is one hike where we recommend you wear hiking boots and carry plenty of water.

Directions:
Drive 3.9 miles north from the South Tahoe *Y* on Hwy. 89 to Road 1306A. The trailhead is one mile up the road.

Special Features:
For those that aren't sure about their ability to make it to the top, you can stop at Floating Island Lake in 1.5 miles up a fairly shaded trail. Three quarters of a mile farther on is Cathedral Lake, another stopping place for a picnic on the lake shore.

Rainbow Trail
Easy. One and a half mile loop trail. Paved with wheelchair access.

Directions:
Drive north on Hwy. 89 from the South Tahoe *Y* 3.2 miles to the U.S. Forest Service Visitor Center.

Special Features:
The Stream Profile Chamber is open after renovation. In the chamber you will have an underwater view of swimming fish and, in October when the kokanee salmon spawn, you can see hundreds of these fish with their red humped backs and strange beak-like jaws making their way up the creek to spawn before they die.

Mount Tallac

Climbing Mount Tallac to 9,735 feet is the experience of a lifetime, for not only have you achieved a true peak climb, but the view is unmatched anywhere. The climb to the base of the bowl that hides Tallac's real peak from view affords another stopping place with spectacular wildflower gardens. Hardy hikers can keep going up the bowl and across the several false tops to the north. It will all be worth the work when you take in the view. Lake Tahoe, Fallen Leaf and Cascade Lakes are to the east, while the granite bowls, peaks and lakes of Desolation Wilderness fill the western horizon.

Rainbow Trail

This nature trail leaves from the Visitor Center. Signs along the way explain the importance of Taylor Creek and the stream ecosystem that helps maintain a healthy forest and Lake Tahoe's water quality. The creek and its riparian zone are nesting and feeding habitats for a myriad of birds. Early in the summer, meadows burst into bloom with buttercups, phlox, wallflower and Indian paintbrush to name just a few.

Special Hikes

Fallen Leaf Lake to Angora Lakes Resort

This is a great hike for those staying at Fallen Leaf Lake. The trail leaves from the church. The hike has many rewards, including unsurpassed views of Fallen Leaf and Lake Tahoe. The first quarter mile is on a trail that crosses a rocky ridge and ascends fairly steeply. The next section uses a set of easy switchbacks through a forest of red fir and western white pine. After reaching the parking lot, you join others who drove to this point to climb gradually on a wide sandy thoroughfare past the first Angora lake until you reach the resort, established in 1917. Children of friends who have long vacationed at Fallen Leaf dubbed this the "Lemonade Lake," because of the famous lemonade the resort serves. Bring your bathing suit for this one. The beach at the resort is open to all and lies along the northwest shore.

Fallen Leaf Lake to Angora Lakes
Dogs allowed on trail, must be on leash at the resort.
Easy. One half mile from Angora Lakes parking lot with 160 feet elevation gain. Moderate. One and a half miles from Fallen Leaf to Angora Lakes with 1,120 feet elevation gain.

Directions to Fallen Leaf Lake:
Drive south 4.6 miles from Hwy. 89 on Fallen Leaf Road. Park at the Marina parking lot. Walk along the shore and frontage road until you come to the church.

Directions to the parking lot:
Parking at Fallen Leaf is very limited and if you're looking for the shorter hike, we suggest that South Shore visitors take Lake Tahoe Boulevard 3 miles from the South Tahoe Y then turn right on Tahoe Mountain Road until it intersects Angora Ridge Road and drive 3.5 miles to the parking lot.

Special Hikes

The Hawley Grade Trail
Dogs allowed.
Easy. Three and a half miles round trip with 700 feet elevation gain.

Directions:
Take U.S. 50 west 5.3 miles from the South Tahoe Y to Upper Truckee Rd. Turn south and drive 3.6 miles to the sign for Hawley Grade National Recreation Trail. Take the single lane road into a small summer home development. Park at the end of the road.

Special Features:
After the Luther Pass road was surveyed in 1854, Asa Hawley set up a trading post in Lake Valley and built an easy ascent from the Luther Pass Road to a point near Echo summit. With money from private sources, he constructed a one-lane wagon road that significantly improved the journey west to Hangtown (Placerville). When the Nevada Comstock mines opened, miners and their suppliers immediately sought a more direct route over the mountains. By 1860 a new road crossed the southern edge of Lake Tahoe and then over Daggett Pass (Kingsbury Grade) down to Genoa. This became the preferred route to Virginia City. Poor Hawley's road became unprofitable. Hawley lived to a ripe old age and wrote in his memoirs that he, Snowshoe Thompson and James Green had taken his boat around Lake Tahoe and discovered its outlet.

The Hawley Grade Trail

The Hawley Grade trail is on the first wagon road built over this portion of the Sierra. Westbound settlers wanted an easier, more direct route than Carson Pass to drive directly to the Hangtown (Placerville) mines. Asa Hawley's road lasted only a few years before it fell into disuse. Today, thanks to the U.S. Forest Service, we are able to hike this road (now a trail) and marvel at his engineering skill.

The trail begins past the last of the houses in a small development. You can hear the Upper Truckee River nearby as you climb past thickets of currant and willow. As soon as the trail turns north, a gradual ascent to the summit begins. The first mile is through deep forest and an area with natural springs that ooze onto the trail, even in late summer. Notice how nature is managing to bring the contours of this slope into alignment, narrowing the width of the trail as you climb. Marvel at the ancient stands of Jeffrey pine and white fir that have been spared the lumberman's axe. After about a mile you cross a rock slide and emerge from the forest to glimpses of Lake Tahoe far to the north beyond Lake Valley.

Special Hikes

Later, you can look south to see the volcanic palisades under Stevens Peak and beyond it, Red Lake Peak. It was from this peak that John Charles Frémont first saw Lake Tahoe. Here you are looking toward the Upper Truckee River's headwaters.

This hike is best in the afternoon when the sun has begun to fall behind Echo Summit. An autumn hike gives vistas of the aspens that paint golden ribbons along the Upper Truckee River.

© Ellie Huggins

Hiking across Big Meadow. The hike is described on the next page.

Special Hikes

Big Meadow and Round Lake
Dogs allowed.
Moderate. Six miles round trip with 800 feet elevation gain.

Directions:
Big Meadow Trailhead parking is 5 miles south of Meyers on Hwy. 89. Turn left off the road about 100 yards past the old roadside parking to a developed trailhead with restrooms and display board.

Special Features:
Families with small children will find this a perfect beginners' hike, for the creek that meanders through the meadow offers plenty of places to safely wade or splash in cool waters. Early in the season you will need mosquito repellant.

Round Lake can also be reached via a wildflower wonderland from Carson Pass over Meiss Pass and through Meiss Meadow. Round Lake is about equidistant from Highways 88 and 89 and affords a good car shuttle opportunity. A description of the hike from Carson Pass can be found on page 209.

Big Meadow and Round Lake

Walk to Highway 89 and cross the highway to find the trail to Big Meadow. The trail begins with a climb of several hundred feet through a forest of Jeffrey pine and white fir until you emerge onto the flat Big Meadow.

To reach Round Lake, continue through the meadow and climb another few hundred feet through wildflower gardens adorning sandy slopes to the crest of the ridge separating Big Meadow Creek and Upper Truckee River drainages. From the ridge you will see Red Lake and Stevens Peaks. The trail descends gradually a mile and a half to Round Lake. The northeast shore has many picnic spots high above the lake. Notice the interesting rock formation that guards the eastern shore. These are volcanic palisades, and debris from them give the water of Round Lake a brownish hue.

lupine

scarlet gilia

Special Hikes

Pacific Crest Trail at Echo Lakes

This is a perfect hike for a family with young children. The trail starts across the dam and goes along the north side of the lake. After a short climb high above the summer homes, the trail contours along the north shore before descending to the forested slopes above Upper Echo Lake. Here you will find a signed trail that leads to the dock and water taxi back to the lodge. This seldom used trail offers an opportunity to hike these beautiful granite slopes for a short distance and return across the water. Use the phone at the dock to call the water taxi.

From Upper Echo Lake there are numerous trails to beautiful lakes nestled in the granite landscape of Desolation Wilderness. We suggest that you consult the appropriate U.S.G.S. map or one of the books listed on page 183 for descriptions of these hikes.

Pacific Crest Trail at Echo Lakes
Dogs allowed.
Fee to ride the boat taxi.
Easy. Two and three-quarter miles to Upper Echo Lake. Less than 100 ft. elevation gain.

Directions:
Drive 8.9 miles west on U.S. 50 from the South Tahoe *Y* to Echo Lakes Rd. Drive north about one mile then turn left and follow signs to Echo Lakes. Park only where allowed.

Summer

Special Hikes

**Tahoe Rim Trail north from
Spooner Summit**
Dogs allowed.

Easy. 800 feet elevation gain, as far
as you want to hike.

Moderately strenuous. Eight-mile hike
returning to Spooner Lake. Car shuttle
necessary.

Strenuous 11 miles to Marlette Lake.
Car shuttle necessary.

Directions:

Parking for the trailhead is on the north
side of U.S. 50 in a signed area off
the road just east of Spooner Summit.
Information about the Tahoe Rim Trail
is on the sign at the trailhead.

Special Features:

If there are two cars in your group, you
can arrange a car shuttle leaving one
car at Spooner State Park. There is a
fee to park here. During the height of
summer, this can be a hot hike, so
bring plenty of water.

Tahoe Rim Trail north from Spooner Summit

Hiking the first miles of this 13-mile
segment of the Tahoe Rim Trail allows
you to get some spectacular views of
Lake Tahoe as well as the Carson
Valley in Nevada. The trail starts at
7,150 feet and climbs gradually into
the Carson Range of the Sierra. As
you round the first bend you will
catch glimpses of Spooner Lake and
Lake Tahoe in the distance. The trail
toward the first vista point passes
through stands of second growth
Jeffrey pine. From a group of granite
boulders you will get your first view of
the Carson Valley and the ranges of
mountains to the south and east. At
the top of the first long climb, in
about two miles, is John's Rock. From
these rocks you see the magnificent
panorama of Lake Tahoe and the
granite peaks of Desolation
Wilderness. If snow is still on the high
peaks, look for the cross of snow on
the southeast bowl of Mount Tallac.
After John's Rock the trail flattens out
and crosses an open plateau where
giant red firs reign supreme. These
beautiful trees were spared in the
logging frenzy of the late 1800s.

Summer

Special Hikes

For those who want to hike the loop, take the Rim Trail across the western slope of Snow Valley Peak until it intersects with an old road and bike trail that descends to North Canyon Road. From these trails you will get your most expansive views of Lake Tahoe and peaks of the western shore.

To hike to Marlette Lake, turn right up North Canyon Road and hike over the next rise and downhill to Marlette Lake. This is a favorite bike trip and the road will be dusty in summer.

Spooner Lake Nature Trail

The trail around Spooner Lake is a natural to include with a family picnic in the park. It is particularly beautiful in autumn when the many aspens surrounding the lake are in full color. Several trails leave the picnic area and descend to the trailhead near the dam. Cross the dam and take the trail in a clockwise direction. Halfway around the lake you walk through aspen groves. These are quaking aspen, whose leaves tremble with the slightest breeze, giving rise to the Latin name *populus tremuloides*. Look closely at a leaf with its flattened stalk. This is what causes the leaf to move in the wind.

Spooner Lake Nature Trail
Fee per vehicle to enter park.
Easy. One and a half miles around the lake.

Directions:
On Hwy. 28 about one-half mile north of U.S. 50.

Special Hikes

**Tahoe Rim Trail Whole Access
Loop at Tahoe Meadows
Dogs allowed.**
Easy. One mile loop.

Directions:
Drive 6.7 miles east on Hwy. 431 to
the paved parking area for the trail.

Tahoe Rim Trail Whole Access Loop at Tahoe Meadows

Families with babies in strollers or those in wheelchairs can enjoy this trail of the Tahoe Rim Trail system. This loop around the high meadows allows you to enjoy a meadow and streamside environment filled with wildflowers and a section of lodgepole pine forest. Among the flowers to be enjoyed up close are bush lupine, asters, alpine daisies, yellow mimulus (monkey flowers), so-called because the face of a monkey to be seen on the flower's petals.

**Mount Rose
Dogs allowed.**
Moderate. Six miles round trip to start
of peak climb with 600 feet elevation
gain. Strenuous. Ten miles round trip
with 1,978 feet elevation gain.

Directions:
Drive 6.9 miles on Hwy. 431 to a
trailhead on the north side of the road.
A pink cement block building is visible
above the road. Park parallel on either
side of the highway.

Climbing to the top of Mount Rose
A trail leaves the road on the right
dipping into the headwaters of Galena
Creek. Crossing the creek drainage,
it climbs north to the final one-mile
ascent east to the summit. It is steep
and can be windy, but the views are

Mount Rose

Like the Mount Tallac climb on the South Shore of Lake Tahoe, one does not have to make the whole trip to enjoy spectacular scenery and views. The first three miles of this hike to the top of 10,778-foot Mount Rose are on an old road with an easy grade and expansive views of Lake Tahoe around every curve. Trailside displays of pink mimulus, delphinium and lupine appear for the first two miles of hiking. When the delphinium are in bloom you may be treated to the sight of many hummingbirds zooming in for drinks of nectar. Deer are also often seen in meadows near the road.

Summer

Special Hikes

In about two miles you come to a pond in a lovely meadow. For those who do not wish to climb the peak, this pond is a perfect picnic spot. Mount Rose is hidden from view at this point as the road curves to the left.

Those not climbing Mount Rose can turn around and return as you came.

Tahoe Rim Trail north from Highway 267

This hike makes a gradual climb from Highway 267 mostly through forest with occasional glimpses of Crystal Bay and Incline Village. After half an hour or so, turn left sharply on a trail uphill to a promontory with expansive views of Lake Tahoe and towards Truckee and beyond. From this vantage point you can pick out Mount Tallac, Rubicon Peak, Freel Peak and the Crystal Range. There are few spots on the Rim Trail with such a vista.

Return to the main trail and turn left to continue toward Martis Peak. This trail passes through red fir forests and meadows with gradual ascents for two and a half more miles to a rocky point at about 8,500 feet, just under the summit of Martis Peak. The view of the entire lake is again spectacular and worth the climb.

Tahoe Rim Trail north from Highway 267
Dogs allowed.
Moderate, two miles round trip with 760 feet elevation gain.
Moderately strenuous, nine miles round trip to viewpoint under Martis Peak.

Directions:
The parking lot for the trail is on the south side of Highway 267 about a quarter mile east of Brockway Summit. The trail starts across the road.

Special Features:
The Tahoe Rim Trail also goes south from this point toward Mount Watson.

Summer

Special Hikes

Winnemucca Lake and Beyond
Dogs allowed.
Easy to moderate. Five miles round trip with 500 feet elevation gain.

Directions:
On Hwy. 88 at Carson Pass, 13 miles west of the junction with Hwy. 89. Park in the lot on the south side of the highway.

Special Features:
Those who wish a longer hike can continue climbing steeply to Round Top Lake (1 mile) and Fourth of July Lake (2 miles).

Short Frog Lake hike:
Take the first part of the trail until you reach the junction to Frog Lake in about a mile. Walk over and take in the view. Families with small children may want to stop here for a picnic and swim.

Winnemucca Lake and Beyond

The trail starts uphill gradually through a red fir forest to the turnoff to Frog Lake. Early in the summer wildflowers of every hue will thrill you along the open slopes. The hike to Lake Winnemucca is an easy grade beyond Frog Lake across an open plateau with views of Round Top Peak and Caples Lake. At the next trail junction, take the right hand fork to Winnemucca, which will come into view from a bluff. Surrounded by the steep cliffs under Round Top Peak (10,300 feet), the lake is a perfect stopping place and creates a day's outing.

© Ellie Huggins

Winnemucca Lake in early summer.

Special Hikes

Meiss Pass, Meiss Meadow to Round Lake or Showers Lake

This section of the Pacific Crest Trail north of Carson Pass offers some of the most expansive views of Lake Tahoe and the Desolation Wilderness peaks anywhere in the region and also has spectacular wildflower gardens. You only have to hike 1.5 miles for the opportunity to see Lake Tahoe as Kit Carson and John Charles Frémont did in 1844. The trail starts gently uphill through a forest of 500-year-old Sierra juniper that are still young enough to keep their form and bark. More gnarled specimens seen on lofty granite slabs can live for more than a thousand years. In the forest, columbine, lupine and scarlet gilia vie for attention, and memorable photographs of these gardens are possible. After crossing a small creek, the trail takes a couple of easy switchbacks past a small glacial tarn (pond) to the crest at Meiss Pass. Hike far enough to take in the view of Lake Tahoe. Red Lake Peak, where Carson and Frémont stood, is to the east. Looking back southwest you can see where the emigrants crossed just south of Thimble Peak above Kirkwood Ski Resort.

The pass area is filled with fields of Douglas iris in midsummer where the

Meiss Pass, Meiss Meadow to Round Lake or Showers Lake
Dogs allowed.
Easy to moderate. Two miles to Meiss Pass, 3.5 miles to Round Lake with 300 feet elevation gain to the pass, 400 feet down to Meiss Meadow or 4 miles to Showers Lake with 400 feet elevation gain from Meiss Meadow to Showers Lake.

Directions:
Park on the north side of Hwy. 88 a few hundred yards west of Carson Pass and the parking for Lake Winnemucca.

Summer

Special Hikes

Showers Lake Hike

To reach Showers Lake, continue straight in Meiss Meadow another mile before a climb of 400 feet brings you over a ridge to a lovely lake nestled among granite boulders. The near shore of the lake has many camping spots, and the lake can be very crowded on summer weekends.

trail continues downhill to the Meiss cabins and meadow, named for Louis Meiss, whose son Benjamin bought these acres in 1901. Cattle have grazed here ever since. Take the right-hand fork at the next junction to hike to Round Lake. You will climb gently uphill through an old growth red fir forest with some fine specimens of this stately giant. The trail reaches Round Lake in another 1.5 miles, which beckons swimmers on a summer day into its surprisingly temperate water. You will want to hike to the northeast shore for good swimming and picnic spots.

View of Lake Tahoe from Meiss Pass.

Just For Kids

Families coming to the region can choose from a variety of free or paid services that can make your kids' vacation like going away to camp. Some ski resorts now have year-round child care as well as special programs for small children and even teenagers. The U.S. Forest Service has interpretive activities that are geared for children and many campgrounds have evening campfire programs for the whole family. We have listed those that are ongoing, but check with the U.S. Forest Service Visitor Center and California State Parks for weekly offerings of hikes and nature programs. The Sierra Nevada Children's Museum in Truckee can provide hours of experiential learning for young people. See page 278 in "Museums" for the description.

Truckee-Donner Recreation and Park District

The District offers a full schedule of activities for all ages, from preschool through junior high. You can check at the district offices in downtown Truckee on Church Street.

Truckee-Donner Recreation and Park District
Truckee
530-582-7720
www.tdrpd.com

Special Features:
The district publishes a brochure in early June that lists all classes. You can call to get your copy.

Tahoe Donner Equestrian Center Horsemanship Camps

The Equestrian Center holds weekly camps Monday through Friday from 9:00 a.m. to 3:00 p.m. Classes are for all levels of Western and English styles and feature basic horsemanship as well as how to care for your horse.

Campers receive special instruction and practice for a show or games on the last day.

Tahoe Donner Equestrian Center Horsemanship Camps
Fee per week.
Enrollment limited.
End of June through August.
530-587-9470

Just For Kids

Northstar-at-Tahoe Minors' Camp
Northstar-at-Tahoe
Reservations required.
530-562-2278

Northstar-at-Tahoe Minors' Camp

If you are staying at Northstar, or just planning to mountain bike, play golf or horseback ride at the resort, you can enroll your 2 to 10-year-olds in Minors' Camp. Children must be completely potty trained, and you must stay at the resort while your child is at camp. The fully licensed child care facility offers a wide variety of activities from off-site field trips to swimming, arts and crafts, creek walks and pony rides.

Resort at Squaw Creek
Reservations required.
530-583-6300

Resort at Squaw Creek

The resort hosts children in their Mountain Buddies program geared to interest, exercise and educate children between the ages of 3 and 13 years. With such activities as "wacky Olympics," rollerblading, ice skating and building snowmen in the winter, there are sports or arts and crafts for children every day all year. There are three sessions daily, and an evening session from 6:00 to 9:00 p.m.

Summer

Just For Kids

Tahoe Trips and Trails

The company that leads adults on hikes of all abilities has an August Family Sampler Tour designed for families with kids six and up. Activities include a hayride breakfast at the Ponderosa Ranch and one evening of kid's activities so the parents can have the night off. Lodging and meals are included in this planned trip.

Tahoe Trips and Trails
Reservations required.
800-581-4453

California State Parks

Junior Ranger Programs are held at Donner Memorial State Park, D.L. Bliss and Sugar Pine Point State Parks. Times vary at each park, so check at the entrance stations for information about family oriented hikes and campfire programs.

California State Parks
July 1 through Labor Day.
Donner Memorial State Park
530-582-7892
D.L. Bliss State Park
530-525-7277
Sugar Pine Point State Park
530-525-7982

U.S. Forest Service Programs

Woodsey Rangers meets at the Fallen Leaf Campground Monday through Friday at 10:00 a.m. Kids between 6 and 12 years old will be treated to games, treasure hunts and storytelling, with different programs each day. Learn about nature's magical environment from knowledgeable Forest Service rangers.

Woodsey Rangers
Fallen Leaf Campground Site 4A
off Fallen Leaf Rd.

Summer

Just For Kids

Camp Tadaka
1180 Rufus Allen Blvd.
South Lake Tahoe
Fee per day.
530-542-6093

Special Features:
There is no need to preregister, just show up before 7:30 a.m. in the morning. If you wish to enroll for a week, drop by the office at 1180 Rufus Allen Blvd. in South Lake Tahoe.

Kirkwood Resort
Fridays, Saturdays and Sundays.
Summer only.
Reservations recommended.
209-258-6000

Camp Tadaka

The South Lake Tahoe Parks and Recreation Department operates a summer day camp for first through sixth graders that is open to any child, whether visitor or resident. The camp features field trips, outdoor activities and games plus arts and crafts. Hours are from 7:30 a.m. to 6:00 p.m.

Camp Radical is for 6th to 8th graders and offers a strenuous set out outdoor activities during the same time period.

Kirkwood Explorers

Kids between 5 and 14 years old can attend this day camp that features everything from fly fishing instruction to nature crafts. Trained naturalists will keep the children happy between 9:00 a.m. and 3:00 p.m. doing a myriad of outdoor activities. On Saturdays there is a family recreation program with dinner followed by a campfire with storytelling and marshmallow roasting. Here's an opportunity to give the kids a day at camp while you hike, fish or relax, then relive your own camp memories with your children in the evening.

Closeup view of a Mariposa lily which your children may learn to identify with the Kirkwood Explorers naturalist.

Ranger Programs

The United States Forest Service conducts many different ranger programs suitable for the whole family. The walks and tours take place at the Visitor Center, at the Tallac Historic Site and at Echo Lakes. The schedule is published in *Lake of the Sky Journal* available at many locations in South Lake Tahoe, at the Meyers Visitor Information Kiosk and at the U.S. Forest Service Visitor Center.

U.S. Forest Service Visitor Center 3.2 miles north of the South Tahoe *Y* on Highway 89. 530-573-2674

U.S. Forest Service Visitor Center

Daily Programs.

A Patio Talk is given daily at the Visitor Center. Subjects of the talks are posted 24 hours in advance.

Weekly Programs

Wonders of Wildflowers walks take you out into the meadows near the Visitor Center. This is a wonderful way to be introduced to the local wildflowers so that you can recognize them on your own walks elsewhere in the basin.

The Creek Walk is a naturalist-led walk <u>in</u> Taylor Creek for two hours of fun. It is not recommended for kids under age 5. Wear old tennis shoes and shorts for this one.

Summer

Ranger Programs

Tallac Historic Site

Guided tours of the Pope Main House are offered Fridays through Mondays. Reservations are required.

The Boats of Tahoe tour at the Pope Boathouse offer a glimpse at the historic working and pleasure boats on Lake Tahoe at the turn-of-the-century.

Washoe Garden Plants tour will introduce you to the plants that the Washoe (sometimes "Washo") used for food and for fashioning into tools and baskets. Following this once-a-week tour, visit the Tallac Museum to learn more about Washoe history.

Tallac Historic Site Tours
Parking is 3.1 miles north of the South Lake Tahoe *Y* on Highway 89.

Echo Lakes

The Echo Lakes Boat Cruise takes place a couple of days a week. A naturalist will describe the glaciated landscape that surrounds the two lakes. This is a great way to become acquainted with this beautiful wilderness above Lake Tahoe.

Echo Lakes

Directions:
Drive 9 miles west on U.S. 50 from the South Tahoe *Y* to Echo Lake Rd. Drive north to the Sno-Park and turn left, following signs to Echo Lakes.

Winter Activities

With mountain peaks reaching 10,000 feet and snowstorms that can dump up to five feet of snow in a few days, the region is well-known for its downhill ski areas.

Before skiing was fashionable, hardy members of the Sierra Skiing Club could be seen schussing down the slopes above Truckee on their 10-foot "Norwegian skis." By 1909 Truckee was hosting a Winter Carnival complete with skiing and jumping exhibitions, sleigh rides, toboggan runs, and a "fantastical" Ice Palace constructed in the middle of town. Soda Springs Ski Area began with a rope tow in 1935. During the 1930s the Lake Tahoe Skii Club (the Scandinavian spelling of ski was used) hosted USSA and state championships at its ski jump. Sugar Bowl opened its Austrian-style resort with the first chairlift in California in December 1939.

Ski hills near South Lake Tahoe were concentrated at Echo Summit before 1955. Chris Kuraisa turned a small ski hill in South Lake Tahoe into Heavenly Valley and opened with one chairlift in 1955.

After the 1960 Winter Olympic Games at Squaw Valley, new downhill ski areas were developed throughout the Lake Tahoe region. Fourteen ski areas now welcome skiers and snowboarders with more than a hundred lifts on thousands of acres of skiable terrain from Donner Summit to Carson Pass. Most resorts have added all kinds of extra mountain activities for all members of the family, including tubing hills with lifts and snowshoe adventures and access to all the new snow toys and even snowmobile tours.

Winter visitors to Lake Tahoe need not be dedicated skiers to enjoy a sojourn here. There is something for every taste and every member of the family. You might consider cross country skiing, ice skating, a snowmobile tour through the forest, or a saucer ride down a snowy hill with the kids. Anyone can snowshoe and most rental shops now rent the new lightweight models so that you can venture out anywhere there is enough snow.

If the weather does not cooperate, try sitting by a cozy fire in one of the area's great restaurants. With museums to visit and casinos for gambling, you might not even find time to shop.

Winter Activities

Winter Driving

Winter travel in the Sierra can be delayed by snowstorms or accidents on the freeway. When driving to the mountains, you are well-advised to do the following:

- Check your antifreeze and windshield washer reservoir.

- Always carry chains, chain repair links, a flashlight, tarp or other cloth to lie on while putting on chains, a shovel and ice scraper or broom for cleaning off snow.

- It is a good idea to have a blanket and extra clothing along in case you are stopped on the road for a long time. Carry some nibbles and a thermos of hot liquid.

Chain Controls

When a storm is in progress, CalTrans requires that drivers use chains or have a four-wheel-drive vehicle with snow tires for portions of mountain roads. Chain installers charge a fee to install your chains. Weather and road conditions change rapidly, thus chain control points change as well.

The posted speed limit when chain controls are in effect is 25-30 miles per hour, and that applies to all vehicles, including four-wheel drives. Most spinouts and accidents involve four-wheel drive vehicles going at speeds greater than the limit.

In California the telephone number for road conditions: 800-427-7623.

In Nevada the telephone number for road conditions: 877-687-6237

Winter

Downhill Skiing and Boarding

The Lake Tahoe region offers the full range of downhill skiing and snowboarding possibilities at 14 ski areas. There are terrain parks for boarders, and some areas have snow tubing, complete with lifts for the uphill ride. See page 257 in "Snowplay." The areas are listed from Donner Summit and Truckee, south on Highway 89 to Lake Tahoe, then Echo Summit and Carson Pass. The descriptions include information about snowboard parks and special programs for children and first-time skiers, along with some of the special ticket rates. Since most areas have two-for-one tickets on certain days as well as women's days and discount tickets through retail outlets, check the Ski Tahoe free tab for this information or call the ski area. All ski areas have a rental shop on the premises. See page 312 for how to order *Mountain Dreamers*, a beautiful book about the pioneers who brought downhill skiing to the Sierra.

Boreal Mountain Playground
Castle Peak/Boreal exit off I-80
530-426-3666
SnoPhone: 530-426-3666
www.borealski.com

Special Features:
With some of the most extensive snowmaking in the region, Boreal is the first to open each season. The resort offers a huge variety of beginning lesson packages. Follow-up lessons are free until the student can ski or snowboard the mountain top to bottom. Kids get a head start learning snowsports at the Animal Crackers and Snow Rangers ski and snowboard schools. Kids even have their own gentle terrain park. Senior rates start at 60 while those over 70 and under 5 ski free.

Boreal has added mini snowmobile rides for youngsters 6-12 on an enclosed course.

Boreal Mountain Playground

Boreal has always been a great family area, with a central lodge that looks out on the mountain and a free chairlift just right for those first runs. Boreal's trail menu includes decent pitches down Ponderosa and Juniper from the top of the mountain. There are plenty of groomed beginner and intermediate runs to explore off the Gold Rush and Accelerator Chairs. It was one of the first resorts to encourage snowboarding, building terrain parks and halfpipes. Serious boarders flock here to the redesigned and improved parks with features for all levels. Serpentine in design, Jibassic Park consists of huge wave hits and radical tabletops. The Night Terrain Park contains a double-barrel halfpipe.

Downhill Skiing and Boarding

Soda Springs Ski Area

Outdoor enthusiasts have been carving turns down Soda Springs slopes since 1935. It has also been the site of the World Snowboarding Championships and each year still hosts the National Longboard Championships. Although small in stature next to its neighboring giants, few resorts provide the unique features offered by this historic winter playground. Two double chairs and two surface lifts access 200 acres of wide open slopes. A one price ticket gives the guest access to snow tubing, skiing, snowboarding, sledding and snowshoe trails. And if you haven't skied enough during the day, your lift ticket gets you several more half-price hours of skiing afterwards under the lights at Boreal.

Soda Springs
530-426-3666
www.skisodasprings.com

Directions:
One mile east of the Soda Springs/ Norden exit off I-80.

Special Features:
Soda Springs also offers four snow tubing flumes at night on weekends. Their Rent A Resort package offers the perfect place for birthday parties, corporate functions, family reunions or special occasions.

© Ellie Huggins

Riding the tubing lift at Soda Springs.

Downhill Skiing and Boarding

Sugar Bowl

Sugar Bowl
530-426-9000
SnoPhone: 530-426-1111
www.sugarbowl.com

Directions:
On Donner Pass Rd. one half mile west of Donner Pass and 3 miles east of I-80 from the Soda Springs/Norden exit. Use the Magic Carpet Gondola to reach the Village Lodge. Mt. Judah parking enters across from Donner Ski Ranch.

Special Features:
Before there was a World Cup, there was the Silver Belt, a hair-raising giant slalom slope that tested the skills of Leo Lacroix, Billy Kidd and Phil Mahre. From the top of Mount Lincoln, it still puts today's skiers to the test. The gully-like slope first funnels down through trees before dropping off the steep face of the Steilhang.

Sugar Bears Child Care Center is a state licensed toddler program for ages 3-6. Included in children's sessions are ski lesson, rental, lunch, indoor activities and a quiet time. For older kids 6-12, Sugar Bowl's Fast Track Program offers an all mountain package focusing on developing skills from beginner through advanced intermediate. Senior discounts start at 60 years old, and there are major discounts for children 12 years old and under, as well as two-for-one lift tickets on Wednesdays.

Sugar Bowl

The oldest of Tahoe's major ski areas, Sugar Bowl has undergone a sizable expansion with a new base area to compliment some of the finest and most scenic pistes in the region. The Donner Pass resort has been a stronghold of San Francisco society since 1939 when Walt Disney and a group of Bay Area investors backed the plans of Hannes Schroll, a famous Austrian skier, to open a European-style resort. The new access road takes skiers directly to the modern 20,000-square-foot Main Lodge at the Mount Judah base area. Sugar Bowl's expanded 1,500 acres of terrain and four mountain peaks are now serviced by 13 lifts, including a new high-speed quad that loads directly in front of the Village Lodge and cruises quickly to the summit of Mount Disney. The venerable Silver Belt Chair to the top of Mt. Lincoln will be a high speed quad for the 2001-2002 season.

Some things never change, however, and Sugar Bowl's terrain remains a tasty selection of cruisers, rolling shoulders, steeps and chutes. Intermediates looking for less challenging terrain can enjoy the wide open slopes off the Crows Nest lift or the Jerome quad on Mt. Judah.

Winter

Downhill Skiing and Boarding

Though Sugar Bowl's nightlife is decidedly low-key, the resort retains a mix of old and new, much to the pleasure of its clientele. The historic Village Lodge is a throwback to a cozy Tyrolean Inn, complete with big stone fireplace and over-stuffed leather sofas. The historic Lodge accommodations are described on page 34. The Belt Room bar is intimate and the dining room still requires appropriate dress.

Donner Ski Ranch

Donner Ski Ranch's mighty little mountain offers 750 feet of vertical and six chairlifts spread over 460 acres. High atop historic Donner summit, the resort receives an annual 35 feet of snowfall. Although relatively small, it offers a wide variety of terrain and an atmosphere that is relaxing and carefree. Guests enjoy uncrowded slopes, scenic splendor and some of the most affordable lift tickets, rentals and lessons in the region. There's plenty of action at the Ranch for snowboarders. Riders have several terrain parks to choose from plus a well maintained halfpipe.

Intermediate skiers enjoy the mile-long Norm's Run. Experts head for the great fall line skiing and steep terrain on the backside off Chair 2.

Donner Ski Ranch
530-426-3635
www.donnerskiranch.com

Directions:
On Donner Pass Road at the pass.

Special Features:
Seniors 66 plus ski for only $5. Midweek Donner Ski Ranch and Boreal have an interchangeable ticket that allows skiers to ride lifts at both resorts. The ski area has rolled back prices to the 1992 level, $10 adult midweek and $20 adult weekend and holiday.

Winter

Downhill Skiing and Boarding

Northstar-At-Tahoe
530-562-1010
SnoPhone: 530-562-1330
www.northstar.com

Directions:
Six miles south of Truckee off Highway 267.

Special Features:
Free lessons are offered daily on Mt. Pluto for intermediate to advanced skiers and riders 13 years and older on a first-come, first-served basis. The resort offers a variety of accommodations, but night life in the village is quiet. Most revelers head to the funky town of Truckee, just six miles north, or over Brockway Summit to the North Shore action.

Senior discounts start at 60, while 70 and over skiers pay only $5.

Northstar-at-Tahoe

Little did George Schaffer realize 130 years ago that the site of his logging camp would become home to some of the Sierra's best skiing. Today, boarders and skiers rocket down mile-long runs from the backside of Northstar's Mt. Pluto or carve turns through stands of lodgepole from the top of Sawtooth Ridge. While the backside of Mt. Pluto, accessed by a high-speed quad, offers everything from ridge line cruising to narrow bump trails, the resort's front side combines lightly forested glades and wide boulevards that stretch to the base. At Polaris Park, guests can try the latest in snow toys, including ski foxes and ski bikes. In 2000 the resort opened new expert runs off Lookout Mountain that plunge toward Martis Valley.

Northstar's family programs are one of its strongest draws. Parents can participate in "Mommy, Daddy and Me" clinics that offer tips on how to enjoy skiing with children. Frequent skiers can join Vertical Plus, an electronic lift-pass system that puts you near the front of the lift lines, automatically charges credit cards, keeps track of vertical feet skied and gives end of season awards. Your pass is good at Sierra-at-Tahoe as well.

Downhill Skiing and Boarding

Tahoe Donner

Tahoe Donner's uncrowded, friendly atmosphere is the perfect place for family fun and learning. Two chairlifts and one rope tow access 125 acres of wide-open slopes that are perfect for keeping the kids in sight. At the Snowflakes Children's Ski School, kids age 3-6 enjoy supervised indoor and outdoor activities. Sessions include equipment, ski instruction, snack and lift ticket. Any weekday, children ages 7-12 learn for free. Tahoe Donner utilizes a conveyor lift for ski school classes. Parents looking for something new might try snow-biking. This relatively new attraction combines skiing and cycling and is easy to learn.

Tahoe Donner
530-587-9444
SnoPhone: 530-587-9444
www.tahoedonner.com

Directions:
On Northwoods Blvd. in the Tahoe Donner development, 4.5 miles from the Donner Pass Rd. intersection.

Special Features:
Senior discounts start at 60 and those 70 and over or 6 years of age and under ski free. For those renting vacation homes in the Tahoe Donner subdivision, a health club, general store and restaurant are each within a short drive if not walk away. Tahoe Donner also offers shuttle buses that run daily from parking lots to the main ski lodge.

Squaw Valley USA

After 50 years Squaw Valley reigns supreme in North America. The imposing geography makes first-time visitors feel as though they're looking through the wrong end of a telescope. Carved from six peaks spread over 4,000 acres and served by 30 lifts, the resort has always been a favorite lair for adrenaline junkies attracted to the area's hair raising chutes and steeps. But the sprawling resort also cradles the novice. Easy rolling shoulders and plateaus offer groomed slopes and calming views below mid-mountain

Squaw Valley USA
530-583-6985
SnoPhone: 530-583-5585
www.squaw.com

Directions:
At the end of Squaw Valley Road off Highway 89.

Special Features:
The Canadian developer Intrawest has completed the first phase of a 14-acre pedestrian village at the base of the Tram. The project features 120,000 square feet of shops, restaurants and nightlife along with underground parking and 640 condominiums. In February 2002 Squaw Valley hosts the return of the Olympic Torch on its way to the Salt Lake City 2002 Winter Games.

Winter

Downhill Skiing and Boarding

More Special Features:

The ski school also has multiple programs to please all groups. The day care center, Children's World, a unique 12,000 square foot facility, offers ski instruction for kids 4-12, equipment rental, and its own ski hill. The Magic Carpet is a safe and easy loading conveyor that cuts down on child fatigue. A toddler program for ages 2-3 provides a full day of licensed day care including a lesson for 3-year-olds, snacks, lunch and equipment. Squaw Valley's junior ski program called Mighty Mites has trained more than 50 athletes who have advanced through the program to make it onto the U.S. Ski Team.

High Camp. The result is that no matter what the ability, guests never feel relegated to a bunny slope next to the parking lot.

Entry level beginners travel to the top by way of the aerial cable car, drink in the same views as the more advanced, have fun and feel like a participant. The Fun in the Sun Adventure Package guarantees satisfaction for first-time skiers. Intermediates warm up in the well-groomed and bump-free Gold Coast bowl above Squaw's other mid-mountain day lodge, Gold Coast. When the legs are ready, it's just up and over the ridge to the Shirley Lake area for even more boulevards of groomed fun.

Kids 12 and under ski for only $5. Senior discounts begin at age 65. Squaw Valley also offers a wide variety of off-slope activities. There are numerous bars and restaurants on the premises as well as shopping, bungee jumping, ice skating, indoor climbing, a movie theater and much more.

Downhill Skiing and Boarding

Alpine Meadows

Alpine Meadows is a cradle of Sierra Nevada carving with its off-piste, wilderness skiing complementing flawlessly groomed cruiser runs. The increasingly popular 2000-acre, 13-chairlift resort offers views of cobalt colored Lake Tahoe from many runs. The resort's five lower lifts disperse skiers to a wide variety of terrain. The Summit Chair accesses four distinct bowls that descend either into wide trails or steep, off-piste drops. Intermediates usually prefer riding nearby Roundhouse Quad, while beginners can ride Hot Wheels, a triple chair that puts them on gentle slopes of manicured snow. "Adventure Zones" provide a backcountry experience within the ski patrolled boundary. Traverses to remote bowls such as Wolverine and Estelle, or the immense High Traverse/Twin Peaks area, are rewarded with steep and often prime untracked snow. The Chalet is located in a nest of pine trees midway up the mountain. It is a great place to rendezvous to sit on the sun deck and enjoy homemade soups, sandwiches, quiche and fresh pastries.

Alpine Meadows
530-581-4232 800-441-4423
SnoPhone: 530-581-8374
www.skialpine.com

Directions:
Two miles off Highway 89 on Alpine Meadows Rd., 4 miles north of Tahoe City.

Special Features:
A new Family Ski Zone provides kids just learning to gain confidence skiing in a safe haven before venturing out onto advanced slopes. Kids 4-6 enjoy their own Sun Kid surface lift and Eco Trail at the Little Mountaineers ski school. For ages 7-12 the Junior Mountaineers have beginner to advanced packages. The ski school will institute all day lessons in 2001. Senior discounts start at 65.

The ski resort offers boarders a Gravity Cavity halfpipe and Roo's Ride terrain park situated near the base of the resort. Snowboarders can find Alpine's Powder Card at local Tahoe Basin snowboard shops. It is a free card that allows 30 days of carving for $30 per day. Alpine Meadows is also home to the second largest school in North America for disabled skiers. Disabled Sports USA has programs all year as well. See page 101 in "Adventures."

Winter

Downhill Skiing and Boarding

Granlibakken Ski Hill
530-581-7533
530-582-4242
www.granlibakken.com

Directions:
On Granlibakken Rd. off Highway 89 a half mile south of the Tahoe City *Y*.

Granlibakken Ski Hill

The story of skiing at Granlibakken, which in Norwegian means "a hillside sheltered by fir trees," dates back to 1928 when the resort became one of Tahoe's first snowplay areas. It built one of the country's best ski jumps in 1930. Today, the historic jump looks over the ski hill and one poma surface lift that continues to evoke old Tahoe charm. There are ski lessons, rentals and a snow play area that makes it a great choice for those who want to ski with their families and avoid crowds.

Homewood Mountain Resort
530-525-2992
SnoPhone: 530-525-2900
www.skihomewood.com

Directions:
Six miles south of the Tahoe City *Y* on Hwy. 89.

Special Features:
The Children's Center offers child care for kids 2-6, Honeybears Ski School for 4 to 6-year-olds and the Snowstars Program for older children 6-12. Supersliders (kids 5-16) can take inexpensive group ski or snowboard lessons. Homewood offers free skiing and snowboarding to accompanied children who are 10 years and under. Frequent Flyer Membership has reduced price tickets and two-for-one tickets on Wednesdays as well as a new partnership with Diamond Peak called a "Lakeview Pass."

Homewood Mountain Resort

A homey atmosphere entertains both skiers and boarders at this one time West Shore gold mining area. Homewood's 56 trails are served by eight lifts spread over 1,260 acres. With its north to northeast exposure, Homewood offers some of the best powder skiing in the Sierra Nevada. Rainbow Ridge Run from the top of the mountain affords spectacular views of Lake Tahoe. Intermediates like the wide runs off the top of the Quad Chair, while the more advanced traverse into the Tahoe Ski Bowl side for the steeps of Quail Face and Hobbit Land.

Downhill Skiing and Boarding

Mount Rose Ski Tahoe

With all the ways to save at Mount Rose, it's nearly impossible to pay full price at this understated Nevada gold nugget. Located just 22 miles from the bright casino lights and economical lodging of Reno, a good time at Mount Rose is never a gamble. While the resort's 900 acres and five lifts qualify it as only a medium-sized resort by Tahoe standards, don't be fooled. There's a lot of skiing here. The trails under Northwest Passage drop 1,400 vertical feet and are steep enough to beat up mid-season legs. The Slide Mountain side is full of wide-open intermediate and advanced runs.

Mount Rose Ski Tahoe
775-849-0704
SnoPhone: 800-SKI-ROSE
www.skirose.com

Directions:
Drive 10 miles east on Hwy. 431 (the Mt. Rose Hwy.) from Incline Village.

Special Features:
What sets Mount Rose apart from all Tahoe ski areas is its base elevation of 8,260 feet, the highest in the Lake Tahoe region. With its cold eastern location, Mt. Rose offers choice snow conditions. The Rosebud Children Center teaches skiing for ages 4-10 and snowboarding for ages 7-10. The "Ski With Me" lesson is designed for one parent and a 3 to 4-year-old child. In a one hour private session, parents learn how to instruct their kids. Seniors ski for half-price and there are two-for-one tickets on Tuesdays.

© John Kelly. Courtesy of Heavenly Ski Resort

A snowboarder rips up some of Tahoe's glorious high altitude powder.

Downhill Skiing and Boarding

Diamond Peak
775-832-1177
SnoPhone: 775-831-3211
www.diamondpeak.com

Directions:
Take Ski Way off Country Club Dr. in Incline Village.

Special Features:
Diamond Peak loves kids. At the Bee Ferrato Child Ski Center, children 7-12 build a strong ski foundation participating in the Sierra Scouts program. Diamond Peak also offers the Incline Kids Klub, a licensed day care program for children 2-6. Children 6-12 and Seniors 60 plus ski for less. The Snowflake Lodge (spruced up for the 2001-2002 season) offers casual fare and outstanding views of the lake in a relaxed sunny setting.

Diamond Peak has teamed with Homewood Mountain Resort across the lake to offer a special "Lakeview Pass." This pass at $299 allows special midweek lift privileges at both ski areas.

Diamond Peak

Incline Village occupies the most northern niche of Lake Tahoe. The town received its name from the grade that was used to carry timber nearly 1,400 vertical feet up from the lake during the 1800s. A century later, the same grade is being used by skiers up and down its slope after the Boise-Cascade corporation developed the golf course and ski resort now called Diamond Peak. With stunning views, affordable pricing, special programs for kids and a variety of terrain, it is one of Tahoe's premier family resorts. Advanced riders and skiers enjoy dropping into Golden Eagle Bowl and Solitude Canyon off the Crystal Quad chairlift. The Lightning is a black diamond run comparable in steepness to Squaw Valley's Headwall. However, almost half of Diamond Peak's terrain is for intermediates. Crystal Ridge Run is over a mile of smooth and wide cruising with magnificent views of Lake Tahoe.

Downhill Skiing and Boarding

Courtesy of Diamond Peak Ski Resort

There are few more glorious views than those from the cruising run off the summit of Diamond Peak.

Downhill Skiing and Boarding

Heavenly Lake Tahoe
775-586-7000
Ski Report: 775-586-7000
www.skiheavenly.com

Directions:
California side: Take Ski Run Blvd. to parking. For the Nevada Side drive 3 miles east on Kingsbury Grade to Tramway. Boulder Base Lodge is the first right turn. Stay straight on Aspen for Stagecoach Base Lodge.

Heavenly runs ski buses all day to both sides of the mountain from the South Shore hotels and casinos so you can start on one side and finish on the other.

Special Features:
A new 3,450 square foot day care facility at the California main lodge now offers fully licensed infant day care for babies as young as six weeks old. Parents can take advantage of the resort's Perfect Turn Children's Center which offers two different day-long activity programs. In the Snow Play Program, 3-4 year-olds accompanied by certified instructors enjoy play time on the snow. Four through 12 year-olds can be enrolled in the Perfect Turn Kids Program from either the California Lodge at the top of the tram or at Nevada side's Boulder Lodge. For adults, Heavenly offers an introductory "Learn To Ski" guarantee. And, if you want to try out the new shaped skis, Heavenly provides a free guided demo program.

Heavenly Lake Tahoe

Twenty square miles of terrain straddle the California-Nevada border, making Heavenly the land of alpine thrills. Killebrews, Motts and the legendary Gunbarrel contain enough steeps and bumps to choke the most courageous. However, it's the resort's long boulevards and unobstructed views of Lake Tahoe that create most of the pleasure for skiers here. Thanks to a multimillion dollar commitment made by Heavenly over the past two decades, the ski area has the largest snowmaking system at Lake Tahoe that blankets almost 70% of the skiable trails. Covered slopes on both the California and Nevada sides include most of the beginner and intermediate trails, plus black diamond runs as well. Heavenly's 82 trails descend 3,500 vertical feet and are accessed by 27 chairlifts (with a 50-passenger tram, 5 high-speed quads, and one high-speed six-pac) which fan out over 4,800 skiable acres including an intermediate 5.5-mile-long descent from its 10,100-foot top elevation. Intermediate skiers looking for other long runs head to the Galaxy and Stagecoach lifts on the Nevada side. The California Trail off the California side Sky Chair and Powderbowl Run off the Waterfall

Downhill Skiing and Boarding

Chair are other favorites. Snowboarders have two terrain parks, a bordercross trail and a halfpipe for thrills. There are seven on-mountain lodges for relaxation and socializing. Heavenly looks to the future with an ambitious, $500 million project that began construction in 2001 bringing hotels, condominiums, restaurants and shops to a new 34-acre base village near the gondola that takes guests to

More Special Features:
The plans for the next seasons include both a winter and summer adventure park and an amphitheater at the top of the gondola, which runs all year from the transportation center near the new Marriott Grand Residence Club.

The winter Adventure Park will feature 5 km of cross country skiing and snowshoe trails. There will also be tubing and snowplay.

© Tom Lippert

Skiing from the California side summit at Heavenly.

Downhill Skiing and Boarding

Sierra-At-Tahoe
530-659-7453
SnoPhone: 530-659-7475
www.sierratahoe.com

Directions:
Take U.S. 50 west 11.5 miles to turnoff. Ski area is 2.1 miles up the access road.

Free shuttle buses make pickups at the casinos and all major motels in South Lake Tahoe.

Special Features:
The Wild Mountain Ski and Snowboard Camps allow parents to take turns on the slopes with their kids. The Family Pack group lesson is a private, introductory ski or snowboard lesson for the family. Available by appointment only, the price includes a two-hour introductory lesson, equipment and beginner lift access for four family members. Toddlers 18 months to 5 years old who are not required to be potty trained, enjoy snowplay, arts and crafts, story time, music and snacks at the day care center. Children ages 6-12 ski all season long for only $99.

Frequent skiers can join Vertical Plus, an electronic lift-pass system that puts you near the front of the lift lines, automatically charges credit cards, keeps track of vertical feet skied and gives end of season awards. This is good at Northstar as well.

Sierra-at-Tahoe

Northstar's sister resort on the south side of Lake Tahoe has plenty of skiing and riding for everyone in the family. Intermediate skiers relish the long roadways of Bashful, Dogwood and Horsetail off the West Bowl chair while experts can head for the trees down Dynamite and Castle. There's plenty of snow and elbow room to go around at the 2,000-acre resort, which averages 450 inches of snowfall annually. Located off the Grand View Express, skiers and riders can enjoy "The Gauntlet," one of three terrain parks containing table tops, gap jumps and more. Powder hounds have five back country access gates off the south side of Summit Grandview. Every Wednesday Sierra hosts free skiercross races in The Gauntlet. At the end of the day, enjoy the views of emerald-hued Lake Tahoe from the Grand View Bar and Grill atop Huckleberry Mountain's 8,852-foot summit.

For powder hounds and experts who want the thrill of back country exploration, there are five back country access gates off the south side of Summit Grandview chairlift.

Downhill Skiing and Boarding

Kirkwood Mountain Resort

Kirkwood has always offered abundant natural snow and richly varied terrain, and now its patrons can enjoy the luxuries of a $13 million, 43,000-square-foot lodge that provides amenities comparable to those of any other major Sierra ski area. Since it opened in 1972, Kirkwood has always been a favorite lair for skiers who are attracted to the resort's narrow chutes, intense steeps and laid-back, unpolished atmosphere. However, the resort's real charm rests in the 2,300 acres that have some of North America's toughest and tamest slopes. Veterans who know the area enjoy the bowl of Thunder Saddle with its four double-black runs. Intermediates enjoy runs off Hole-n-Wall, The Reut and Caples chairs. In 2001 the first high-speed chairlift was installed to reach the top of Thimble Peak. With a base elevation of 7,800 feet, it's not unusual for the snow to reach depths of 20 feet at the base and 35 feet at the summit.

The special young adult rate (12-24) offers affordable skiing for boarders and powder hounds. Seniors rates start at 65 with a special rate for seniors 70 plus. The Avid Skier program offers every fifth day free.

Kirkwood Mountain Resort
209-258-6000
SnoPhone: 888-KIRKWOOD
www.skikirkwood.com

Special Features:
In 2000 the $18 million Mountain Club condominium hotel, a quarter-ownership hotel, provides guests with spa, gym, sauna, ski check and full concierge services. The plaza houses retail shops and restaurants as well. Two other new complexes, Snowcrest Condominiums and Lost Cabin Townhouses, will help raise Kirkwood's present bed-base of under 1,000 pillows to more than 5,000 at completion (approximately 5-7 years).

The new Mountain Village features numerous attractions, including an ice skating rink, a swimming pool and tennis courts.

Although the new village offers a variety of attractions, the historic Kirkwood Inn, built in the late 1800s, still serves hearty fare and cocktails. See the photo on page 70 and the description in "Dining Out" on page 90.

At Seawood Child Care Center for ages 2-6 (diapers OK), kids enjoy art, games, snowplay and stories.

Winter

Cross Country Skiing

Cross country (sometimes called nordic) ski areas are listed below from the Truckee area south to Lake Tahoe and Carson Pass. Distances are given in kilometers (1 km = .6 mile) at most cross country areas. All of the ski areas groom trails with a skating lane next to the tracks.

Many cross country areas open their trails to snowshoers and rent equipment. For those in your party who feel uncomfortable on skis, this is an excellent way to enjoy the trails and get a great workout.

Eagle Mountain
One mile south of I-80 at the Yuba Gap exit.
530-389-2254 800-391-2254

Special Features:
The comfortable lodge and the roaring fire beckon for a cup of coffee before you depart, or a cup of homemade soup and burger or sandwich at the end of your tour. Eagle Mountain Resort also operates a bicycle park and camp in the summer. See page 152 in "Bicycling" for details.

Although a forest fire roared through the resort in 2001, the owners feel that they will be able to have better trails now and you can watch the forest regenerate.

Clair Tappaan Lodge
530-426-3632
www.sierraclub.org/outings/ lodges/tappaan.asp

Directions:
On Donner Pass Rd. 2 miles east of the Soda Springs exit off I-80.

Special Features:
Use of trails is free to lodge guests. Others are asked for a minimal ($7.00) donation.

Eagle Mountain

Eagle Mountain is the closest ski resort to Sacramento and only a half-hour drive from Truckee via I-80. You will find more than 86 kms of trails that travel through beautiful forests and meadows of moderate pitch and elevation. Excellent novice terrain is found on The Juniper Forest and California Dreamer trails. Experienced skiers and snowshoers will want to climb Eagle Mountain or take the six-mile Cisco Trail out to Cisco Butte. The 360 degree views are very special.

Clair Tappaan Lodge

Since 1935, this Sierra Club lodge has offered enveloping warmth, affordable bedding and surprisingly good food for the winter recreationist. The lodge provides 12 km of novice and intermediate trails that access miles upon miles of back country skiing. Come spring lodge guides offer hut to hut backcountry ski outings.

Cross Country Skiing

Royal Gorge Cross Country Ski Resort

Royal Gorge is the largest nordic ski area in the country with 330 km of groomed track. Four lifts aid access to more difficult uphill portions of some trails. The network of 90 trails includes the gently rolling terrain of Palisade Trail or the steep challenge of Devil's Peak. Ten warming huts and four trailside cafés complement your day's adventure. A new 17 km round trip ski from Summit Station takes you to Sugar Bowl ski area, where you can dine on the deck. On weekends novice skiers can enjoy the easier Van Norden Meadow trails. Snow conditions permitting, experienced skiers in good condition can try the 22-km Rainbow Interconnect to Rainbow Lodge at Big Bend. A free shuttle that operates on weekends takes you back to your car.

Weekend rates are more expensive than weekdays. Seniors 65 and over ski for the afternoon rate.

Royal Gorge Cross Country Ski Resort
Soda Springs
530-426-3871 800-634-3086
www.royalgorge.com

Directions:
Take I-80 to the Soda Springs/Norden Exit. Drive east to Soda Springs Rd. Lake Van Norden Meadow parking is on the left after crossing the RR tracks. Follow signs to the Summit Station parking.

Special Features:
For the ultimate experience, consider two nights at the Wilderness Lodge complete with a sleigh ride in on Sunday, Wednesday or Friday evening, two days of instruction and French country gourmet dinners at the lodge. Add to this hot mulled wine and the promise of a hot tub or sauna for tired muscles at the end of the day, and you have a ski vacation you won't soon forget. Two cabins for two, each with queen bed, have been added for a special romantic getaway.

Courtesy of Royal Gorge

Skating up the trail at Royal Gorge.

Winter

Cross Country Skiing

Tahoe Donner Cross Country
530-587-9484
www.tahoedonner.com

Directions:
Take Northwoods Blvd. off Donner Pass Rd. in Truckee to Fjord, turn right to Alder Creek Dr. and left one-half mile to the parking lot.

Special Features:
Senior discounts are given any day for skiers 60 and over. If you are 70 years or older you ski for free.

The Donner Party Café in the day lodge serves both breakfast and lunch daily. Try one of their delicious soups. On weekends, a limited choice of food and beverage is available at the Cookhouse in Euer Valley.

Tahoe Donner Cross Country

This area has 75 km of trails on 5,000 acres with extensive beginner terrain. Tiny Tracks Snow School is open for children on weekends and holidays. The Meadow Loop is an excellent place for your first experience. Children can join parents on the North Fork or Pony Express Loops. Skiers with some skill will find a ski to Euer Valley exhilarating, while experts and skaters can enjoy the climb to Donner Ridge at 7,800 feet where telemark opportunities abound in the Sunrise Bowl. Tahoe Donner Cross Country offers more vertical than its sister downhill area.

Euer Valley overlook at Tahoe Donner Cross Country.

© Ellie Huggins

Winter

Cross Country Skiing

Squaw Creek Cross Country Ski Center

The 30 km of trails around the meadow in Squaw Valley are designed with the beginner in mind. It is also a great place to spend an afternoon, even if it's snowing. You can leave children 4 to 13 at the Mountain Buddies day camp while you ski.

Squaw Creek Cross Country Ski Center
Squaw Valley
530-581-6637

Special Features:
After skiing, try lunch on the deck at the resort or at the Ristorante Montagna. Valet parking is free if you eat at any restaurant. You can also arrange for a gourmet picnic to take along. Seniors 62 and over ski free.

Granlibakken Resort

Granlibakken has 3 km of beginner trails and an access trail to Paige Meadows for intermediate skiers who want to venture into the back country. You can also reach the Paige Meadows trail from the top of the lift at the ski hill.

Granlibakken Resort
Granlibakken Road off Highway 89 just south of the Tahoe City _Y._
530-583-6203

Special Features:
The snowplay area is next to the ski hill.

Tahoe Cross Country

The former Lakeview Cross Country Ski Area is now managed by a nonprofit group that operate the area with only two staff and a corps of volunteers. The 65 km of trails on 3,600 acres are groomed to perfection with wide skating lanes. Beginners will find gentle hills on trails that wander through the forest. A great intermediate tour follows the yellow trail to the green and orange in a counterclockwise direction.

Tahoe Cross Country
Tahoe City
530-583-5475
www.tahoexc.org

Directions:
From the Tahoe City _Y_ drive east 2.5 mi. to Fabian Way and follow signs to the ski center via Village Rd. and Country Club Dr.

Special Features:
There is a special trail for skiers and their dogs. Tahoe Cross Country is the starting point for the Great Race between Tahoe City and Truckee, an annual race with hundreds of participants.

Winter

Cross Country Skiing

Northstar-at-Tahoe Cross Country and Telemark Ski Center
Six miles south of Truckee via Hwy. 267.
530-562-2475

Special Features:
For those wishing to learn or practice telemark techniques, the close proximity to the downhill area makes this the telemark capital of the Tahoe area. You can purchase 3,4 and 5-day interchangeable passes with all the cross-country ski centers in the area. They also rent snowshoes.

A new program called The Parent's Predicament ticket lets the first parent ski in the morning and the second in the afternoon.

North Tahoe Regional Park
National Ave.
Tahoe Vista
530-546-5043

Northstar Cross Country and Telemark Ski Center

The trails leave from the mid-mountain Day Lodge. A trail pass includes the ride up on the gondola. A total of 65 km of trails fan out from mid-mountain. The greater number of trails are laid out on the east side of the Big Springs Day Lodge. The Sawmill Flat trail, an easy round trip of 5 km leads to the Caboose Warming Hut, a remodeled train caboose complete with pot bellied stove and couch. A smaller system of trails leave from the Nordic Center west of the Day Lodge that include the experts only Psycho climb to views of Lake Tahoe followed by a 5 km downhill pitch aptly called The Black Hole.

North Tahoe Regional Park

This is good place to take the whole family. Fifteen kilometers of groomed trails are just right for a few hours of skiing. Non-skiers can frolic with their sleds and saucers on a nearby snowplay hill. The park rents all equipment.

Winter

Cross Country Skiing

Spooner Lake Cross Country Ski Area

Situated eleven miles from Incline Village and only ten miles from either Carson City or Stateline, Spooner Lake Cross Country's trail system begins at 7,000 feet and rises all the way to Marlette Lake and Hobart Reservoir at 7823 feet. Most of Spooner's 90-km trail system loops through Aspen groves and heavily wooded forests until giving way to high country panoramas of Lake Tahoe. Seniors over 60 ski for only $5 while those over 70 or under 7 ski free. Tuesday is half price and on Wednesdays skiers can rent equipment for half price. Free lessons are offered on Thursdays. Innovative children's programs are available weekends.

Camp Richardson Cross Country Ski Center

Camp Richardson Resort has created the perfect family cross-country ski center across the road from the resort. There are 15 km of easy groomed trails through the woods plus 35 km of more difficult skier-packed trails.

Spooner Lake Cross Country Ski Area
Spooner Lake Nevada State Park
775-749-5349 888-858-8844
www.spoonerlake.com

Directions:
On Highway 28 a half mile north of Highway 50, and 12.5 miles south of Incline Village.

Special Features:
Two overnight cabins provide enthusiasts with a wonderful wilderness experience. The Wildcat Cabin off the intermediate North Canyon Trail sleeps four and provides warmth, comfort, cooking stove, kitchen supplies and free 100% Kona coffee. The Spooner Lake Cabin sleeps six and rests on a knoll off the west end of Spooner Lake itself, only 2 kms from the resort's lodge.

Camp Richardson
Emerald Bay Road (Highway 89) two miles north of the South Tahoe Y.
530-542-6584

Special Features:
On Friday nights they lead a moonlight ski from the Beacon Bar and Grill, weather permitting.

Winter

Cross Country Skiing

Hope Valley Outdoor Center
Highway 88 just east of
Sorensen's.
530-694-2266

Special Features:
The Center rents ski and other gear. They will also give you a map of the Hope Valley trails.

Hope Valley Cross Country

The Hope Valley Cross Country trails are marked and skier groomed. Best of all, they are free. Beginners can take the Sawmill trail to the Burnside Lake trail, returning when the climb becomes too steep. Intermediate skiers will enjoy the climb to Burnside Lake, a perfect day's outing. This is truly wilderness skiing. Advance skiers can take the Indian Head trail that leaves directly behind Sorensen's Resort.

Kirkwood Cross Country
209-258-6000

Directions:
On north side of Hwy. 88 just east of the entrance to Kirkwood Ski Resort. The Schneider trailhead is on Schneider Cow Camp Rd. 2 miles east of the Day Lodge.

Special Features:
If you don't want to pack a lunch, or if the weather is not conducive to a picnic in the snow, try the lunch special or one of the delectable burgers at the historic Kirkwood Inn. See page 90 in "Dining Out."

Kirkwood Cross Country

Kirkwood Cross Country has 80 km of trails on 4,200 acres in three trail networks. There is a special children's area near the Cross Country Day Lodge. Beginners and families will find the miles of trails around Kirkwood meadow perfect for that first experience. The summit trails accessed from the Schneider trailhead take you up onto the high crest with magnificent views in all directions. There are 9 km of easy trails and about 30 km of more difficult terrain in this location. Advanced skiers can also access these trails from the main loop near the lodge via the Agony and Ecstasy trails. The Caples Creek loop offers skiing where the silence is broken only by the sound of water in Caples Creek or wind in the pines.

Cross Country Skiing

Back Country Skiing

If you are looking for a back country experience, or only want to ski a few hours, there are many locations in the area where you can ski free. Some trails are accessed from California Sno-Park trailheads (see following pages). Each trail description indicates the degree of difficulty.

Sno-Park Ski Trails

The California Department of Transportation maintains a number of Sno-Park areas at certain trailheads. You must buy a permit for these from November through May. One-day or season Sno-Park permits are available at locations listed opposite.

Father and son enjoy a Spring day touring.

Donner Memorial State Park:
Donner Lake.
530-582-7892
Mountain Hardware:
11320 Donner Pass Rd., Truckee.
530-587-4844
Sierra Mountaineer:
Jibboom and Bridge Sts., Truckee.
530-587-2025
Homewood Hardware:
5405 West Lake Blvd., Homewood.
530-525-6367
CSAA office:
7717 North Lake Blvd., Kings Beach.
530-546-4245

Meyers Shell and Food Mart:
2950 Hwy. 50, Tahoe Paradise.
530-577-4533
Old MacDonald's Enterprise:
1060 Ski Run Blvd., So. Lake Tahoe.
530-544-3663
South Lake Tahoe Chamber of Commerce:
3066 Hwy. 50, So. Lake Tahoe.
530-541-5255
U.S. Forest Service:
870 Emerald Bay Rd., So. Lake Tahoe.
530-573-2600
Kirkwood Cross Country Center:
Highway 88, Kirkwood.
209-258-7248

© Ellie Huggins

Winter

Cross Country Skiing

Castle Peak
Donner Summit
Intermediate to Advanced

Directions:
Take I-80 to the Castle Peak/Boreal exit. Drive east on the frontage road to the Sno-Park. Limited parking is available on the north side of the freeway at the exit.

Donner Memorial State Park
Beginner and Intermediate

Directions:
On Donner Pass Rd. just west of the Donner State Park I-80 exit.

Special Features:
A winter visit to the Donner Museum to see the slide show about the Donner Party ordeals in 1846 reminds us all of the courage needed to emigrate to California in those days.

Sno-park permits are no longer required to use the trails.

Blackwood Canyon
Beginner to Intermediate

Directions:
The Sno-Park is on the west side of Hwy. 89 four miles south of the Tahoe City Y.

Castle Peak Sno-Park

You will need to walk to the trailhead on the north side of the freeway. This trail begins at 7,000 feet and leads to the Sierra Club Peter Grubb Hut over the 7,800-foot shoulder of Castle Peak. The trip is only recommended for those with good downhill skills.

Donner Memorial State Park

The park is an excellent choice for families and beginners. An easy, marked trail follows the road to the beach at China Cove and through the forest around the perimeter of the park. From the beach you can also ski along the lakeshore returning to the road near your starting point. Intermediate skiers will find a groomed trail into Coldstream Valley and back.

Blackwood Canyon Sno-Park

The trail follows the road into Blackwood Canyon on gentle terrain. This is a perfect place for a sunny spring outing with lunch in the snow or a place to escape cabin fever during a storm. More ambitious skiers may want to climb toward Barker Pass but are warned to avoid steeper terrain in the canyon as it is prone to avalanches.

Cross Country Skiing

Taylor Creek Sno-Park

One ski trail leaves from the south side of the parking lot. Blue diamonds or blue signs with a skier mark the trails. The trail follows an old road that skirts the west shore of the lake until you reach an old log cabin and picnic site. The return part of this loop passes the cabin uphill and returns through the woods until it intersects the unplowed Cathedral Road taking you back to the parking lot. Another trail on the north side of Highway 89, about 200 yards east, leads to the Tallac Historic Site and the shore of Lake Tahoe. This is an excellent trail for beginners.

Taylor Creek
South Lake Tahoe
Beginner to Intermediate

Directions:
West side of Highway 89, about 3 miles north of the South Tahoe Y.

Special Features:
Maps of the trails are usually available at the Sno-Park. Snowmobiles are permitted only on the south side of Highway 89 toward Fallen Leaf Lake.

Echo Summit Sno-Park

The trails in this area are laid out near the former Echo Summit Ski Area. From the parking lot follow the marked trail around the former ski lodge then south toward Benwood Meadow, a tour of 4 miles round trip. The Echo Summit to Kirkwood race starts here, and advanced skiers might wish to continue the climb to Upper Benwood Meadow. This trail follows the Pacific Crest Trail and traverses avalanche prone terrain, so check the weather and snow conditions before embarking on this tour. Beginners may try the trail to Lake Audrain, heading northwest from the parking lot.

Echo Summit
South Lake Tahoe
Beginner to Intermediate

Directions:
The Sno-Park is 8 miles west of the South Tahoe Y on the south side of U.S. 50.

Special Features:
No snowmobiles allowed. This is an excellent snowplay area.

Winter

Cross Country Skiing

Echo Lake
South Lake Tahoe
Beginner to Intermediate

Directions:
Off U.S. 50 on the road to Echo Lake, one mile west of Echo Summit.

Special Features:
No snowmobiles allowed. There are many private cabins surrounding both lakes. Please respect this private property, and do not picnic on cabin porches.

Echo Lake Sno-Park

This is a very popular cross country ski excursion. The trail to Lower and Upper Echo Lakes climbs gradually until you are overlooking Lower Echo Lake. There is a fairly steep descent to the lake. Once you have negotiated this, when conditions permit, you can ski across the lake toward Upper Echo Lake, which is usually frozen from January through March. Be sure to assess the conditions before skiing on the lake. In spring, skiing along the south shore is safest.

Carson Pass
Intermediate to Advanced.

Directions:
The Sno-Park is at Carson Pass on Hwy. 88, 25 miles south of Lake Tahoe via Hwy. 89 and Luther Pass.

Carson Pass Sno-Park

The most popular trail in the region is to Winnemucca Lake. Marked by blue diamond signs, it climbs steeply to Frog Lake then more gradually along a great open ridge toward Winnemucca Lake. If you want to make a loop, descend to Woods Lake campground, then follow an unplowed road in gentle grades back to the parking lot.

Winter

Skiers climb above Schneider Sheep Camp at Kirkwood Cross Country.

Striding out in the meadow at Kirkwood Resort.

Winter

Cross Country Skiing

Other Back Country Ski Trails

Old Henness Pass Road East
Beginner to Intermediate

Directions:
From I-80 drive 19.7 miles north on Highway 89. A few parking spaces are plowed on the right at the beginning of the Kyburz Flat Rd.

Old Henness Pass Road East

Park in the space that is plowed. The road up to Kyburz Flat is skier groomed and affords an easy uphill ski to a U.S. Forest Service interpretive area. The road turns gently downhill to Kyburz Flat and a bridge across a creek. Follow the road as far as you wish as it passes through a forest over gentle hills and vales. This is a great trail after a snowstorm, for it is little used and you can make your own tracks through the powder.

Martis Peak
Beginner to Intermediate

Directions:
Parking is on the east side of Highway 267 just one-half mile north of Brockway Summit.

Special Features:
Snowmobiles use this road, which means that some of your track will be packed.

Martis Peak

The trail leaves the parking area for a steady climb. There are signs on the trees to guide you in a generally northwesterly direction around the shoulder of Martis Peak to the overlook. When the snow is fresh this is a spectacular trip to lunch on the porch of the fire lookout with its expansive views of Martis Valley, Truckee and the peaks of Donner Summit and Castle Peak in the distance. The descent back to your car is only steep at the end and, unless the tracks are icy, can be maneuvered by novices.

Winter

Cross Country Skiing

Paige Meadows

The drive to the trailhead is up a very steep hill and may require chains or a 4WD. The trail leaves from the end of the road and descends through a forest. Take the first trail off to the right through the woods toward the meadow. Once in the meadow there is lovely flat terrain to explore. Rank beginners will find the first descent somewhat steep. The meadows may also be accessed from a trail that is marked from Granlibakken Ski Hill. See page 228 in "Downhill Skiing and Snowboarding" for a description.

Paige Meadows
Beginner to Intermediate

Directions:
Take Highway 89 south from Tahoe City for 2.3 miles to Pine Ave. Turn right, then right on Tahoe Park Heights Dr., right on Big Pine Dr. and left on Silver Tip Dr. to the end of the road.

Sugar Pine Point State Park

The state park maintains a groomed ski trail in the General Creek section west of the highway. The terrain is perfect for beginners. You may also ski across Highway 89 into the Ehrmann Mansion and the banks of the lake. This is a perfect snowshoe locale.

The California State Parks Sierra District offers courses in cross country skiing, so you might want to check with the nearest park headquarters to pick up the fall/winter schedule of ski classes and snowshoe trips.

Sugar Pine Point State Park
Fee per vehicle
Beginner

Directions:
Drive 9.3 miles south of the Tahoe City Y on Highway 89. The park entrance is on the west side of the road.

Winter

Cross Country Skiing

Tahoe Meadows
Beginner

Directions:
There is parking along Highway 431 (Mt. Rose Highway) on both sides 6.7 miles from the intersection with Highway 28 in Incline Village.

Special Features:
Snowmobiles allowed and there are snowplay areas.

Tahoe Meadows

Open meadows on both sides of the highway invite snowmobilers and skiers. Hills on the north side of the highway are perfect for sledding as well. The meadows are at about 8,500 feet above sea level with excellent snow during a long season. The area on the south side beckons skiers of all abilities, but is particularly good for families with small children just learning to walk on their skis and for beginners who wish to practice striding. More advanced skiers will want to climb the mountain through the trees to the south. The east end of this climb affords magnificent views of the Carson Valley.

Climb to Mount Rose
Intermediate to Advanced

Directions:
Drive about a half mile east of Tahoe Meadows. Parking is located on the south side of the road.

Climb to Mount Rose

The trail ascends the ridge on the north side of the road. This is a route for intermediate skiers who want to ski as high as they feel like and enjoy a wonderful long run downhill at the end of the day. Advanced skiers will find ample terrain off the road to test their telemark skills.

Winter

Cross Country Skiing

Grass Lake Meadows on Highway 89 at Luther Pass

The endless meadow terrain just west of Luther Pass is the perfect place for a spring outing. Ski as far as you wish to find a picnic spot and return across the meadow using another route. You can't get lost here, as Highway 89 is always somewhere near the meadow. If you climb south toward Luther Pass, you will be in the Hope Valley watershed. Combine a morning here with an afternoon at Hope Valley and follow it with a trip to Grover Hot Springs (page 103 in "Excursions") to ease tired muscles. To finish off the day in style, make a reservation for dinner at Sorensen's Resort described on page 90 in "Dining Out."

Grass Lake Meadows
Beginner to Intermediate

Directions:
Take Highway 89 south from Meyers about 6.5 miles. There is official parking just at the pass, although there are turnouts along the way which you can use.

For more information about back country skiing:

Experienced cross country skiers who are confident of their abilities to handle a variety of terrain should buy a copy of Marcus Libkind's *Ski Tours in the Sierra Nevada*. *Volume One* includes all of Lake Tahoe while *Volume Two* describes tours in Carson Pass, Bear Valley and Pinecrest.

Winter

Ice Skating

Squaw Valley High Camp
Top of the cable car in Squaw Valley.
Fee to ride the cable car.
Information: 530-583-7246

Special Features:
The rink is covered for great summer season skating from June to September. See "Excursions" on page 100 for information about all the High Camp summer activities.

Resort at Squaw Creek
Squaw Valley
Reservations required.
530-583-6300

Kirkwood Resort
209-258-6000

The ice rink was being completed at the time of printing. You will need to check with the resort regarding times of operation and skate rentals.

Squaw Valley High Camp

The Olympic-size ice rink at High Camp is a high-altitude skating experience with a view. There are two-hour sessions throughout the day and into the evening. You can rent both figure and hockey skates, or bring your own. If you buy a ski lift ticket, you can come up the mountain at night at no extra charge. You might even decide to spend the whole day at High Camp, with dinner followed by skating. Try this at full moon. The hot tubs are open in mid-March and the pool weather permitting.

Resort at Squaw Creek

A small round rink is located above the swimming pools. The sessions generally last two hours. The fee is minimal if you bring your own skates.

Kirkwood Resort

Kirkwood has added a 60 by 100-foot ice rink between the Mountain Club and the lodge near the edge of the Village Plaza. Due to open for Christmas 2001, it will not be far from the new recreation center which will include an outdoor heated swimming pool with lap lanes, a play area and a spa sun deck.

Winter

Snowmobiling

Northstar-at-Tahoe

Northstar has added snowmobile tours three times daily. These guided wilderness tours include your helmet. No children under five are allowed and drivers must be at least 16 years old. They also feature "full moon" tours.

Northstar-at-Tahoe
Reservations required.
Minimum number of participants also required.
530-562-2267

North Tahoe Regional Park

The snowmobile track on a quarter-mile course makes a good place to learn or to determine if you are ready for an all-day trip. The snowplay area and cross country trails are adjacent, making this park a good choice for groups wishing to try different activities.

North Tahoe Regional Park
National Avenue in Tahoe Vista
530-546-7248

Snowmobiling Unlimited

This group operates the track at the Regional Park but trips leave from Brockway Summit on Highway 267. Their groomed trails offer exceptional views of Lake Tahoe, so bring your camera and take a wilderness tour.

Snowmobiling Unlimited
530-583-7192

Winter

Snowmobiling

**Eagle Ridge Snowmobile
Reservations required.
530-546-8667**

Eagle Ridge Snowmobile Outfitters

Directions:
The meeting point is 20 miles north of I-80 on Highway 89 North at the snowmobile staging area of the U.S. Forest Service.

Special Features:
They also offer overnights to Bassett's Station where three basic rooms are available, or you can upgrade to stay at the High Country Inn Bed and Breakfast nearby.

Eagle Ridge leads guided wilderness tours on groomed trails. You can go for 2 hours, 3 hours, half day, all day or overnight. There are 175 miles of trails over 650 square miles of snowbound wilderness. Their new machines are easy to drive and they provide snacks and hot drinks.

© Ellie Huggins

Getting ready to leave on a tour with Eagle Ridge.

Winter

Snowmobiling

Tahoe City Golf Course

A snowmobile track is laid out on the golf course. This is a good place to practice driving before going on a longer ride. Rentals are available at the clubhouse.

Tahoe City Golf Course
251 No. Lake Blvd.
Tahoe City
530-583-1516

High Sierra Snowmobile

A small track is operated on the Brockway Golf Course. Here you can try your hand at driving before taking one of the longer tours. This is a great place to fill an hour or two with the whole family.

High Sierra Snowmobile
Brockway Golf Course
530-546-9909

Directions:
At the corner of Highways 267 and 28 in Kings Beach.

T C Sno Mo's

Your two-hour guided tour leaves from downtown Tahoe City. They take small groups on a very scenic drive above the lake.

T C Sno Mo's
Tahoe City
530-581-3906

Lake Tahoe Snowmobile Tours

Tours leave from Highway 267 just south of Northstar and drive to 6,800 feet on the summit of Mt. Watson. You'll enjoy the incredible views of the region so be sure to bring a camera. The tours meet at the Crystal Bay Visitor Center.

Lake Tahoe Snowmobile Tours
Crystal Bay
530-546-4280 775-831-4202

Winter

Snowmobiling

Lake Tahoe Winter Sports Center
Lake Tahoe Golf Course
Highway 50 south of the Airport.
Sports Center
3071 Highway 50
Tahoe Paradise
530-577-2940
Reservations required for the wilderness tours.

Lake Tahoe Winter Sports Center

Before taking this wilderness tour, you can try your hand driving at the Center's track course on the Lake Tahoe Golf Course. Rentals are by the half hour on a single or double-rider machine.

The special two-hour wilderness tours begin with a shuttle bus ride to Blue Lake in beautiful Hope Valley. Special overnight tours can be arranged as well. They rent clothes and provide you with the finest snowmobiles available that feature backrests and handlebar heaters.

Zephyr Cove Snowmobilin'
Zephyr Cove
775-588-3833
Reservations required.
Free shuttle bus from the casinos and hotels.

Zephyr Cove Snowmobilin'

Riders sign up at Zephyr Cove and are bused to Spooner Summit. The tours last two hours with several stops for photos. Groomed trails lead to a high point where on a good day you have spectacular views of Lake Tahoe, the Sierra and the Carson Valley. Single or double-rider machines and warm clothing are available for rent. First-time riders are welcomed and given instructions.

Winter

Snowplay

Tubing at Kingvale

On your way to the slopes or on your way home, try this tubing hill at Kingvale. Four different runs twist down from the top.

Kingvale Tubing and Sledding Center
Kingvale Exit off I-80
Weekends and Holidays only.
530-426-1941

Boreal Mountain Playground

The snowplay area is at the west end of the ski area parking lot. The fee includes saucer rental but you must drag your saucer up the hill.

Boreal Mountain Playground
I-80 at the Castle Peak/Boreal exit.
Fee to use the hill.
530-426-3666

Soda Springs Ski Area and Tubing

Soda Springs has introduced family fun with tubing. Everyone in the family will want to try the three different runs from the top of the lift. Tubes are large enough so that small fry can go with an adult.

Soda Springs Ski Area and Tubing
One mile east of the Soda Springs/Norden exit off I-80.
530-426-1010

Special Features:
An all-day lift ticket is also good on the tubing hill.

Winter

© Ellie Huggins

Riding the lift at Soda Springs is almost as much fun as the ride.

Snowplay

Northstar-at-Tahoe
Highway 267
Truckee
Fee per hour.
530-562-2267

Northstar-at-Tahoe

Northstar has tubing runs uphill from the Day Lodge. A tow brings you to the top of the hill.

Squaw Valley USA
Highway 89 south of Truckee.
Fee to ride the cable car.
530-583-6985

Squaw Valley USA

The snow tubing area operates every day from 2:00 to 9:00 p.m. off Bailey's lift near High Camp. Here is fun for the whole family at the end of the day, or a place where non-skiing members of the group can play in the snow with the help of a lift to the top. This would be a great way to spend an afternoon, followed by skating and dinner at Alexander's. This just may be the highest place you've ever slid down the hill, and the view is spectacular.

Tahoe Donner
Northwoods Blvd. near
the Clubhouse.
Fee to rent saucers.
Weekends and holidays only.
530-587-9400

Tahoe Donner

The broad hill with protective fences at the bottom is operated by the Tahoe Donner Association. This is a good place for a large group to play. The fee includes saucers.

Granlibakken Resort
Granlibakken Rd.
Tahoe City
Weekends and holidays only.
530-583-6203

Granlibakken Resort

Granlibakken operates a snowplay area next to the ski hill. The hill is fenced for safe runouts. The fee includes saucer rental.

Snowplay

North Tahoe Regional Park

The snowplay area has good protection for runouts. Because it is next to the cross country ski area, families can engage in both activities. Equipment rentals are available, but no sleds with metal edges are allowed.

North Tahoe Regional Park
National Ave.
Tahoe Vista
530-546-5043

Incline Village Golf Course

The snowplay hill is on the golf driving range next to The Chateau. Bring your own equipment. There is no supervision. The hill has different spots for short or long runs. Small children will be safe here.

Incline Village Golf Course
Fairway Drive
Incline Village

Hansen's Resort

Hansen's fee covers tubes and saucers to use on their hill with banked turns and a groomed trail to walk to the top. For families with skiers at Heavenly, this is a wonderful choice for the little ones.

Hansen's Resort
1960 Ski Run Blvd.
South Lake Tahoe
Fee to rent equipment.
530-544-3661

Unofficial Snowplay Areas

There are unofficial snowplay areas in Truckee, on Highway 267, Tahoe City just south of the Tahoe City *Y* and at the intersection of Highways 50 and 28 near Spooner Summit. You must bring your own saucers or tubes and parking is very limited at these locations.

Winter Adventures

Sleigh Rides

You can plan a sleigh ride for your group or take part in regularly scheduled departures. You can even charter a wedding sleigh with one outfit. So dress warmly and take the family for a memorable experience.

Northstar-at-Tahoe
Highway 267
Truckee
Fee per person.
530-562-1230

Northstar-at-Tahoe

The resort offers daily sleigh rides from the golf clubhouse, weather permitting. Dress warmly and bring the family out for this unique adventure.

Camp Richardson's Corral
Fee per person.
Reservations required.
530-541-3113

Directions:
On the west side of Highway 89 just north of the main entrance to Camp Richardson.

Camp Richardson's Corral

The corral offers sleigh rides along the shores of Lake Tahoe or through mountain meadows. Dinner rides include a one-hour trip through the forest at sunset followed by a barbeque at the ranch house. Their special six-person, hand-painted sleigh rents out for weddings or other special occasions.

Borges Sleigh Rides
Lake Parkway across from
Caesars Tahoe.
Stateline
Fee per person.
Reservations recommended.
530-541-1953
Cellular 530-957-6338

Borges Sleigh Rides

Borges famous Belgian Blonds and Baskir Curleys from Russia are hitched to their sleighs and ready to take you for a one-hour tour over the meadow and through the woods and to one of the most spectacular views of Lake Tahoe. Or you can schedule a private ride for a romantic evening.

Winter

Winter Adventures

A romantic sleigh ride with Borges.

© Tom Kelly, Courtesy of Heavenly Ski Resort

Kirkwood Resort

Kirkwood Stables will take groups by appointment, weather and snow conditions permitting. The sleigh is drawn around the meadow by two Clydesdale draft horses. Kids in the Mighty Mountain Ski School will often get a noon ride as part of the day's activities.

Kirkwood Resort
Highway 88 five miles west of Carson Pass.
Fee per person.
Reservations required.
209-258-7433

Winter Adventures

Special Ski Classes

Alpine Skills International
P.O. Box 8
Norden, CA 95724
530-426-9108
www.alpineskills.com

Special Features:
Corporate team building classes and back country snowboarding are available. Their instructors offer guide training in all the mountaineering skills.

Alpine Skills International

If you have ever dreamed of skiing the Haute Route from Chamonix, France, to Zermatt, Switzerland, or you want to hone your skills for skiing extreme slopes in the back country, this is the place to start. ASI teaches everything you need to know about ski touring, ski mountaineering, telemark and randonnée techniques as well as ice climbing. They lead back country tours around the Tahoe area and in the Eastern High Sierra.

North American Ski Training Center
P.O. Box 9119
Truckee, CA 96162
530-587-4772
www.skinastc.com

Special Features:
Lodging is not included in the local ski improvement clinics. Other courses include lodging and transfers.

North American Ski Training Center

Chris and Jenny Fellows have started an organization for intermediate and advanced skiers. Ski improvement clinics will ingrain skills and techniques to last a lifetime. The courses offer intensive immersion into the world of skiing. Jumpstart Your Skiing clinics include all-day classes, on the snow video and drills plus evening indoor clinics. The all conditions, all terrain, adventure skiing and back country skills are offered at one of five great mountains in the West and Canada. They also offer international tours.

Winter Adventures

Sierra Ski Touring

Dave Beck of the Husky Express leads special instructional telemark classes and avalanche training to Meiss Hut above Carson Pass. The Meiss Hut trips have a limit of eight people. He and Dottie Dennis also lead combined ski and mushing weekends to the same hut. They provide all the food in what they call hut cuisine. Adventurous back country skiers can also choose from three high country five-day trips. These trips are limited to six skiers.

Dog Sled Rides

The Husky Express Dog Sled Rides

Dottie Dennis and her team of huskies are waiting to take you on a one-hour sled ride across the Hope Valley. If you've ever watched the Iditarod sled dog race on television, here's your chance to experience the thrill of mushing behind Aspen, Abby, Alexis, Rainy, Ski and the rest of the pack. Husky Express has been featured in *Bay Area Backroads*.

Sierra Ski Touring
775-782-3047
www.highsierra.com/sst

The Husky Express
Fee per person.
Reservations recommended.
775-782-3047
www.highsierra.com/sst

Directions:
Rides leave on the north side of Highway 88 a few miles west of the junction with Highway 89.

Winter

The former C.B. White House in Truckee, now Jordan's Collectibles.

Year Round

Kids at Casinos

Since no children under 18 years old are allowed in the casinos, the casino hotels have special arcades where youngsters can play video games. A parent or older child must accompany any children under 12.

Cal-Neva Resort, Crystal Bay Club and the Tahoe Biltmore Lodge and Casino

Cal-Neva Resort
775-832-4000
Crystal Bay Club
775-832-0512
Biltmore Lodge and Casino
775-832-0660

Each casino has a video arcade to amuse the kids while you hit the tables. Your small children must be accompanied by an older child or a parent.

Hyatt Regency Lake Tahoe Resort and Casino

Hyatt Regency Lake Tahoe Resort
Reservations required.
Children must be guests of the resort.
775-832-1234 x3214

Camp Hyatt is a program designed just for kids 3 to 12 years old. From mid-June to Labor Day your children can participate in their own indoor and outdoor activities, from trips to Ponderosa Ranch or scavenger hunts to bingo and arts and crafts. The camp operates in Summer from 9:00 a.m. to midnight in two sessions. The rest of the year day sessions are on weekends only. One other caveat, your three-year-old must be potty trained with no pull-ups. This is an activity oriented program to stimulate kids, not a baby-sitting service and is open only to guests of the hotel.

Year Round

Kids at Casinos

Caesars Lake Tahoe
Fee for all games.
775-588-3515

Caesars Lake Tahoe

Caesars has a state-of-the-art video arcade with all kinds of games and virtual reality rides to keep junior guests occupied.

Harrah's Lake Tahoe
Fee for all games.
775-588-6066

Harrah's Lake Tahoe

Harrah's Family Fun Center offers an indoor playground featuring ball pools, climbing areas and two levels of slides. At the video and pinball games kids can win points to redeem for gifts. This is a safe, well lit, non-smoking and alcohol-free place. Harrah's offers bonded babysitting for hotel guests.

Harvey's Resort Hotel
Fee for all games.
775-588-2411

Harvey's Resort Hotel

There is no doubt that this is the most up-to-date and fancy arcade at South Shore. It is centrally located in its own grotto near the hotel. There are special extra fee attractions as well as a family fun center with virtual reality games.

Horizon Casino Resort
Fee for all games.
775-588-6211

Horizon Casino Resort

The Horizon Hotel has an arcade in the convention center. There are games for all ages, but your youngest children will need supervision.

Art Galleries

There is an extensive art community in the Truckee-Lake Tahoe region and many galleries show the works of local artists. In order to find out what is showing, check the local newspapers for information about current shows. *Artifacts*, a free publication about the arts scene, is published quarterly and is distributed around the lake. Galleries are listed below starting in Truckee. Every July, Tahoe ARTour holds a three-day, self-guided tour of 30 artists' studios in the North Tahoe-Truckee area. Some artists welcome visitors by appointment.

Artruckee

Artruckee located in the Loading Dock building features the works of local artist, Audrey Dygert, and others. Interesting carved bears, jewelry and other gift items are also for sale.

Artruckee
Downtown Truckee
530-587-5189

Daily, 10:00 am to 5:30 pm.

The White Buffalo

This shop features authentic Southwest Indian art, jewelry and pottery as well as clothes, moccasins and cookbooks for hot chili food.

The White Buffalo
Downtown Truckee
530-587-4446

Daily, 10:00 am to 5:30 pm.

The Backstreet Framers and Gallery

The store is upstairs and sells posters and Edward Curtis prints, plus works of local artists.

Backstreet Framers and Gallery
Jibboom St., Truckee
530-587-1409

Monday through Saturday, 10:00 am to 5:30 pm.

Year Round

Art Galleries

Kathleen Curtis Studio
Studio: 530-823-8334
in Pilot Hill.

Kathleen Curtis Studio

Kathleen Curtis, longtime Truckee resident artist, has moved her studio to Pilot Hill south of Auburn off Highway 49.

Thomas Kinkade Lake Tahoe
Galleries
10076 Donner Pass Rd.
Truckee
530-550-1395

Daily, 10:00 am to 6:00 pm.

Thomas Kinkade Lake Tahoe Galleries

Framed paintings, prints, books, calendars and plates of the Artist of Light, one of the most collected artists in America.

James Hacker Sculpture
Frank Rossback Glasforms
Capitol Building
Downtown Truckee
530-587-8460

Daily except Tuesday,
10:00 am to 5:00 pm.

James Hacker Sculpture

The bronze cast and welded sculptures are designed to hang on walls and over fireplaces. His outdoor pieces and fountains will enhance your garden.

Frank Rossback Glasforms

The custom glass blowing and sculpture of Frank Rossback shares the space in the upstairs room of the Capitol Building.

Vrooman Woodcarvings and
Wildlife Gallery
The Loading Dock
Truckee
530-587-8104

Daily, 10:00 am to 6:00 pm.

Vrooman Woodcarvings and Wildlife Gallery

The lifelike woodcarvings of birds and trout are in his gallery along with jewelry, prints and work of local artists celebrating nature and wildlife.

Year Round

Art Galleries

Squaw Valley Trading Post

Here's your chance to see the largest and best collection of Zapotec Indian rugs in the country and at wholesale prices.

Squaw Valley Trading Post
1600 Squaw Valley Road
Squaw Valley
530-583-6468

Wednesday through Sunday, 10:00 am to 6:00 pm.

James Harold Gallery

Discerning collectors can find an eclectic and exciting collection at this gallery located in the shopping arcade. They carry traditional oil landscapes as well as modern impressionists and colorful contemporary cowboys by Thomas Charles. They also sell old photos of the Tahoe-Truckee area.

James Harold Gallery
Resort at Squaw Creek
Squaw Valley
530-581-6639

Weekends: 10:00 am to 10:00 pm.
Weekdays: 10:00 am to 6:00 pm.

Pogan Gallery

This upstairs gallery features ceramic pieces, contemporary and traditional realism, and original fine art in a variety of media. They display local and national artists.

Pogan Gallery
255 No. Lake Blvd.
Tahoe City
530-583-0553

Daily, 10:00 am to 5:30 pm.

North Tahoe Art Center

The works of local artists are displayed in changing exhibits at the art center. The shop and gallery are run by volunteer artists who are members of the cooperative. Special art classes open to anyone are held during the summer.

North Tahoe Art Center
380 No. Lake Blvd.
Tahoe City
530-581-2787

Thursday through Sunday, 11:00 am to 4:00 pm.

Year Round

Art Galleries

Frames by Ryrie
Cobblestone Mall
Tahoe City
530-583-3043

Monday through Saturday,
10:00 am to 5:00 pm.

Mother Nature's Wildlife Art
521 No. Lake Blvd.
Tahoe City
530-581-4278

Monday through Saturday,
10:00 am to 6:00 pm.
Sunday, 10:00 am to 5:00 pm.

High Country Silverworks
600 No. Lake Blvd.
Tahoe City
530-583-1600

Daily, 10:00 am to 6:00 pm.

Freeman Photo Gallery
620 No. Lake Blvd.
Tahoe City
530-581-4310

Monday through Saturday,
10:00 am to 5:30 pm.

James Harold Galleries
Boatworks Mall
Tahoe City
530-581-5111

Summer: 10:00 am to 10:00 pm.
Winter: 10:00 am to 6:00 pm.

Year Round

Frames by Ryrie

An exciting gallery with posters, etchings of the Sierra, wood blocks and original water colors. They also do custom framing.

Mother Nature's Wildlife Art

This gallery next to Porter's sells fine art prints, photos and sculptures of wildlife by such artists as Lyman Doolittle, Redlin, Wysocki, Bateman, Brenders, Franca Calley and more.

High Country Silverworks

A working jewelry studio plus gallery, they carry the work of 60 artists using different media and materials.

Freeman Photo Gallery and Custom Framing

The gallery has original photographs and hand-colored black and white archival prints, pen-and-ink sketches and vintage Tahoe photographs.

James Harold Galleries

This is a large gallery that features the original paintings, sculpture, and limited edition graphics of local, national and international artists. They also show wildlife photography of Jim Stamate.

Art Galleries

Thomas Kinkade Lake Tahoe Galleries

Thomas Kinkade is one of America's most collected living artists. The gallery is devoted to his light-filled landscapes, gardens and street scenes from around the world.

**Thomas Kinkade Lake Tahoe
Galleries
Boatworks Mall
Tahoe City
530-581-0880**

Monday through Thursday,
10:00 am to 7:00 pm.
Friday, Saturday, 10:00 am to 9:00 pm.
Sunday, 4:00 to 6:00 pm.

Douglas Taylor-Art and Framing

Douglas Taylor shows the works of over 20 contemporary print makers and photographers along with works in other media, vintage Tahoe photographs and unique gifts. There are shows three times a year featuring various artists and occasional art workshops.

**Douglas Taylor - Art and Framing
6883 No. Lake Blvd.
Tahoe Vista
530-546-7794**

Monday through Friday,
10:00 am to 6:00 pm.
Saturday, 10:00 am to 5:00 pm.

Kilim Hand Woven Rugs

This store is not unlike an art gallery with its handmade old and new Oriental rugs, contemporary rugs, kilims, mats and wall hangings.

**Kilim Hand Woven Rugs
8675 No. Lake Blvd.
Kings Beach
530-546-4011**

Daily, 10:00 am to 5:30 pm.

Lakeside Gallery and Gifts

Established in 1978, the gallery shows landscapes, seascapes, impressionist paintings and still lifes, as well as fine art prints and gift items.

**Lakeside Gallery and Gifts
8636 No. Lake Blvd.
Kings Beach
530-546-3135**

Monday through Saturday,
10:00 am to 5:00 pm.

Year Round

Art Galleries

The Potter's Wheel
8331 No. Lake Blvd.
Kings Beach
530-546-8400

Thursday through Monday,
10:00 am to 6:00 pm.

Artists of Tahoe An Arts Desire
761 Northwood, Incline Village
775-831-3011

Monday through Saturday,
10:00 am to 6:00 pm.

Art Attack Gallery
Christmas Tree Village
Incline Village
775-832-7400

Monday through Saturday,
10:00 am to 6:00 pm.

The Potter's Wheel

The Potter's Wheel, in business since 1976, features water colors by Betty Layton, designer ceramic sinks and other handcrafted pottery as well as glass, woodwork and gift items.

Artists of Tahoe An Arts Desire

Cynthia Ashe frames art work in her studio and shows originals by local artists.

Art Attack Gallery

The gallery in the Christmas Tree Village features the work of William and Judith Vrooman as well as an "Artist of the Year." There are special exhibits with lectures by visiting artists throughout the year. Watch the *North Tahoe Truckee Week* or *Artifacts* for listings of these shows.

Year Round

Art Galleries

Hanifin's Art and Antiques

Hanifin's features oils and watercolors by local artists and interesting sculptures. He also sells fine oak and pine European and American antiques.

Hanifin's Art and Antiques
855 Emerald Bay Rd.
South Lake Tahoe
530-542-4663

Tuesday through Sunday,
10:00 am to 5:00 pm.

Eagle Valley Frames and Art Gallery

This gallery features investment art as well as prints and posters with particular emphasis on local scenes and artists.

Eagle Valley Frames and Art Gallery
2660 Lake Tahoe Blvd.
South Lake Tahoe
530-544-4099

Monday through Saturday,
10:00 am to 6:00 pm.

Wyland Gallery

Appropriately located in the Ski Run Marina building at lake's edge, the gallery sells paintings, prints and photographs of the sea, by the world-famous Wyland plus works of local artists and others from California and Hawaii.

Wyland Gallery
900 Ski Run Blvd.
South Lake Tahoe
530-541-8865

Summer: Daily, 10:00 am to 10:00 pm.
Rest of the year: Daily, 10:00 am to 5:00 pm.

Year Round

Art Galleries

Sierra Galleries
Caesars at Tahoe
775-588-8500

Daily, hours vary.

Addi Galleries
Harrah's Casino Hotel
775-588-1505

Daily, 9:00 am to 10:00 pm.

Legends
Horizon Casino Hotel
775-588-8598

Daily, 10:00 am to 4:00 pm.

A Frame of Mind Gallery
Harvey's Resort
775-588 8081

Daily, 11:00 am to 4:00 pm.
Some evenings.

Sierra Galleries

The gallery is filled with original paintings, limited-edition sculpture and antique carousel horses.

Addi Galleries

The Addi Galleries features works by Red Skelton, their celebrity artist for 15 years. They also publish the work of marine artist David Miller. Other unique items here are burlwood furniture and clocks.

Legends

Here you will find limited edition prints of wildlife and wilderness. They also do framing.

A Frame of Mind Gallery

A Frame of Mind features the stunning photographs of Tahoe by its owner, J.T. Ravisé. His work has been bought by Vice President Al Gore, Senator Feinstein, Senator Reed and others. His exhibit about the Tahoe basin has been shown in Carson City, Sacramento and Washington D.C. and has just been released as a book. His work has been influential in the efforts to secure the funding to save Lake Tahoe.

Shopping

Truckee

Historic Downtown Truckee along Donner Pass Road is a perfect place to spend a morning or afternoon looking for unusual gifts. Among the many offerings are: **The Cooking Gallery** with everything imaginable for the cook and kitchen; **Cabona's** selling casual clothing since the early 1900s; and **Truckee River Llama Ranch** with imported sweaters and clothing. **Joanne's Stained Glass** sells fascinating gifts of glass. There's a Christmas shop and homemade candy store, as well as places for T-shirts, ice cream and numerous restaurants. Across the main drag at the Loading Dock you will find **Jackass Ridge** with a complete line of Brighton accessories as well as **Vrooman's Woodcarving and Wildlife Gallery**. Model train enthusiasts will want to visit **Truckee Train and Toy**. **Jordan's Collectibles** in the C.B White House sells antiques and women's clothing.

The **Gateway Shopping Center**, at the corner of Donner Pass Road and Highway 89, is home to Safeway and Payless Drugs. Stores of interest are **Florian's Fine Wines and Specialty Foods** and **The Bookshelf at Hooligan Rocks**, a full service bookstore with books on tape, cards and magazines. Visit **Pacos Truckee Bike and Ski** for all your biking and cross country skiing needs.

Mountain Hardware and Sports is more than a hardware store, carrying kitchenware and linens, sports supplies for fishing and hunting, snowshoes and skis to rent or buy, plus books and maps.

Next door, the former Ace Hardware is now **Granite Chief**, the Truckee store for the famous Squaw Valley ski service center. They sell bikes and other mountain gear and clothing in the summer.

The Factory Stores are located on Donner Pass Road just east of the Donner State Park Interstate 80 exit. The shops offer clothing, household items, jewelry and shoes at marked-down prices.

Shopping

Squaw Valley

Currently **Squaw Valley Olympic House Mall** features boutiques and ski shops, but with the Christmas 2001 opening of the first phase of Intrawest's **Village at Squaw Valley** pedestrian mall, the shops and restaurant choices will multiply. At the time of printing it was announced that **PlumpJack Balboa Café** will open a ski-in/ski-out restaurant offering American brasserie fare. **Starbucks Coffee** will be there, along with **Mountain Hardware** of Truckee fame, plus **Occhiali** for Italian designer eyewear, **Y.B. Uglee** with personalized cosmetics and **Nantucket Natural Oils**.

The **Resort at Squaw Creek** shopping promenade offers upscale shopping for clothing, art and jewelry. **Sweet Potato Deli** has delectables to eat and a full line of cookbooks as well. Even if you don't buy, it's a great place to window-shop.

Tahoe City

For plants and other garden items, books, house decorations and Jeb's Mountain Gallery of nature and wildlife prints, don't miss the **Tahoe Tree Company** at 401 West Lake Boulevard south of the Tahoe City Y. Nearby, look in at **Girasole** that sells Irish country furniture, dishes and other decorations for the home.

Four malls offer a variety of shopping experiences. **Cobblestone Mall** shops sell clothing, jewelry, quilts and art. The **Boatworks Mall** has a collection of gift and clothing shops, galleries and the **Bookshelf at Boatworks.** The **Tahoe Marina Mall,** west of the Boatworks also has a variety of shops including **Sports Tahoe** featuring beautiful resort wear. Next door to Safeway in the **Lighthouse Mall, The Store** sells gifts, cards, books and other necessities.

The Watermelon Patch is an interesting gift shop at 3225 North Lake Boulevard near Dollar Point. It features unusual clothing, gifts and cards. In the summer they sell plants for your garden and are the site for a farmers' market that sells fresh produce every Thursday.

Shopping

Incline Village

You'll find **Hallmark Village Cards and Books** has a large collection of books and of course cards for all occasions, while **The Potlatch** offers a complete line of Southwest and Indian art, artifacts and jewelry. **The Christmas Store** in The Christmas Tree Village is the perfect place to pick up decorations and other gifts all year.

South Lake Tahoe

If you are visiting the **Tallac Historic Site** you will definitely want to check out the Art Store in front of Valhalla that sells unusual artifacts and jewelry by local artists along with interesting ornaments from around the globe.

You will find numerous **Factory Stores** around the South Tahoe *Y*. **Mikasa** is a nice place to look for bargains in china and pottery and chocolate lovers will want to visit the **Rocky Mountain Chocolate Factory**. Well-made knits at **Cape Isle Knitters** and **Oneida Silver** are among the many outlets on both sides of Highway 50.

At the *Y*, on the west side of Highway 50, you'll also find the **Sierra Bookshop**, crammed full of books, cards, games and calendars and an excellent collection of hiking and skiing guides and maps.

The casinos have shopping galleries that offer everything from sports essentials to sculptures and paintings by renowned artists, as well as T-shirts and other attire. Be sure to visit **Heavenly Sports** across the street from Harvey's Casino for all your sporting gear and attire.

The redeveloped **Ski Run Marina** features a stylish shopping area next to the Riva Grill that includes a gallery, womens clothing and jewelry shops.

Museums

The area's history is rich in tales of pioneer grit and Bunyanesque feats to fell and transport lumber and build the first transcontinental railroad across the granite slopes of the Sierra Nevada. Whether you want a diversion on a winter afternoon or are curious about the colorful history of the region, there are many museums and historical sites worth a visit.

The Western America Ski Sport Museum
Boreal Mountain Playground
530-426-3313

Hour:
Wednesday through Sunday,
10:00 am to 4:00 pm.

The Western America Ski Sport Museum

The Western America Ski Sport Museum, operated by the Auburn Ski Club, features the history of winter sports. The exhibits include old photos of the days when skis, called snowshoes, were just wooden boards strapped to your boots, and examples of the evolution of boots to today's high-tech models. There are photos of the West's greatest skiers and, on weekends, old ski movies are shown continuously to provide an afternoon of entertainment.

Sierra Nevada Children's Museum
The Kid Zone at Truckee High School
Truckee
530-587-KIDS (587-5437)
Fee to enter.

Hours:
Wednesday through Saturday,
10:00 am to 5:00 pm.

Sierra Nevada Children's Museum

The museum reopens in October 2001 in The Kid Zone next to the teen center on the High School grounds. With exciting new exhibits, you may have to drag your child away from the fascinating hands-on activities that help children learn about their natural environment. Helpful volunteers guide children in art and computer activities.

Museums

Donner Memorial State Park and Museum

The park is a memorial to the Donner Party and all pioneers who made the trek west. The Emigrant Trail Museum's exhibits display artifacts from the Donner Party and show the life of the Paiute tribes who summered in the area for several thousand years. Dioramas depict the construction of the Central Pacific Railroad over the Sierra Nevada between 1864 and 1869. A slide show about the tragic story of the Donner Party is shown several times a day. The bookstore in the museum sells a wide variety of titles on natural history of the area as well as many books about the Donner Party and other emigrant history.

The park is open all year. Information about other activities at the park is in "Beaches," "Bicycling," "Special Hikes," "Cross Country Skiing," "Just for Kids" and "Ranger Programs."

Donner Memorial State Park
Fee per person.
530-582-7892

Directions:
Donner Pass Rd. just west of the Donner State Park exit off I-80.
Hours:
Summer: Daily, 9:00 am to 5:00 pm.
Winter: Daily, 10:00 am to 4:00 pm.
Slide shows on the hour.

Special Features:
The imposing Pioneer Monument just east of the museum was built to commemorate all who struck out across the trackless land to reach California. Note the height of the monument's base. The snow was that deep in 1846-47, when the Donner Party camped here.

A trail from the museum leads to the site of the Murphy family cabin, one of the families of the Donner Party. A bronze plaque attached to the rock that formed one wall of their shelter lists the survivors and deceased of that ill-fated group. Of eighty-nine who had set out from Missouri in May 1846, only forty-seven lived to see California's fertile valleys.

Year Round

Museums

Donner Day Camp
Summer only.

Directions:
On the east side of Highway 89 three miles north of I-80.

Special Features:
There is a Commemorative Emigrant Trail built by the U.S. Forest Service that leads north to Prosser Dam. You might want to consider a short hike on this. The whole trail — open to hikers, cyclists and equestrians — traverses 12 miles between the Donner Camp and Stampede Reservoir and is described in "Bicycling" on page 155.

Donner Day Camp of the U.S. Forest Service

The tragedy of the Donner Party has fascinated historians and tourists ever since C.F. McGlashan, editor of the *Truckee Republican*, published his *History of the Donner Party* in 1880. A sign at the edge of the parking lot tells the tragic story of the Donner Party. The sites of makeshift shelters of the families of Jacob and George Donner are marked along a path around the meadow.

During the summer of 1990, volunteers under the guidance of the University of Nevada, Reno undertook an intensive archeological search to uncover artifacts that might confirm the exact locations of the Donner family camps. Bone fragments, pieces of china and metal wagon parts were unearthed in the meadow nearby confirming the presence of the group here. However, nothing was found under the fire-scarred pine tree that was originally thought to be the location of George Donner's family tent.

Year Round

Museums

The Gatekeeper's Cabin

This museum, operated by volunteers of the North Lake Tahoe Historical Society, tells the story of Lake Tahoe. Exhibits include exquisite Washoe baskets and several collections of obsidian arrowheads. You can learn about important pioneer settlers of the area and buy books and items of historical interest at the museum store. The newest exhibit at the museum is an accurate scale model of the steamer *Tahoe* that plied the waters of Lake Tahoe delivering mail and passengers to destinations around the lake before roads were built.

Next door, the Marion Steinbach Indian Basket Museum displays the $1.5 million collection that was donated to the Historical Society upon Marion's death in 1991. In addition to the baskets she collected between 1935 and 1957 from Alaska to the Plains, there are over 100 Indian dolls, examples of basket starts, carvings and other art.

The Gatekeeper's Cabin
530-583-1762

Directions:
On Hwy. 89 just south of the Tahoe City Y.

Hours:
Summer: Daily, 11:00 am to 5:00 pm. May 15 to June 15 and Labor Day to October 1: Wednesday to Sunday 11:00 am to 5:00 pm.

Special Features:
Between 1916 and 1968 the Gatekeeper's log cabin served as home for the official regulator of Lake Tahoe's water level. After 1968, the Federal Watermaster's Office in Reno controlled the dam. However, it is still necessary for someone to hand turn the gates of the dam. Special agreements between California and the Nevada irrigation districts determine the amount of water to be released into the Truckee River. The water flows downstream to Reno and its reservoirs. The river finally turns north at Wadsworth, east of Reno, and empties into Pyramid Lake.

Year Round

The Watson Cabin
560 No. Lake Blvd.
Tahoe City
530-583-8717

Hours:
Summer: Daily, noon to 4:00 pm.
Rest of the year: Weekends and
holiday weeks only.

Special Features:
The cabin was built by Robert
Montgomery Watson, a Tahoe City
pioneer and its first constable. He
served the town for 28 years and could
often be seen riding around town on
his horse Pinto. His son Rob moved
into the cottage with his bride in 1909.
The Watsons were one of the first
families to live in Tahoe City year
round. Their daughter Mildred lived in
the cabin until 1950.

The Watson Cabin Living Museum

This turn-of-the-century log cabin
stands on its original site overlooking
the Commons Beach in Tahoe City.
In 1979 the North Lake Tahoe
Historical Society purchased the
building and placed it on the National
Register of Historic Places. The cabin
has been restored as a "living museum"
depicting the life of a Tahoe pioneer
family.

For more information about Tahoe
City's past, you may wish to purchase
a copy of *Tahoe City's Yesterdays*,
gathered and edited by Carol Van
Etten. The book is available at both
museums and local bookstores.

The Watson cabin in Tahoe City.

© Ellie Huggins

Year Round

Museums

California State Parks Museums

During the summer, at Sugar Pine State Park and Emerald Bay, the state parks open two mansions for your enjoyment. Step back to Victorian times in the **Ehrman Mansion** in Sugar Pine State Park. The house is open with living history docents to show you around the rooms of this elegant summer residence built in 1902 by Isaias W. Hellman, a San Francisco financier. For a description of the bicycle ride to the park, see page 148 in "Bicycling."

See page 194 in "Special Hikes" for the hike to **Vikingsholm** on the shores of Emerald Bay. Tours are held during the summer months of this replica of a 9th century Norse fortress, built by Mrs. Lora J. Knight in 1929. Her tea house on Fannette Island can be visited on a Tahoe Whitewater Tours kayak trip to Emerald Bay described on page 124 in "Boating."

Sugar Pine Point State Park
Summer only.
Fee per vehicle.
530-525-7982

Directions:
Nine miles south of the Tahoe City *Y*.

Emerald Bay State Park
Summer only.
Fee to park.
530-541-3030

Directions:
Parking: Eight miles north of the So. Tahoe *Y*. You must hike one mile downhill to the mansion or come by boat.

Year Round

Lake Tahoe Historical Society Museum
3058 Hwy. 50
South Lake Tahoe
Fee to enter.
530-541-5458

Hours:
Summer: daily, 11:00 am to 4:00 pm.
Winter: weekends, 11:00 am to 4:00 pm.

Lake Tahoe Historical Society Museum

Step back in time for an hour or two with Lake Tahoe's interesting history, from the time when Washoe tribes called the lake their summer home to Stateline's first gambling casinos. The museum is the product of dedicated volunteers of the Lake Tahoe Historical Society who have assembled exhibits depicting all periods of the area's history. Learn about Washoe Indian basketry and pioneers who settled here when Lake Valley was a crossroads for the Bonanza Road from California to Nevada's silver mines. There is an exhibit about the Pony Express and the story of the lake's famous steamers and lumber operators of the late nineteenth century who felled, shipped and flumed their logs to Nevada to shore up the silver mines of Virginia City. There are oral histories on tapes and three different videos for hours of interesting viewing. The museum shop sells books and posters about Lake Tahoe. When you leave, be sure to look at the two buildings behind the museum: the oldest log cabin in the region which was the Society's first museum and Osgood's Tollhouse, built in 1859.

Museums

Tahoe Douglas Chamber of Commerce Visitor Center

Be sure to drop in and see the interpretive panels. Here you can learn the story of Lake Tahoe, from the earliest Washoe settlements to the new casinos. You can read about the success story of Harvey's Casino Resort that started in 1947 as a small coffee shop with a few slot machines. Harvey's wife Lewellyn brought the food over from their home next door.

Tahoe Douglas Chamber of Commerce Visitor Center
775 588-4591

Directions:
In the Round Hill shopping center.

Hours:
Monday through Friday, 9:00 am to 6:00 pm.
Weekends, 9:00 am to 5:00 pm.

Celio Ranch

The Celio family has been in Lake Valley since 1863, when Carlo Celio established a ranch south of present day U.S. 50. The family expanded their holdings in 1903 when they purchased most of the land of today's Meyers and Yank's Station Hotel. They operated a lumber company here from 1905 until 1952, furnishing much of the lumber for summer homes in the surrounding areas. They also raised beef cattle and operated a dairy. Across the road is the original milk house. The present-day Celio ranch house was built in 1915 on the foundations of the old house that had worn out.

Celio Ranch

Directions:
Drive west on U.S. 50 from the So. Tahoe *Y* to Upper Truckee Rd. then south on Upper Truckee Rd. about one mile. The Celio Ranch is on both sides of the road. A historic marker is on the right side of the road.

Special Features:
Descendants of the Celio family still live in this lovely structure with its encircling porch that provides shade in summer and protection from snow in the winter. So please respect their privacy.

Year Round

Photo and Vista Points

Donner Lake Vista Points

Vista points are located off Interstate 80 about three miles east of Donner Summit and three miles west of Truckee. The two vista points on the interstate east or west offer magnificent views of Donner Lake, Donner Pass and Schallenberger Ridge. Display maps point out the railroad line, old roads and the emigrant wagon routes used between 1844 and 1870.

Donner Lake Overlook and McGlashan Point

Drive west on Donner Pass Road from Donner Lake to the overlook just before the Rainbow Bridge. This classic view of Donner Lake makes a wonderful sunset photo. The range of mountains to the east is the Carson Range, a spur of the Sierra Nevada. The Rainbow Bridge has been restored and rebuilt and if you walk up the road, you can frame the lake through the bridge.

Logan Shoals Vista Point

The Logan Shoals Vista Point is on U.S. 50, north of Stateline 7.2 miles. Here you can frame a photo of the lake with one of the many beautiful Jeffrey pines at this spot. You may want to climb around on the point to find the perfect location for your photograph.

Memorial Point

About two miles south of Incline Village on Highway 28, the Lake Tahoe Nevada State Park has built a beautiful vista point. Interpretive signs describe the lake, its history and locations of the various overlooks along the lake. Several paths get you close to the emerald water, where your photographs may be able to reflect the granite boulders shimmering just beneath the surface.

Mount Rose Highway Overlook

Take Mount Rose Highway (Highway 431) east from Highway 28 in Incline Village. Drive 3.5 miles to the overlook. The vistas from this point are among the best in the region.

Photo and Vista Points

Stateline Fire Lookout

From Highway 28 in Crystal Bay take Reservoir Road, across from the post office, and turn right on Lakeview. The Forest Service road is on the left in about one half mile. One of the gates on the road may be closed, but the half-mile walk to the top is worth it. At the end of the road is the region's most spectacular view of Crystal Bay and south to high peaks behind the South Shore. A nature trail with interpretive panels encircles the Fire Lookout Station. Plan to spend an hour taking in the views here and learning some history, too. The Lookout has been adopted by local citizens.

Emerald Bay Overlook

The overlook parking area is nine miles north from the South Tahoe *Y* on Highway 89. The photo images from this spot are unlimited. If you feel like taking a short hike, continue to the Eagle Falls parking lot and take the trail up to the falls and on to Eagle Lake. There are spots above Eagle Lake where your vista of Emerald Bay is exceptional. The description of the hike is in "Special Hikes" on page 195.

Carson Pass Region

Several vista points on the south side of Highway 88 as it climbs west toward Carson Pass capture views of Red Lake and the Hope and Charity Valleys below. If you are lucky enough to drive this road during the fall when the aspens splash gold across the valleys, some beautiful photos are possible. Driving west on Highway 88 from Highway 89, autumn foliage will provide colorful backdrops for the meandering Carson River.

Summer visitors will find wildflower gardens that produce a palette of color across the landscape. The best and easiest trail to photograph flowers is the Pacific Crest Trail just north of Highway 88 at Carson Pass. Park in the lot just west of the pass on the north side of the highway. The trail is described in "Special Hikes" on page 209. You don't have to hike far before your camera will be clicking around every corner. Don't miss the opportunity to photograph the giants of the Sierra, those gnarled forms of Sierra juniper that have been around for many centuries.

Special Events

The North Tahoe-Truckee area promotes many annual special events. The North Shore and Truckee papers each list events in their special entertainment sections. Dates vary from year to year, so check with the Visitor Bureaus or the *North Tahoe Truckee This Week* magazine for exact dates of the events listed. The South Lake Tahoe and Carson Pass area offer a bonanza of special events including a summer-long music festival. Since specific dates vary from year to year, check the *Tahoe Daily Tribune* "Lake Tahoe Action" section as well as Tourist Information Centers for exact dates. The list below was current at printing time, but new events are planned each year, so this may only be a partial list of the possibilities. Ski areas in the region have so many ski and snowboard events during the season that it is impossible to include them here. We have listed only those that have been held at the same time during the last few years. In addition, more and more mountain bike races are being scheduled at the resorts with mountain bike parks. If you are interested in these kinds of events, check with the resorts for information.

March
Heavenly Ski Resort

Coors Light Top Gun on Gunbarrel at Heavenly

Billed as one of the top mogul competitions in the country you can watch how the pros of bump skiing do it on the famous Gunbarrel run.

March
North Lake Tahoe and Truckee

Snowfest

A week-long winter carnival for North Lake Tahoe and Truckee starts with a torchlight ski parade at Squaw Valley and is followed by races, spaghetti feeds and pancake breakfasts, plus dances and dress-up contests.

Special Events

The Great Race

March during Snowfest
Tahoe City to Truckee

This 30 km cross-country race from Tahoe City to Truckee attracts locals and world-class skiers alike. The finish can be watched at Hilltop in Truckee.

Windows on History

Memorial Day weekend
Truckee

Downtown Truckee becomes a stage with a wandering barbershop quartet, the Virginia City Gunslingers and Saloon Girls and other acts.

Renaissance Festival

Early June
Camp Richardson's Resort

Come participate in medieval festivities with food, dancing and art at Camp Richardson's Resort.

Donner Lake Triathlon

July
Around Donner Lake

Watch them swim, run and ride bicycles up Donner Pass Road. This event draws hundreds of competitors.

Northstar-at-Tahoe Beer Festival

July
Northstar-at-Tahoe

Spend an evening tasting beer from Northern California's microbreweries.

Valhalla Summer Arts and Music Festival

June to August
South Lake Tahoe
Tallac Historic Site

A summer-long festival of art and music. There is music every Thursday night at Valhalla and a Potpourri Concert every Tuesday.

Year Round

Special Events

**July Fourth
Truckee, Squaw Valley,
Lake Tahoe**

July 4th Celebrations

Truckee has a real, small town parade with floats, drill teams and horses. Fireworks are produced at Squaw Valley, North and South Lake Tahoe.

**Second Saturday in July
Markleeville**

The Death Ride

Bicycle riders gather in Markleeville for a 128-mile death ride over five alpine passes returning to the start. The riders are off at 6:00 a.m., but if you can't get there at that hour, come in the afternoon and stay to see the first riders return.

**July
Start at Squaw Valley**

Western States 100-mile Endurance Run

Watch runners leave from the base of Squaw Valley ski area and run up the mountain on the first leg of this demanding marathon that ends in Auburn.

**July
Tallac Historic Site
South Lake Tahoe**

Wa She Shu Edeh Native American Festival

Come to the Tallac Historic Site for basket weaving demonstrations, art exhibits and traditional dances.

Year Round

Special Events

Truckee Regional Park

Bring the family, a blanket and a picnic to listen to different groups throughout the summer.

July and August
Every Wednesday 6:30 to 8:00 pm.
Truckee Regional Park
Amphitheater
Hwy. 267, Truckee

Lake Tahoe Summer Music Festival

Classical, jazz and popular music at various locations around the lake including High Camp at Squaw Valley.

July and August
Various locations around Truckee
and Lake Tahoe
530-581-3101
www.tahoemusic.org

Shakespeare at Sand Harbor

Shakespearean plays are presented in an outdoor theater on the beach at Sand Harbor. Bring a blanket, picnic and warm jacket to enjoy the Bard's plays under the stars.

July and August
Sand Harbor
1-800-747-4697
www.laketahoeshakespeare.com

Great Gatsby Festival

Relive Lake Tahoe's gilded era at the Great Gatsby Festival at the Tallac Historic Site.

August
Tallac Historic Site

Wooden Boat Week

Enjoy a Concours d'Elegance of Lake Tahoe's antique wooden boats.

August
Tahoe City

Truckee Championship Rodeo

Serious rodeo competition with out-of-town as well as Truckee riders.

Second Weekend in August
Truckee

Year Round

Special Events

August
Northstar-at-Tahoe

Northstar Splendor of the Sierra Fine Arts Show

Artists from around the West display their work for sale

September
North Lake Tahoe
530-587-FEST
www.tahoefilmfestival.com

Tahoe International Film Festival

Now five years old, the festival has grown to include juried selections from hundreds of entries on a different theme each year. A gala black tie opening and film screenings are shown to sponsors. VIP tickets are usually available in early spring.

September
Truckee
www.truckeerailroaddays.com

Truckee Railroad Days

Celebrate Truckee's connection to the railroad since its founding in the 1860s. Hand car races, model railroads, a parade and more fill the weekend.

End of September
Northstar-at-Tahoe

Autumn Jubilee Food and Wine Festival

California wines are matched to food from 30 local restaurants for tasting and comparing.

Year Round

Special Events

Donner Party Hike Weekend

October
Truckee

Learn more about the Donner Party history on hikes and presentations in the Truckee/Donner Summit area.

Oktoberfest

October
Alpine Meadows

Dining, dancing and fine Bavarian libations are offered at Alpine Meadows.

Kokanee Salmon Festival

October
U.S. Forest Service Visitor Center
South Lake Tahoe

When the salmon are spawning at Taylor Creek, you can watch the strange behavior of these fish as they return to the creek to lay their eggs.

Genoa Christmas Faire

December
Genoa, Nevada

On the first weekend in December the town of Genoa welcomes you to their Christmas Faire.

Tiny Tim's Christmas Fair

December
Truckee

Arts and crafts are on sale at the Community Center, a good place to do some early Christmas shopping.

Year Round

Index

Index

Index

Index

Index

Index

Index

Index

Index

Index

Index

Index

Index

Index

Index

Index

Index

Notes

Note from the Publisher

Lake Tahoe and Truckee are tourist communities, and as such, shops can change owners or go out of business, or chefs can leave and restaurant menus change.

We have tried to be as complete and up-to-date as possible for the revised and expanded 5th edition of *What Shall We Do Tomorrow at Lake Tahoe*. If you find something that could be included in the next edition, please write and let us know. If you would like to order a copy of this book for a friend, use the order blank on the next page or visit our website.

Other Books by Coldstream Press

All Roads Lead to Yosemite: Where to Stay and Play In and Near the Park released in Spring 1999. It is a complete guide to lodging, dining and recreation for the gateway communities of Oakhurst, Mariposa, Groveland, Lee Vining/June Lake and Yosemite National Park.

Coldstream Press has three books about ski history in the Sierra Nevada, two released in Fall 1999.

Mountain Dreamers: Visionaries of Sierra Nevada Skiing by Robert Frohlich, with photographs by Carolyn Caddes and Tom Lippert chronicles the memories of 26 extraordinary men and women who share with us their deep love for skiing in the Sierra Nevada.

Magic Yosemite Winters: A Century of Winter Sports by Gene Rose for the first time tells the story of winter in America's most beautiful park. It is illustrated with more than one hundred historical and modern photos, some never before published. The book won the 2000 Benjamin Franklin Award.

Skiing with Style: Sugar Bowl 60 Years by Robert Frohlich and S.E. Humphries commemorates the 60th anniversary of California's first ski resort. It is lavishly illustrated with photographs from personal collections and the archives of this venerable ski area.

Northwest Passages from the Pen of John Muir in California, Oregon, Washington and Alaska is a reprint of the 1988 Benjamin Franklin Award book featuring original woodcuts by Andrea Hendrick that illustrate Muir's inspirational words.

Coldstream Press

P.O. Box 9590
Truckee, CA 96162

I wish to order:

____ What Shall We Do Tomorrow at Lake Tahoe $14.95

____ All Roads Lead to Yosemite: Where to Stay and Play
      In and Near the Park $14.95

____ Mountain Dreamers: Visionaries of Sierra Nevada Skiing $40.00

____ Magic Yosemite Winters: A Century of Winter Sports $40.00

____ Skiing with Style: Sugar Bowl 60 Years $40.00

____ Northwest Passages from the Pen of John Muir $15.00

        Subtotal $_____

        California residents add 7.875% sales tax $_____

        Shipping $ 5.00

        Total $_____

Please charge my Visa or MasterCard

Card No. _____

Expiration Date _____   Phone _____

Signature _____

Name _____

Address _____

City _____State ____Zip _____

Or order by phone toll-free: 800-916-7450, by fax: 530-587-9081 or on the
internet at www.coldstreampress.com

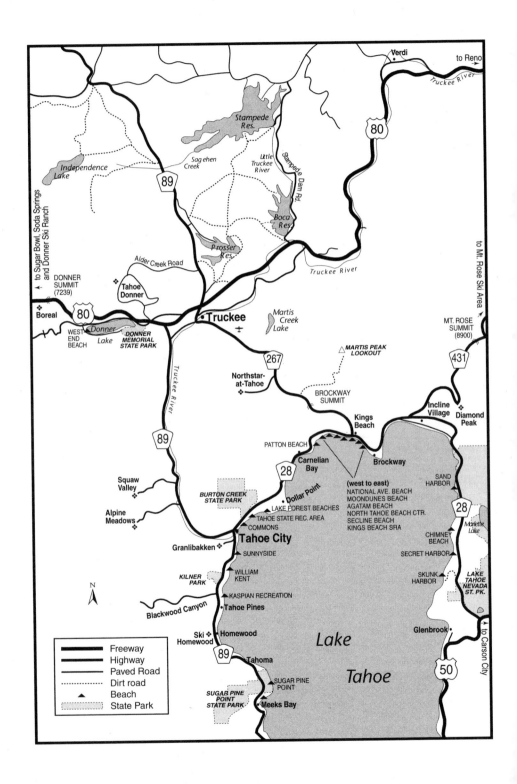